POCKET MONEY MUSEUMS
IN
ENGLAND

700 museums to visit
with over 340 free admission

Melvyn and Angela Davies

First Published in 1998
by Nuthatch Agencies
Fernlea, Barton Road, Carlton, Nuneaton, Warwickshire CV13 0DB

This publication has been prepared with the help of all the museums whose names appear in the guide which is greatly acknowledged.

All entries correct at the time of publication.

Editors: Melvyn and Angela Davies
Principal Researcher: Melanie Siddon
Researcher: Brenda Kinson
Photography: Peter Siddon
Front and back cover photographs: Wayside Museum, Zennor, Cornwall

Printed by: Echo Press, Loughborough

British Library Cataloguing in Publication Data
A catalogue record for this book is available from the
British Library

ISBN 0 9532549 0 9

Distributed by:
Nuthatch Agencies
Fernlea, Barton Road,
Carlton, Nuneaton, Warwickshire CV13 0DB
Telephone: 01455 291204 Fax: 01455 292659
E-Mail: nuthatch@internet-uk.net

CONTENTS

Guide to Symbols

£ Admission charges
O Opening Times
P Parking
C Activities for children
R Refreshments
T Toilets
D Facilities for the disabled
• Brief summary in the museum's own words of their star attractions

If the symbol has been omitted then the facility is not available.

INTRODUCTION

One very wet and windy day in the Easter holidays of 1996, whilst on holiday with our 4 children we came across a small museum full of treasures and interest that kept us amused and enthralled for hours and yet did not cost a fortune. Having discovered one, we thought there must be further sources of untapped delight in other small museums but the problem was how to find them and so began our search.

The result is this guide and we hope that the museums will give you as much pleasure as they have us.

PS. If you have come across a museum that you think should be included in our guide, please do let us know.

DEDICATIONS

This book is dedicated to our children
Eleanor, Gillian, Susannah and William

AVON & SOMERSET

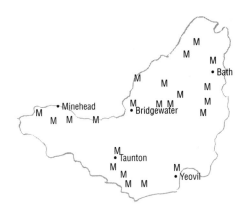

AXBRIDGE

Axbridge Museum
King John's Hunting Lodge, The Square, Axbridge, Somerset BS26 2AP. Tel 01934 732012
£   Free
O   Easter-end Sept daily 14.00-17.00
P   Axbridge Square Meadow Street
T   Close by
D   Access to ground floor
•   Mediaeval merchant's house which now houses the museum of local history and archaeology

BATH

Bath Postal Museum
8 Broad St, Bath BA1 5LJ Tel 01255 460333
£   A £2.50 C £1 Con £1.75 Fam £6
O   All year Mon-Sat 11.00-17.00 March-Dec Sun 14.00-17.00
P   Podium and Broad Street car parks
C   Questionnaires, games at points throughout museum, activity room
R   Light refreshments available
T   Yes
D   Wheel chair access to ground floor, toilet facilities
•   This museum's theme is 4,000 years of communication. Special exhibitions, airmail room, Valentines, postcards and social history.

Book Museum
Manvers Street, Bath BA1 1JW. Tel 01225 466000
£   A £2. Con £1
O   Mon-Fri 09.00-13.00. 14.00-17.00. Sat 09.30-12.30

P   Nearby
D   Museum is down a flight of stairs
•   History of bookbinding. Exhibits on authors who lived in or visited Bath, incl Jane Austen and Charles Dickens, Dr Johnson, Pepys, etc. Also first and fine editions of their books, portraits and memorabilia.

Herschel House & Museum

19 New King Street, Bath BA1 2BL. Tel 01225 311342
£   A £2.50. Con £1. Fam £5.
O   Mar-Oct, daily 14.00-17.00. Nov-Feb, weekends only 14.00-17.00
P   Charlotte Street
T   Yes
D   Access difficult as museum is on 3 levels
•   18th century town house, home of William & Caroline Herschel, depicting their lives as astronomers, musicians & composers.

Police Museum

Avon & Somerset Constabulary, The Police Station, Manvers Street, Bath BA1 1JN. Tel 01225 842415
£   Free but donations to charity appreciated
O   By appointment only
P   Yes

Roman Baths Museum

Pump Room. Stall Street, Bath BA1 1LZ. Tel 01225 477785
£   Charge for Museum but free to pump room, costume museum, art gallery garden
P   Avon Street
C   Hands-on, questionnaires, activity sheets
R   Yes
T   Yes
D   Admitted free to terrace overlooking Bath. Toilets
•   Great Roman temple and bathing complex. One of Britain's most spectacular ancient monuments built around the country's only hot springs 2000 years ago. Free personal audio guides in 6 languages.

Victoria Art Gallery

Bridge Street, Bath BA2 4AT. Tel 01225 477772
£   Free
O   All year, Mon-Fri 10.00-17.30. Cl Suns & BHS
P   Charlotte Street/Avon Street
T   Yes
D   Wheelchair access to ground floor only. Toilets
•   The art gallery houses the city's collection of British and European art from 17th century to present day.

BRIDGWATER

Admiral Blake Museum

Blake Street, Bridgwater, TA6 3NB. Tel 01278 456127
£   Free
O   Tue-Sat 10.00-16.00. Cl Xmas - New Year

P   150 metres
C   Yes
R   Nearby
T   Nearby
D   Limited access to ground floor
•   Local history & archaeology featuring Battle of Sedgemour, Bridgwater shipping & 18th century local portraiture. Exhibitions.

BRISTOL

Bristol Industrial Museum

Princes Wharf, City Docks, Bristol BS1 4RN. Tel 0117 925 1470
£   A £1. Con 50p. Under 16s & pre-booked educational groups free
O   Tue-Sun 10.00-17.00. Cl Mon except BHS
P   Yes
C   Hands on
R   Nearby
T   Yes
D   Full access for wheelchairs. Toilets
•   Hundreds of exhibits relating to Bristol's industrial history incl much transport. Working exhibits give rides most weekends. Beautiful dockside location

John Wesleys Chapel

36 The Horsefair, Bristol BS1 3JE. Tel 01179 264740
£   Donation requested of £1.50 per adult. Child up to 13 free. Guided tours for groups £2.50 each
O   Mon-Sat 10.00-13.00. 14.00-16.00. Cl Weds Oct-Apl
P   200 metres. On street parking for disabled
R   Nearby
T   Yes
D   Access for wheelchairs via Broadmead entrance. No adapted toilet
•   The oldest Methodist chapel in the world, built 1739. Above are living rooms where the first Methodists worked and studied

CASTLE CARY

Castle Cary District Museum & Preservation Society

1st Floor, Market House, Market Square, Castle Cary, Somerset BA7 7LX. Curator, Mrs P M Schiffer 01963 351334
£   Free but donation appreciated
O   Apl-Sept, Mon-Fri 10.30-12.30. 14.30-16.30. Cl Tue p.m & Sats.unless by appt.
P   Nearby
C   Hands-on artefacts, questionnaires
R   Nearby
T   Yes
D   Difficult for disabled due to spiral staircase
•   Victoriana, country & domestic; geology; John Boyd only horsehair manufacturing company in Europe, library - maps, photographs etc. Changing presentations throughout the season.

CHARD

Chard and District Museum
Godworth House, Chard TA20 1NR Tel 01460 65091
£   A £2 C 80p OAP £1.50 Fam £5
O   May-Oct Mon-Sat 10.30-16.30 July and Aug -Sun
P   Public car park pay and display 400 metres
C   'Touch' table
T   Yes
D   Access to all parts except first floor
•   Displays illustrating social and industrial history of Chard, plus by-gone farming and rural industries, also important exhibitions of work of pioneers of powered flight (John Stringfellow) and artificial limbs (James Gillingham)

CREWKERNE

Crewkerne Museum
9 Manor View, Crewkerne
Opening Easter 1998.

DUNSTER

Dunster Dolls Museum
Memorial Hall, High Street, Dunster TA24 6SF. Tel 01643 821220. Correspondence to Curator, Mrs C Dore, 31 West Street, Dunster TA24 6SN
£   A 50p. C 25p
O   Gd Fri-to 1st wk in Oct. every day, 10.30-16.30. Evening & out of season by arrangement, phone C Dore
P   Nearby
R   Nearby
T   Nearby
D   No lift to museum on first floor
•   Mollie Hardwick's fascinating unique collection of dolls from many countries and many periods. Over 700 dolls in varied costumes, a doll's house and baby gowns. Sure to bring back happy memories.

FROME

Frome Museum
1 North Parade, Frome, BA11 1AT.
£   A 50p. C 10p
O   Mar-Dec Wed-Fri, 11.00-15.00. Sat 10.00-13.00
P   Nearby
T   Upon request
•   Frome geology, architecture, industry, local history. Local books for sale. Local archives available. Help with family histories.

GLASTONBURY

Glastonbury Lake Village Museum
Tourist Information Centre, The Tribunal, 9 High Street, Glastonbury BA6 9DP. Tel 01458

832954
£   A £1.50. Child/OAP 75p. Con £1. English Heritage, free
O   Easter-end Sept, Sun-Thur 10.00-17.00. Fri-Sat 10.00-17.30. Oct-Easter, Sun-Thur 10.00-16.00. Fri-Sat 10.00-16.30. Cl Xmas & Boxing days.
P   Yes
D   No access to museum, only to tourist information on ground floor
•   Fascinating insight into life in an Iron-Age settlement, brought to life through exciting displays and artists' reconstructions. Well preserved remains of a wooden dug-out canoe.

Somerset Rural Life Museum
Abbey Farm, Chilkwell Street, Glastonbury BA6 8DB. Tel 01458 831197
£   A £2. OAP £1.50. C 50p. Fam £5.
O   Easter-end Oct, Tue-Fri 10.00-17.00. Sat/Sun 14.00-18.00. Nov-Easter, please phone
P   Yes
R   Summer only
T   Teas
D   Wheelchair access. Toilet.
•   Magnificent medieval Abbey barn and Victorian farmhouse. Displays on Somerset's rural history. Temporary exhibitions, craft and farming demonstrations and special events.

ILMINSTER

Perry's Cider Mills
Dowlish Wake, Ilminster TA19 0NY. Tel 01460 52681
£   Free. Coach parties £1 per person incl talk & cider tasting
O   Mon-Fri 9.000-13.00, 13.30-15.30. Sat 9.30-13.00, 13.30-16.30. Sun 10.00-13.00. BHs 9.30-16.30. Cl Xmas & NY
•   16th century thatched barn where cider is made in autumn; collection of old farm tools, cider making equipment; horse harness, farm wagons and implements. Cider making video. Fine range of ciders for sale

MINEHEAD

West Somerset Rural Life Museum
The Old School, Allerford, Minehead TA24 8HN. Tel 01643 862529
£   A £1. OAP 70p. C 30p.
O   Gd Fri-mid Oct. Mon-Fri 10.30-13.00. 14.00-16.30. Sat 14.00-16.30. Aug Suns 14.00-16.30.
P   Yes
C   Dressing up. Quizzes
R   Yes
T   In car park
D   Limited wheelchair access. Toilet in car park
•   Victorian schoolroom, photo collection, craft demos, picnic area, croquet

PORLOCK

Dovery Manor Museum
High Street, Porlock TA24 8PS No tel
£   Free

P   Public car park nearby
O   May-Oct Mon-Fri 10.30-13.00 14.00-17.00 Sat 10.30-12.30 14.00-16.30
P   Public car opposite museum-charge
C   Questionnaires and activity sheets
R   None on site. Refreshments available in village
T   None on site. Nearest toilet is in public car park
D   Access to ground floor only
•   Concentrating on social and natural history of Porlock Vale. Each year museum aims to present a display on different theme eg "1997-Porlock in 1500". The Manor is the most significant secular building in the village.

Porlock Methodist Church
High Street, Porlock. Correspondence to Church Steward, Mr C O Corner, Tyrol, Villes Lane, Porlock, Somerset TA24 8NQ
£   Free
O   Suns 12 noon or by appt.
P   Yes
R   In village
T   Yes
D   Steps to museum
•   Museum showing history of Porlock Methodism from 1810, incl photos, pictures and press cuttings

RADSTOCK

Radstock Museum
Barton Meade House, Haydon, Radstock, Bath BA3 3QS. Tel 01761 437722
£   A £1.50. Con £1.
O   Sat 10.00-16.00. Sun 14.00-17.00. BH Mons 14.00-17.00. Cl Dec & Gd Fri. Pre-booked groups by appt.
P   Yes
C   Hands on
R   Yes
T   Yes
•   Local history museum depicting life in the old north Somerset coalfield. See how a miner lived and worked, where they shopped and went to school and much more.

STREET

Shoe Museum (C & J Clark)
40 High Street, Street, Somerset BA16 0YA. Tel 01458 842169
£   Free
O   Mon-Fri 10.00-16.45. Sat 10.00-17.00. Sun 11.00-17.00
P   In Clarks Village
R   In Clarks Village
T   In Clarks Village(5 mins away)
D   Facilities for disabled

TAUNTON

Bakelite Museum
Orchard Mill, Off Bridge Street, Williton, Taunton TA4 4NS. Tel 01984 632133
£   A £2. C £1.
O   Mar-Oct, Sat Sun Tue Thu Fri BHs, 10.30-18.00. Wed & Mon (exc BHs) 15.30-18.00
P   Yes also for coaches
C   Play area. Questionnaire for parties
R   Yes
T   Yes
D   Limited access for museum, free for ground floor viewing. Access for tea rooms & gardens
•   Britain's first museum of vintage plastics brings hundreds of these fascinating and nostalgic objects under one roof. Patrick Cook's personal collection represents three decades on the subject.

Sheppy's Cider Farm Museum
Three Bridges, Bradford on Tone, Taunton TA4 1ER. Tel 01823 461233
£   A £1.75. OAP £1.50. C £1.25
O   All year, Mon-Sat 8.30-18.00. Easter-Xmas, Suns 12.00-14.00
P   Yes
R   Yes, May-Oct
T   Yes
D   Most of attraction at ground floor level. Toilets.

Somerset Cricket Museum
7 Priory Avenue, Taunton TA1 1XX. Tel 01823 275893
£   A 60p. Con 40p. Party rate by arrangement
O   Apl-Oct, Mon-Fri 10.00-16.00. Other times by arrangement
P   Yes except on first class cricket days
R   Yes
T   Yes
D   Access to ground floor only
•   Collection of cricket memorabilia housed in 15th century converted barn

Somerset County Museums Service
Taunton Castle, Taunton TA1 4AA. Tel 01823 320200
£   A £2. OAP £1.50. C 50p. Fam £5.
O   Tue-Sat 10.00-17.00. Cl Gd Fri. Xmas & Boxing days
P   Nearby
C   Quiz sheets
T   Yes
D   Limited access. Toilet
•   Toys, dolls, fossils, silver, pottery & archaeological items. Follow the fortunes of the Somerset Light Infantry.

THORNBURY

Thornbury Museum
4 Chapel Street, Thornbury. Correspondence to Thornbury & District Heritage Trust, c/o The Town Hall, High Street, Thornbury BS12 2AR. Tel 01454 412103(Town Hall)

£   Free
O   Wed-Fri 13.00-16.00. Sat 10.30-16.00. Cl BHs & 2 wks either side of Xmas
P   Nearby
D   Facilities
•   Social history collection. Exhibitions of local interest change approx every 8 weeks.

WATCHET

Somerset & Dorset Railway Museum
Washford Station, Watchet TA23 0PP. Tel 01784 640869
£   A £1. Con 50p. Fam £2.50
O   Mar-Oct, daily, 10.00-17.00
P   Yes
R   Pub next door
T   Yes
•   Mechanical, pictorial and documentary collection of the paraphernalia which went to make up an important transport system in the west country.

Watchet Market House Museum
Market Street, Watchet TA23 0AN. Tel 01643 707132(Sec). 01984 631345(Curator)
£   Free
O   Easter then daily from May-Sept 10.30-12.30. 14.30-16.30. Also 19.00-21.00 Jul & Aug.
P   Off Market Street
C   Historic Watchet colouring sheet
R   Nearby
T   Nearby
D   Ramp available on request, otherwise 2 steps.
•   History of this ancient seaport incl fossils, archaeological finds, Saxon mint, maritime history, railways, mining, Victoriana, photos, paintings, models. Video-'The Watchet Story'

WELLINGTON

Wellington Museum & Historical Society
28 Fore Street, Wellington, Somerset TA21 8AQ. Tel 01823 664747
£   Free
O   Easter-Oct, Mon-Sat 10.00-16.00. Nov-Xmas, Sat 10.00-12.00
P   Opposite
T   Yes
•   Displays of historical interest and crafts.

WELLS

Wells Museum
8 Cathedral Green, Wells BA5 2UE. Tel 01749 673477
£   A £2. C £1. Con £1.50. Fam £5. (valid for one year)
O   Easter-Oct, daily 10.00-17.30. except Jul & Aug 10.00-20.00. Nov-Easter, Wed-Sun 11.00-16.00
P   Nearby
C   Activities during specific times of year, i.e Museums week/Xmas
R   Coffee morning every 3rd Thur Mar-Dec.

T   Yes
D   Access and toilet
•   Displays showing past and present life of Wells and Mendip area incl archaeology, geology, mining, statues, samplers, caves and the witch of Wookey Hole.

WESTON SUPER MARE

Time Machine
Burlington Street, Weston Super Mare BS23.1PR Tel 01934 621028.
£   A £2. OAP £1.50. C £1. Fam £4.50
O   Mar-Oct, 10.00-17.00. Nov-Feb, 10.00-16.00
P   5 mins walk away
C   Hands-on, questionnaires activity sheets plus holiday comps and quizzes
R   Yes
T   Yes
D   Yes
•   Children friendly museum with art gallery and peoples collections

YEOVIL

Ilchester Community Museum
c/o The Caretaker, Town Hall & Community Centre, High Street, Yeovil BA22 8NQ. Tel 01935 841247
£   Free
O   Easter Sat-Sept, Thur & Sat 10.00-16.00
P   Nearby
C   Touch table
R   In village
T   Near Limington Rd car park
D   By prior arrangement with caretaker when facilities are available and access through Town Hall for wheelchairs.
•   History of the village from pre-history to 20th century. An Iron Age Lowland Oppidum, Roman Civitas
    Capital & the County Town until mid 19th century.

Museum of South Somerset
Hendford, Yeovil BA20 1UN. Tel 01935 424774
£   Free
O   Apl-Oct, Tu-Sat 10.00-16.00. Nov-Mar, Tue-Fri 10.00-16.00. Mon by appt.
P   Yes
C   Quizzes & activity sheets. Summer programmes. Handling sessions
R   Nearby
T   Yes
D   Wheelchair access 1st floor. Stairlift to 2nd floor. Toilets in theatre next door.
•   History of South Somerset from prehistoric and Roman occupation to agricultural and industrial revolutions.

BEDFORDSHIRE

BEDFORD

Bedford Museum

Castle Lane, Bedford MK40 3XD. Tel 01234 353323

£ Free
O Tue-Sat 11.00-17.00. Sun 14.00-17.00. BH Mons 14.00-17.00. Cl Gd Fri & Xmas
P Public car parks adjacent
C Quiz sheets available. Hands-on activities generally available
T Yes
D Wheelchair access to ground floor at all times. Access to first floor by lift subject to staff availability. Toilet.
• Museum has displays of local and national history from Bedford and surrounding area. Of particular interest to children are the displays of toys and games and the natural history gallery.

ELSTOW

Moot Hall

Church End, Elstow, MK42 9XT

£ A £1. Con 50p. Special rates for groups
O Apl-Oct, Tue-Thur 14.00-17.00. Sat & BH Sun 14.00-17.30.
P Yes
C Questionnaires available
T Yes
D Wheelchair users admitted free but access may be difficult to downstairs
• Housed in old timberframed medieval market house. Fine display of 17th century furniture. Exhibitions of cottage crafts and small amount about John Bunyan.

LUTON

John Dony Field Centre
Hancock Drive, Bushmead, Luton LU2 7SF. Tel 01582 486983
£   Free
O   Mon-Fri 09.30-16.45. Sun 09.30-12.45
P   Yes
C   Regular workshops(please phone for details)
R   Nearby
T . Yes, also baby changing facilities
D   Car parking and toilets, wheelchair access throughout
•   Displays of wildlife and countryside in and around Luton. Centre for conservation of sites of natural history interest in Luton.

Luton Museum & Art Gallery
Wardown Park, Luton LU2 7HA. Tel 01582 746722
£   Free
O   Mon-Sat 10.00-17.00. Sun 13.00-17.00. Cl Xmas,Boxing & N.Y days
P   Yes
C   'One upon a Time - 100 years of Childhood' (permanent) children's gallery exploring the history of childhood and including games, dressing-up boxes and other hands-on exhibits
R   Yes
T   Yes, also baby changing facilities
D   Car parking and toilets. Wheelchair access incl lift to first floor displays
•   Displays of local history, archaeology, natural science, art, costume, lace, childhood, Beds & Herts Regiments; gallery with changing exhibitions. Occasional events organised (please phone for details)

Stockwood Craft Museum & Gardens
Stockwood Park, Farley Hill, Luton LU1 4BH. Tel 01582 387
£   Free
O   Apl-Oct, Tue-Sat 10.00-17.00. Sun 10.00-18.88. Nov-Mar, Sat, Sun 10.00-16.00. Cl Xmas-N.Y.
P   Yes
C   'The Wheel' hands-on display in transport gallery; observation bee hives, animal corner and stables
R   Yes
T   Yes, also baby changing
D   Car park and toilets. Wheelchair access virtually throughout.
•   Displays of Bedfordshire rural life, crafts and trades. Mossman collection of over 60 horse-drawn vehicles. 20th century transport gallery. Period gardens re-creating 900 years of English garden history.

BERKSHIRE

NEWBURY

Newbury District Museum
The Wharf, Newbury RG14 5AS. Tel 01635 30511
£   Free
O   Apl-Sept. daily 10.00-17.00. Sun & BH 13.00-17.00. Oct-Mar -daily 10.00-16.00. Cl Sun
    & BH.
P   Yes
C   Prehistoric trail & nature quiz
D   Wheelchair access to ground floor only
•   Displays include archaeology, natural and local history, rural crafts, costume, ceramics,
    pewter, silver, games & pastimes. Audio-visual displays tell the story of Newbury's two
    civil wars battles and the history of ballooning

OLD WINDSOR

British Balloon Museum and Library
75 Albany Road, Old Windsor SL4 2QD Tel 0175 862977
•   Displays at Newbury District Museum, Shuttleworth Collection, Old Warden and
    Museum of Berkshire Aviation at Woodley. Library based at Cranfield University. Please
    telephone for more details.

READING

Blake's Lock Museum
Gasworks Road, off Kenavon Drive, Reading RG1 3DH. Tel 0118 939 0918
£   Free
O   Tue-Fri 10.00-17.00. Sat, Sun & BH 14.00-17.00. Cl Xmas, Boxing & Easter days
P   Limited. Public car park nearby
C   Year round programme of childrens events and activities

T   Yes.
D   Access to all areas & toilets
•   Situated on banks of river Kennet, the museum of industrial heritage explores the history of 19th and early 20th century Reading, including reconstruction's of Victorian shops and a restored gypsy caravan.

Calleva Museum
The Rectory, Bramley Road, Silchester, Reading RG7 2LU
£   Free
O   09.00-dusk
P   Yes but please don't block the lane
•   Pictorial record of the Roman town of Calleva Atrebatum. Walk to the site from Bramley Road or drive from museum to Wall Lane and start the walk from there.

Museum of Reading
Belgrave Street, Reading RG1 1QH. Tel 0118 9399800
£   Free
O   Tue-Sat 10.00-17.00. Sun & BH Mon 14.00-17.00.
P   Queen's Chatham Station/Gerrard Street
C   Interactivities/videos - galleries aimed at children and adults. Low level trail in gallery. Holiday activities.
R   Yes except Suns.
T   Yes
D   Few parking spaces in front of museum. Ramped access and lift. Toilets(radar key)
•   Full sized replica of the Bayeux tapestry. The story of Reading from Saxon times to present day and the Silchester gallery housing fascinating Roman artefacts from the nearby site of Calleva Atrebatum.

REME Museum of Technology
Isaac Newton Road, Arborfield Garrison, Arborfield, Reading RG2 9NJ. Tel 0118 97633384
£   Free
O   Mon-Fri 8.30-17.00 (Fri 8.30-16.30). Cl BHs
P   Yes, also parking for coaches
C   Hands-on. Questionnaires available to take people around and explain things
T   Yes
D   Parking to front of museum. Good access to all buildings.
•   Attractions include life-size exhibits of electronic equipment dioramas, some hands-on attractions.

Ure Museum of Greek Archaeology
Dept of Classics, Faculty of Letters, The University, Whiteknights, Reading RG6 2AA. Tel 0118 9318420
£   Free to individuals but £20 for school group
O   Term time 09.00-17.00 also often open during holidays
P   Yes
C   Questionnaires
T   Yes
D   Wheelchair access
•   Museum holds the fourth largest collection of Greek antiquities in the country with special exhibitions for children showing the development of vase painting styles, beauty and ancient Greek parties.

WINDSOR

Museum of Eton Life
Eaton College, Windsor SL4 6DW Tel 01753 671177
£   A £2.50 C £2 Tours A £3.70 C £3
O   March-Early Oct 10.30-13.00 14.00-16.30 Holiday times 14.00-16.30 Term time Cl 27th
     May 1998
P   In Windsor or Eaton High Street.
C   Could be available from June 1998
R   Tea prebooked only, shop sells sweets
T   Yes
D   Toilet facilities and ramps but not to College Chapel
•   Over 400 exhibits illustrating the life and history of Eaton since its foundation in 1440.

BUCKINGHAMSHIRE

AMERSHAM

Amersham Museum
49 High Street, Amersham HP7 0DD. Tel 01494 725759

£   A 75p. C free
O   Easter-end Oct, Sat, Sun & BH Mons. Weds from last week in Jul-first week in Sept, 14.30-16.30
P   On street(if you're lucky!) otherwise public parking nearby
C   Questionnaire
T   Yes
D   Very old building with physical limitations therefore difficult for disabled and impossible for wheelchairs beyond first room.
•   Housed in part of medieval hall house c1450; displays of local history, fossils, Roman finds, dairying bygones, lacemaking etc. Material relating to Amersham's WW II naval connections and much more.

AYLESBURY

Buckinghamshire County Museum
Church Street, Aylesbury HP20 2QP. Tel 01296 331441

£   Main museum free. Dahl Gallery-A £1.75. C £1.50.(Peak)
    A £1.25. C £1.00 (Mon-Fri term time)
O   Mon-Sat 10.00-17.00. Sun & BHs 14.00-17.00. Cl Xmas & Boxing days. Dahl Gallery, school parties have priority term time 10.00-15.00 otherwise as above(please phone to check during term time)
P   Public parking within walking distance (signposted)
C   Quiz sheets
R   Yes
T   Yes
D   All parts accessible. Toilets

Buckinghamshire

BLETCHLEY

Bletchley Park
Bletchley Park Trust Ltd, The Mansion, Bletchley Park, Wilton Avenue, Bletchley MK3 6EF. Tel 01908 640404
£ A £3. Con £2. Under 8's free
O Alternate weekends throughout year 10.30-17.00(last admission 15.30), also groups of 20 or more during the week by appt.
P Yes, also parking for coaches
C Toys
R Yes
T Yes
D Reasonable access but no special toilet
• See how the 12,000 personnel worked in Bletchley Park on World War II Codebreaking. A guided tour takes you round the wartime buildings and the 40 acres of grounds. Extensive collection of Churchillian memorabilia, toy collection, wartime vehicles.

BUCKINGHAM

The Old Gaol Museum
Market Hill, Buckingham MK18 1EN. Tel 01208 823020
£ A £1. Con 50p. Unders 5's free
O Apl-Dec, Mon-Sat 10.00-16.00. Sun 14.00-16.00.
P Off High Street, Western Avenue and short term in town centre
C Quiz sheet
T Yes
• Museum reflects aspects of Buckingham's past, the story of the building with an audio-visual display and the county's military history.

HIGH WYCOMBE

History & Chair Museum
Priory Avenue, High Wycombe HP13 6PX. Tel 01494 421895
£ Free
O Mon-Sat 10.00-17.00. Cl Sun & BH except for special events
P Yes
C Interactive local history quiz, activity sheets
R Drinks machine
T Yes
D Wheelchair access to ground floor only.
• Set in historic house with attractive garden, the museum houses a nationally important collection of regional furniture, local history displays and a stimulating range of changing exhibitions

OLNEY

Cowper & Newton Museum
Orchard Side, Market Place, Olney MK46 4AJ. Tel 01234 711516
£ A £2. Con £1.50. C £1. Fam £5. Parties 12 or over £1.50
O 1st Mar-23 Dec, Tue-Sat 10.00-13.00. 14.00-17.00
P Opposite on Market Place (except Thur). or Cattle market car park adjacent

C   Hands-on in archaeology room. questionnaire
R   Yes
T   Yes
D   Wheelchair access to ground floor only. Firm paths in two gardens.
•   Literary museum of memorabilia of poet, William Cowper. Bobbin lace collection, Victorian kitchen and wash-house. Collection of dinosaur bones.

CAMBRIDGESHIRE

CAMBRIDGE

Cambridge University Collection of Air Photographs
The Mond Building, Free School Lane, Cambridge, CB2 3RF Tel 01223 334578
- £   Free
- O   Mon-Tue 09.00-13.00, 14.00-17.00 Fri 09.00-16.00. Cl weekends, Easter and Xmas
- P   Lion Yard
- T   Yes
- D   Wheelchair access, no adapted toilet
- •   Private collection of air photographs; public consultation permitted; copies made to order; all Cambridgeshire in a colour survey made in 1988.

Cavendish Laboratory
Madingly Road, Cambridge CB1 2QF Tel 01223 337200
- £   Free
- O   Mon-Fri 08.30-17.00 except BH, Cl Xmas to New Year
- P   Yes - No charge
- R   Common Room open 1030-1130, 1230-1345, 1530-1630
- T   Yes
- D   Lift Access and Toilets
- •   Selection of original instruments and background information on the laboratory research since it opened in 1971 including Maxwell's dynamical top, JJ Thompson's E/M tube, Wilson's Cloud Chamber and Crick and Watson's DNA model.

The Fitzwilliam Museum
Trumpington Street, Cambridge CB2 1RB Tel 01223 332900
- £   Free, donation appreciated. Guided tours available, 10+ £3.00 pp, booking req.
- O   Tue-Sat 10.00-17.00, Sun 14.15-17.00. Cl Mon except summer BH
- P   None on site
- C   Phone Education officer 01223 332993
- R   Museum cafe - light lunches and coffee
- T   Yes, facilities for the disabled

D   Wheelchair access - please give prior notice.

Museum of Archaeology and Anthropology
Downing Street, Cambridge CB2 3DZ Tel 01223 333516
£   Free
O   Mon-Fri 14.00-16.00 Sat 10.00-12.30 except June 16th-Sept 5th Mon-Fri 10.30-17.00
    Sat 10.00-12.30
P   Lion Yard
C   Activity sheets on Romans and Anglo Saxons for children aged 7-11 years
R   Cafes nearby
T   Yes
D   Lift available
•   Local antiquities. World archaeology. Anthropolgy from all continents. Special
    exhibitions.

University Museum of Zoology
Downing Street, Cambridge, CB2 3EJ Tel 01223 336650
£   Free
O   Mon-Fri 14.15-16.45 Cl for 1 week Easter and Xmas
P   Lion Yard
T   Yes
D   Wheelchair access to upper floor, lift to lower floor.
•   A light spacious museum displaying zoological specimens on two floors. Cambridge
    District's 'Natural History Museum'.

The Whipple Museum of the History of Science
University of Cambridge, Free School Lane, Cambridge., CB2 3RH Tel 01223 330906/334545
£   Free
O   Mon-Fri 14.00-16.00 except BH
P   Lion Yard
R   Cafes nearby
T   Yes in departmental building
D   Yes if prior notice given.

Cambridge Museum of Technology
The Old Pumping Station, Cheddars Lane, Cambridge CB8 8LD. Tel 01223 368650.
£   Steaming £3. non steaming £1.50. Reduction for cons.
O   Please telephone for steam days and non steam days
P   Yes
C   Hands-on and water pumps
R   Yes
T   Yes and disabled
D   With assistance from staff
•   Preserved Victorian pumping station with original plant. Exhibits of area's industrial
    history.

Cambridge & County Folk Museum,
213 Castle Street, Cambridge CB3 0AQ. Tel 01223 355159.
£   A £1. Child & Cons 50p. Under 5's free
O   Tue-Sat 10.30-17.00. Sun 14.00-17.00 (last admissions 16.30)
P   Pay & display in surrounding roads

C   Activity sheets. Trails.
D   No access for wheelchairs. Tapes available for the blind
•   Museum housed in 15th century building near the river Cam. Collection reflects everyday life of local people from 17th century to present day. Themes include trades, homelife, childhood and the fens.

Sedgwick Museum of Geology
Dept of Earth Sciences, University of Cambridge, Downing Street, Cambridge CB2 3EQ Tel 01223 333456
£   Free
O   All year except Xmas - New Year and Easter weekend
P   Opposite in Lion Yard
C   Activity sheets/questionnaires Structured visits/talks for booked school parties
D   Lift access available, staff will help
•   Largest display of fossils in Britain incl mounted skeletons, special displays incl new 'Jurassic Sea Life' Small mineral gallery.

Kettle's Yard
Castle Street, Cambridge CB3 0AB Tel 01223 352124
£   Free
O   House Tue-Sun 14.00-16.00. Gallery Tue-Sat 12.30-17.30. Sun 14.00-17.30
P   Pay & display-Pound Hill
T   Yes
D   Full wheelchair access to exhibition areas and toilet. Limited access to house.
•   20th century art exhibitions alongside the house created by M S 'Jim' Ede incl paintings by Ben & Winifred Nicholson, Christopher Wood, Alfred Wallis, David Jones. Sculptures by Henri Raudier, Bazeska, Brancusi, Motre, Hepworth.

ELY

Ely Museum
The Old Gaol, Market Street, Ely CB7 4LS. Tel 01353 666655
£   A £1.80. Con £1.25. Under 6's free
O   Tue-Sun & BH Mon, 10.30-16.30
P   Public car parks in and around Ely town centre
C   As appropriate
R   In town centre, 2 mins walk
T   Yes
D   Ramps; stairlift to first floor; toilet
•   Fascinating history of Ely and the Isle from the Ice Age to present day. Displays include geology, archaeology, domestic, rural and military bygones. Also temporary exhibitions and events.

MARCH

March & District Museum
High Street, March PE15 9JJ Tel 01354 655300
£   Free, donations appreciated
O   Wed 10.00-12.00. Sat 10.00-12.00, 14.00-16.30. Cl mid Dec to mid Jan. Parties by arrangement.
P   City Road car park nearby

T   Public toilets on adjacent car park
D   Wheelchair user would need assistance with awkward entrance. Museum is all on one
    level
•   Exhibits from homes, shops, societies, railway and both world wars. George Cross won
    by local railwayman Benjamin Gimbert in 1944.

PETERBOROUGH

Peterborough Museum

Priestgate, Peterborough PE1 1LF Tel 01733 343329
£   Free
O   All year Tue-Sat 10.00-17.00 Cl Xmas week and Gd Fri
P   Public car parks nearby
C   Varies with exhibitions
T   Yes
D   Yes
•   The story of Peterborough from dinosaurs to the present day

RAMSEY

Ramsey Rural Museum

Wood Lane, Ramsey. Tel 01487 815715
£   A £1. Con 50p
O   Apl-Sept, Thur & Sun 14.00-17.00
R   Yes
T   Yes
D   Wheelchair access and toilets
•   Rural life exhibits incl a large display of agricultural implements, carts and tractors.
    Special events incl craft fair, May BH, and Plough Sunday, normally last weekend in Sept.

ST NEOTS

St Neots Museum

The Old Court, 8 New Street, St Neots PE1S 1AE
£   A £1.50 C (5-16) 75p under 5 free
O   Wed-Sat 10.30-16.30
P   Town centre pay and display
C   Yes
T   Yes
D   Yes, wheelchair available. Toilet
•   A new museum telling the story of this historic market town on the River Ouse. Attractive
    displays housed in the town's former police station-and court building complete with
    original Edwardian cells.

WHITTLESEY

Whittlesey Museum

Town Hall, Market Street, Whittlesey PE7 BD
£   A 50p C 20p
O   Fri & Sun 14.30-16.30 Sat 10.00-12.00 All year
P   Free parking nearby

P   Free parking nearby
C   Occasional competition forms
T   Yes
D   Wheel chair access but no toilet facilities for disabled
•   Small social history museum with current theme of village post office-corner shop set in 1950's plus local industry, domestic artefacts, photographs, forge and costume.

WISBECH

Fenland & West Norfolk Aviation Museum
Old Lynn Road, West Walton, Wisbech PE14 7DA. Tel 01553 841049.
£   A £1. C 50p.
O   Mar-Oct, Sat, Sun & BH 09.30-17.00. For out of hours visits contact Mr Mason 01945 585808.
P   Yes
C   Hands-on, questionnaires
R   In garden centre
T   In garden centre
D   Wheelchair access.
•   Collection of aviation archaeology, memorabilia of several wars, uniforms, aircraft engines. Exhibits include 747 jumbo jet simulator and Jet Prost systems trainer. Access to cockpits of aircraft on display outside, when museum is open.

Wisbech and Fenland Museum
Museum Square, Wisbech, PE13 1ES Tel 01945 583817
£   Free
O   Oct-March 10.00-16.00. Apl-Sept 10.00-17.00
P   The Crescent and St Peter's car park
C   Yes during some school holidays, handling sessions for school groups.
•   A purpose built Victorian Museum with displays on the Fens, agriculture, geology, archaeology, ceramics, Egyptians, social history and the contents of a village Post Office.

HESHIRE

M
• Warrington
M
M• Mouldsworth
M
• Macclesfield
M
Chester
M
M
• Crewe
Nantwich •

HESTER

heshire Military Museum
he Castle, Chester CH1 2DN. Tel 01244 327617.
   A 50p Con 30p
   Daily 10.00-17.00(doors close 16.30) Cl 22 Dec-2 Jan.
   City centre
   Quiz, questionnaires etc
   On request
   Wheelchair access
   Displays of regiments connected with the county of Cheshire. Tableaux, art and the army, WW1 and WW2. Story from 1689 to present. How the Victorian army packed for travelling.

On The Air' Broadcasting Museum
2 Bridge Street Row, Chester CH1 1NN. Tel 01244 348468
   A £1.95. OAP £1.50. C £1. Fam £5.50
   Mon-Sat 10.00-17.00. Sun 11.00-16.30. Cl Sun & Mon from Xmas-Easter
   City centre parking nearby
   Hands-on
   Wheelchair accessible
   The story of radio and TV from the cat's whisker to present day. Lots to see, hear and do.

hester Toy Museum
3a Lower Bridge Street, Chester CH1 1RS. Tel 01244 346297
   A £2. Con £1. Fam £4.
   Every day except Xmas
   Nearby
   Activity sheets/info brochure

- Largest collection of Matchbox toys in the world. Working amusement machines. 1950' jukebox.

CREWE

Englesea Brook Chapel & Museum of Primitive Methodism

Englesea Brook, Crewe, CW2 5QW. Tel 01782 810109.
£   Free, donations welcome
O   Easter-Sept, Thur-Sat & BH Mon 10.30-17.30. Sun 12.00-17.30.
P   Roadside parking
C   Build a chapel with jigsaw and building bricks. Quiz. Treasure hunt (inside museum an across open country)
R   Tea, coffee, orange. Bring own sandwiches to eat inside or out
T   Yes
- Pipe organ and printing press used by primitive Methodists, both played/worked o special occasions

MACCLESFIELD

Silk Museum

The Heritage Centre, Roe Street, Macclesfield SK11 6UT. Tel 01625 613210.
£   A £2.50. Con £1.75. Joint incl Paradise Mill, A £4.40. Con £2.50. Fam £6.75.
O   Mon-Sat 11.00-17.00. Sun & BHs 13.00-17.00. Cl Xmas, Boxing, NY & Gd Fri days.
P   Yes
C   Trail/quiz sheet
R   Yes
T   Yes
D   Fully accessible
- Fascinating story of silk told through audio-visual programme, exhibitions, models and silk articles.

Paradise Mill

Park Lane, Macclesfield SK11 6TJ. Tel 01625 618228
£   A £2.50. Con £1.75. Joint incl Silk Museum, A £4.40. Con £2.50. Fam £6.75
O   Tue-Sun & BH Mon 13.00-17.00. Cl Xmas, Boxing ,NY & Gd Fri days
P   Yes
R   Yes
T   Yes
D   Fully assessible
- A short distance from the Silk Museum, Paradise Mill is now a living museum, the handlooms are restored and guides illustrate the intricate production processes. Exhibitions and room settings show mill life in the 1930's.

West Park Museum

Prestbury Road, Macclesfield SK10 3BJ. Tel 01625 619831.
£   Free
O   Tue-Sun & BH Mon 13.30-16.30. Cl Xmas, Boxing, NY, days & Gd Fri.
P   Adjacent
C   Activity sheets
R   Yes
T   Yes

Accessible. Toilet
A wide range of fine and decorative art material and objects relating to local history. Egyptian antiquities take the visitor on a journey through life in ancient Egypt. Process of mummification and objects buried with the dead.

MOULDSWORTH

Mouldsworth Motor Museum

Smithy Lane, Mouldsworth CH3 8AR. Tel 01928 731781(answerphone)

A £2.50. C £1

Feb-Nov, Sun & BHs 12.00-17.00. Wed in Jul & Aug 12.00-17.00.

Yes

Brass rubbing, tables(car badges), set of steering wheels, free quiz with prizes

Close by in Delamere forest

Yes

Easy wheelchair access, ramp to entrance. No specific toilet

Housed in an amazing 1930's art deco building, this unique collection of over 60 motor cars, motor cycles and early bicycles nestles in the heart of the Cheshire countryside. Excellent children's quiz with prizes.

NORTHWICH

The Salt Museum

162 London Road, Northwich CW9 8AB. Tel 01606 41331

A £1.75. C 85p. Fam £4.35.

Tue-Fri 10.00-17.00. Sat-Sun 14.00-17.00

Yes

Interactive gallery, activity sheets

Yes

Yes

Disabled access. Toilet

Britain's only salt museum tells the fascinating story of something we all take for granted - salt.

RUNCORN

Norton Priory Museum and Gardens

Tudor Road, Manor Park, Runcorn WA7 1SX. Tel 01928 569895

A £2.90. Con £1.60. Fam £7.95

Apl-Oct, weekdays 12.00-17.00. Weekends & BHs 12.00-18.00. Nov-Mar, daily 12.00-16.00

Yes

Replica tiles and carved stone to rub, puzzle, activity booklets for purchase

Yes

Yes

Dedicated parking, wheelchairs, adapted toilet, tactile maps, audio tapes

Welcoming staff will help you enjoy your visit to this unique haven of nature, art and beauty with it's thoughtful displays, fascinating priory remains, relaxing walled garden and peaceful woodland.

WARRINGTON

Warrington Museum & Art Gallery

Bold Street, Warrington WA1 1JG. Tel 01925 442392.

£   Free

O   Mon-Fri 10.00-17.30. Sat. 10.00-17.00. Cl Sun & BHs.

P   Multi-storey parks in town centre, 5-10 mins walk.

C   Activity sheets to cover temporary exhibitions, museum trails being planned, 'cabinet of curiosity'.

R   Drinks machine

T   Yes, plus baby changing room

D   Ramp to entrance. Lift to 1st and 2nd floors. Ambulant & wheelchair toilets.

•   Eclectic mix from Victorian toys to fossils of Chirotherum, our local dinosaur, footsteps plus a selection of artefacts from other eras and cultures incl natural history and refurbished specimens in geology gallery.

CLEVELAND

HARTLEPOOL

Museum of Hartlepool
Jackson Dock, Hartlepool TS24 0XZ. Tel 01429 222255.
£   Free
O   Daily 10.00-18.00. Cl Xmas, Boxing & NY days.
P   Yes
C   Hands-on exhibits, activity sheets
R   Cafe on board the museum's largest exhibit, the paddle steamer 'Wingfield Castle'
T   Yes
D   Level access with all displays on one floor. Toilet.
•   The museum tells the story of Hartlepool from prehistoric times to present day and includes many original artefacts, models, touchscreen computer and inter-active display.

MIDDLESBROUGH

Captain Cook Birthplace Museum
Stewart Park, Marton, Middlesbrough TS7 6AS. Tel 01642 311211.
£   A £2. Con £1.
O   Tue-Sun, Summer, 10.00-17.30. Winter 09.00-16.00. Last entry 45mins prior to closing.
P   700 metres away
C   Various items
R   Yes
T   Yes
D   Access to all areas. Parking outside museum.
•   Follow the life of Captain Cook from his birth in Marton to his voyages of discovery in the south seas.

Dorman Museum

Linthorpe Road, Middlesbrough TS9 6LA. Tel 01642 813781.
£   Free
O   Tue-Sat 10.00-17.30. Sun 14.30-17.00.
P   On-street parking outside and nearby
C   Various items
T   Yes
D   Access to ground floor only. Toilet.
•   Changing temporary exhibition programme, educational activities, lecture programme.

REDCAR

Kirkleatham Old Hall Museum

Kirkleatham, Redcar TS10 5NW. Tel 01642 479500.
£   Free
O   Summer, Tue-Sun 10.00-17.00.
P   Yes
C   Some items
R   Yes
T   Yes
D   Ground floor access. Toilets.
•   Wide ranging collection of items covering archaeology and social history. Art, photos, maps, etc.

Zetland Lifeboat Museum

5 King Street, Redcar TS10 3AH. Tel 01642 494311
£   Free
O   May-Sept, daily 11.00-16.00
P   Yes
C   Hands on facilities
T   Public toilets 200 metres
D   Wheelchair access to ground floor only
•   Museum houses oldest lifeboat in the world, built in 1802, which saved over 500 lives. Other local and maritime artefacts

SALTBURN

Margrove Heritage Centre

Margrove Park, Boosbeck, Saltburn TS12 3BZ. Tel 01287 610368.
£   Free
O   Summer, Mon-Thur 10.00-16.30. Sun 12.00-17.00.
P   Yes
C   Some special items
R   Yes
T   Yes
D   Ground floor access. Toilets
•   Wide ranging collections of archaeology and social history. Art, photos, maps etc.

The Tom Leonard Mining Museum

Deepdale, Skinningrove, Saltburn TS13 4AA. Tel 01287 642877.

£   A £2.50 C£1. Party rate(min 12 pre-booked) A £1.25 C 75p.
O   Apl-Oct, daily 13.00-17.00 (last admission 15.45). Schools & parties admitted all year.
P   Yes
C   Some tools can be handled. Questionnaires may be available.
T   Yes
•   The only museum in the country dedicated to the ironstone industry. We have an underground visit to a working face 'experience' complete with explosion, smoke, etc. The tour lasts approx 1hr 30mins.

STOCKTON-ON-TEES

Green Dragon Museum

Theatre Yard, Stockton-on-Tees TS18 1AT. Tel 01642 674308.

£   Free
O   Mon-Sat ,09.00-17.00, excl BHs & Xmas-NY.
P   In town centre
C   Victorian handling activities by arrangement. Saturday morning craft club. Holiday prize cryptic quizzes. Occasional hands-on.
R   Town centre cafes nearby
T   Yes
D   Limited wheelchair access. Activities will be arranged to meet needs of disabled visitors.
•   Discover Stockton's past, present and it's people, from Big Ben to Britain's first beauty star, and from locomotion to local pottery. Also school room, historic films and exhibitions.

Preston Hall Museum

Yarn Road, Stockton-on-Tees TS18 3RH. Tel 01642 781184.

£   A £1. Con 50p. Fam £2.50.
O   Easter-Sept, Mon-Sun 10.00-17.00. Oct-Easter, Mon-Sat 10.00-16.30. Cl Xmas-NY/Gd Fri.
P   In Preston Park.
C   Holiday quizzes and craft activity sessions. Regular museum activity for all the family.
R   Cafe in park.
T   Yes
D   Ground floor access only for wheelchair users. Handling sessions by prior arrangement for blind/visually impaired visitors. Toilet.
•   Displays of social history in Georgian house incl costume, toys, arms and armour, period room displays and recreated Victorian period street. Working craft displays and changing exhibitions.

CORNWALL

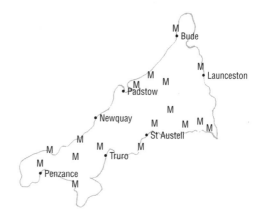

BODMIN

Bodmin Town Museum
Mount Folly, Bodmin PL31 2HQ.
£ Free
O Easter-Oct.
P Yes
C Hands-on
D Limited
• Large collection of fossils, stones from medieval local buildings, Victorian kitchen, Bodmin Moor display, historical and hands-on displays for children. Costumes of Victorian police, local hospital, mayors, Cornish bards, etc.

BUDE

Stratton Museum
The Castle, Bude EX23 8LG. Tel 01288 353576.
£ A 50p. OAP 25p. Under 16's free. Terms for parties(min of 12) by arrangement.
O Gd Fri-end Sept. daily 11.00-16.30. Thur & Sat during Oct 11.00-16.30.
P Adjacent
C Working model of inclined plane. Questionnaires.
R Cafe next door
T Yes
D Wheelchair access and low level displays
• Bude's maritime history - ships and shipwrecks, lifesaving. Bude canal and railway history. Many objects, photos and artefacts. T.V. audio display on shipwreck and railway. WW2 display.

CAMELFORD

British Cycling Museum
The Old Station, Camelford PL32 9TZ. Tel 01840 212811.

£ A £2. C 5-17 years £1.50.
O All year, Sun-Thur 10.00-17.00.
P Yes
C Fun activity sheets
T Yes
D Wheelchair accessible, all on ground floor
• The nation's foremost museum of cycling history from 1818 to present day with over 400 various cycles, over 1,000 medals and badges. Displays of gas, candle, battery and electric lighting.

North Cornwall Museum & Gallery
The Clease, Camelford PL32 9PL. Tel 01840 212954.

£ A £1.25. C 75p. Con £1.
O Easter-Sept, Mon-Sat 10.00-17.00
P Free parking opposite museum
R In Camelford
T Yes
D Access for small wheelchairs. Toilet in town park.
• The museum ,housed in building originally used for making coaches and wagons, covers many aspects of north Cornwall life incl farming, dairy, cidermaking and wagons. Reconstructed moorland cottage Tools of various trades. Many other exhibits.

HELSTON

Helston Folk Museum
Market Place, Helston TR13 8TH. Tel 01326 564027.

£ Free
O Mon-Sat 10.30-13.00. 14.00-16.30. Wed 10.30-12.00 only. Closed Xmas week & Easter weekend
P Wendron Street, Tyacke Road, Trengrouse Way.
R Cafes nearby
T Adjacent to museum
D Steps to front door but side access available. Toilet adjacent.

LANREATH

Lanreath Folk & Farm Museum
Lanreath PL13 2NX. Tel 01503 220321.

£ A £2.50. C £1. Party rates by arrangement.
O Daily, Gd Fri-June, 11.00-17.00. Jul-Sept 10.00-18.00. Oct 11.00-17.00.
P Yes
C Hands-on, questionnaires and fun sheets on request
R Yes(cream teas a speciality)
T Yes
• Partly housed in ancient parish tithe barn, vast range of farming, engineering, office and household exhibits. Lambs, chickens & rabbits to be fed. Telephone play system. Picnic and recreation area for children.

LAUNCESTON

Launcester House Museum
9 Castle Street, Launceston PL15 8AY. Tel 01566 773277.
£ Free
O Apl-mid Oct Mon-Fri 10.30-16.30. Other times by appt.
P Public parking nearby
T Yes
D Limited access, museum on 3 floors.
• Local History, Victorian kitchen and costumes, garden. Small shop.

Potter's Museum of Curiosity
Jamacia Inn Courtyard, Bolventor, Launcester PL15 7TS. Tel 01566 86838.
£ A £1.95. Con £1.50. Fam £4.90. Party rates for 10 or more.
O Nov. Dec. Feb. Mar. daily 11.00-16.00. Sept. Oct. Apl. May, June 10.00-17.00. Jul. Aug. 10.00-20.00.
P Yes
C Puzzle book.
R Hot and cold food in Inn 09.00-21.00
T Yes
D Good facilities but access to ground floor only.
• Smugglers museum also to open 1998.

LISKEARD

Liskeard Muesum
West Street, Liskeard PL14 4BU. Tel 01579 345407.
£ Free but donations towards upkeep are welcomed
O May-Oct, daily 10.00-12.00. 14.00-16.00. Sat 10.00-12.00.
P Pay & display 100 metres
C Possible for juniors with prior notice
T Yes
D Fully assessable. Toilet
• Displays of artefacts, Victorian clothes etc. Local photos, Boer War, WW1, WW2. Documents. Henry Rice plans. General items of interest re Liskeard.

LOOE

Old Guildhall Museum
Higher Market Street, East Looe, Looe, PL13 1BP 01503 263709
£ A £1 C 50p Groups of students 30p each
O Easter, then cl until Spr B.H.-Sept
P Public car parks in town
• 15th Century building - Old Court House - Small museum about Looe and Hinterland. Fishing, smuggling, minerals etc. History of Looe, original stocks. Reputedly haunted.

LOSTWITHIEL

Lostwithiel Museum
Fore Street, Lostwithiel PL22 0BW
£ Free, donations welcomed

O   Easter wk, Whitsun-Sept Mon-Sat 10.30-12.30 14.30-16.30.
P   Two car parks nearby
D   Wheelchair access
•   Situated on ground floor of Guildhall dated 1740, was once Corn Exchange and Lock up. Large collection of photographs, pictures and objects relating to Lostwithiel-domestic, trade and agriculture.

MEVAGISSEY

Mevagissey Folk Museum
East Quay, Mevagissey. Tel 01726 843568.
£   A 50p. Con 30p. Special rates for parties on request.
O   Easter-Sept, Mon-Fri 11.00-17.00. Sat-Sun 13.00-17.00.
P   In village
C   Facilities available
T   Nearby on quay
D   Access to ground floor only. Toilets on quay.
•   Historic exhibits of Mevagissey and district from prehistoric times to present day incl many interesting photos showing fishing harbour and boats.

PADSTOW

Padstow Museum
Market Place, Padstow. Tel 01841 532574.
£   A 50p. Con 30p.
O   Easter-end Sept. and Autumn half-term.
P   Nearby on quay.
D   Not really suitable as there are steps to negotiate.
•   Small museum of local history, the Padstow lifeboat, harbour and fishing. 'Obby Oss' celebrations on May Day. Items on railway and geology.

PENZANCE

Cornwall Geological Museum
Alverton, Penzanze TR18 2QR Tel 01736 332400
£   A £2 C and OAP £1.25
O   All year Mon-Sat 10.00-16.30 Cl Xmas, Boxing & NY Days
P   Public car park next door to museum
C   Sometimes, telephone first
T   Yes
D   Yes, wheelchair lift and toilet facilities
•   Wholly dedicated to the earth sciences, the museum features displays of rocks, fossils and minerals. The geological history of Cornwall is graphically illustrated.

Levant Mine Steam Engine
Trewellard, Pendeen, Penzance. Tel 01736 786156.
£   A £3. Student £1.50. Con £2.50. Fam £7.50.
O   Easter ,May, Spr BH, Sun, Mon. June, Wed.Thu. Fri. Sun. Jul-5 Oct. Fri. Sun.
P   Yes

National Lighthouse Centre

Wharf Road, Penzance TR18 4BN. Tel 01736 360077.

£   A £2.50 C£1. Con £1.50. Children free when accom by 2 adults
O   Easter-end Oct, daily, 11.00-17.00.
P   No on-site parking. Main harbour car park 400 metres.
C   20 question sheets available, aimed at school parties. Several hands-on items.
T   Yes
D   Wheelchair access to 80% of museum. No disabled toilets.
•   The world's finest collection of lighthouse equipment. Optics, fog signals, models. etc. Video history of the first rock lighthouses. Reconstructed living quarters of a tower light complete with original curved furniture.

Penlee House Gallery & Museum

Morrab Road, Penzance TR18 4HE. Tel 01736 363625.

£   A £2. Con £1. free on Sats. U 16's free. Pre-booked school parties free.
O   Mon-Fri 10.30-16.30. Sat 10.30-12.30.
P   200 metres.
C   Interactive computer screen on archaeological sites in the area and data base on collections.
R   Coffee shop with sun terrace.
T   Yes, also baby changing facilities.
D   Wheelchair access to all parts of building. Toilets and dedicated parking.
•   Victorian merchant's house in a lovely parkland setting which houses fascinating displays on the history and art of the area. Ancient sites, farming, fishing, tourism, 'Newlyn school' painting, exhibitions.

Pendeen Lighthouse

Pendeen Watch, Pendeen, Penzance TR19 7ED. Tel 01736 788418.

£   A £1.50. C/stud 75p. Con £1. Fam £4.
O   28 Mar-2 Nov, daily except Sun. Mar-May & Sept-Oct, daily except Mon &Tue.
P   Yes

Porthcurno Museum of Submarine Telegraphy

Porthcurno, Penzance TR19 6JX. Tel 01736 810966.

£   A £3. C £1.50. Con £2.50. Fam £8.
O   28 Mar-end Oct. Fri 11.00-17.00. 2 Apl-29 Oct. Wed 11.00-17.00.
P   Local public car park.
T   Yes, also disabled toilet

PERRANPORTH

Perranzabuloe Folk Museum

Oddfellows Hall, Ponsmere Road, Perranporth TR6 0HX.

£   Free
O   Whit-early Oct.
P   Public car parks on prom and in village.
•   Local collection showing activity and development in the parish i.e. mining, agriculture, fishing, also natural history and archaeology.

REDRUTH

Camborne School of Mines Museum & Art Gallery
Camborne School of Mines, University of Exeter, Pool, Redruth. Tel 01209 714866.
£   Free
O   Mon-Fri(exc BHs & Xmas-NY) 09.00-17.00.
•   Museum showing the historic mining area around Pool. Many show cases of gemstones, crystals, structures, volcanic rocks, local mining, radioactive and fluorescent minerals.

Cornish Engines
Pool, Redruth TR15 3EB. Tel 01209 216657.
£   A £2.50. C £1. Con £1.50. Fam £6.
O   28 Mar-2 Nov, daily, 11.00-17.00.
P   Adjacent and Safeway car park opposite
R   At Safeway cafe
T   At Safeway cafe
•   2 beam engines, one for winding is operated by electric power; the other for pumping is now static. The centre is being converted into a major centre for Cornwall heritage tourism.

Tolgus Tin
Cornish Goldsmiths, Portreath Road, Redruth TR6 4HN. Tel 01209 219786.
£   50p.
O   All year exc Xmas day, Mon-Sat 09.30-17.30. Sun 10.30-16.30.
P   Yes, also for coaches
R   Restaurant and picnic areas
T   Yes

SALTASH

National Maritime Museum Outstation
Cotehele Quay, St Dominic, Saltash PL12 6TA. Tel 01579 350830.
£   30p in honesty box for Quay Museum.
O   Apl-Oct, daily 09.30-18.00
P   Yes
C   Educational project-moving heavy loads. Activities on board sailing barge 'Shamrock' Both by prior arrangement.
R   Yes
T   Yes
D   Wheelchair access. Toilets.
•   Exhibits concern mainly 19th century use of River Tamar, shipping, salmon fishing, ship building, mining/quarrying, local industry. 'Shamrock' is berthed at the quay.

ST IVES

Wayside Folk Museum
Zennor, St Ives TR26 3DA. Tel 01736 796945.
£   A £2. Over 60's £1.75 C(5-16) £1.50(incl free quiz trail & certificate) Group rates on request.
O   Easter-Sept. daily, 10.00-18.00. Oct, Sun-Fri 11.00-17.00
P   In village

C   Apart from quiz trail(incl in admission cost), many items can be handled or operated.
R   Light refreshments in tea garden
T   Next door
D   Limited, according to disability
•   Cornwall's oldest private museum, founded 1937, has over 5,000 items in 14 display rooms, covering all aspects of life in the area from 3,000 BC to 1930's. Step back in time and enjoy the museum with a difference.

TINTAGEL

Tintagel Toy Museum

Fore Street, Tintagel PL34 0DD. Tel 01840.770354.
£   Free
O   Summer 09.00-18.00(dusk in peak holiday period). Nov-Feb 10.00-16.00.
P   Pay & display within 150 metres.
R   Available within 100 metres
T   Available within 100 metres
D   Access for wheelchairs
•   Museum includes a 1950's toy shop full of toys by Dinkie, Corgi. Minic, Tri-Ang, Budgie, Spot-On, Victory etc. Also large sales area.

TRURO

Royal Cornwall Museum

River Street, Truro TR1 2SJ. Tel 01872 272205.
£   A £2. Con £1 C free
O   All year exc BHs, Mon-Sat 10.00-17.00.
P   NCP nearby
C   Activity sheets, schools workshops, interactive displays.
R   Cafe
T   Yes
D   Ramps, lifts, toilets.
•   Cornwall's leading museum of archaeology, local history, art, ceramics, geology. Natural history gallery

CUMBRIA

BARROW- IN-FURNESS

The Dock Museum
North Road, Barrow in Furness LA14 2PW. Tel 01229 870871.
£   Free
O   Easter-Oct, Wed-Fri 10.00-17.00. Sat-Sun 11.00-17.00. Nov-Mar, Wed-Fri 10.30-16.00.
    Sat-Sun 12.00-16.00.
P   Yes
C   Interactive display, filmshow, quiz.
T   Yes, plus baby changing room
D   Wheelchair access.(wheelchair available). Toilet.
•   Spectacular modern museum built over an original Victorian graving dock with
    fascinating displays and high-tech filmshow. Adventure playground and landscaped
    dockside site.

CARLISLE

Birdoswald Roman Fort
Gilsland, Carlisle CA6 7DD. Tel 016977 47602.
£   A £1.95. OAP £1.45. C £1. Fam £5. Group rates available.
O   End Mar-end Oct, daily, 10.00-17.30.
P   Yes
C   Topographical model of Hadrian's wall and Birdoswald, noughts & crosses game, audio-
    visual presentation, activity sheets.
R   Yes
T   Yes
D   Dedicated car parking, access to exhibitions, shop and tea-room, Toilets.
•   Overlooking Irthing Gorge, Birdoswald brings together all the components of the frontier
    system. Learn also about border raids in the middles ages, about the Victorians and
    about 20th century archaeology.

Border & King's Own Royal Border Regiment Museum

Queen Mary's Tower, The Castle, Carlisle CA3 8UR. Tel 01228 32774.

£   A £2.70. Con £2 C(u 16) £1.40. U 5's free. Group rates for 11+

O   Apl-Sep, Mon-Sun 09.30-18.00. Oct Mon-Sun 9.30-18.00(or dusk if earlier). Nov-Mar Mon-Sun 10.00-16.00.

P   Nearby in Devonshire Walk(west side of castle)

T   Yes

D   Parking for disabled. Wheelchair access to ground floor with assistance. Toilet in Tullie House museum opposite castle.

•   Museum relates Cumbria's military history with uniforms, weapons, equipment, medals, memorabilia, video presentations and anti-tank guns Outside is a 25 Pounder Filed gun and a Ferret Scout Car.

COCKERMOUTH

Cumberland Toy & Model Museum

Banks Court, Market Place, Cockermouth CA13 9NG. Tel 01900 827606.

£   A £2. OAP £1.80. C(4-15) £1.(U 4's free). Fam £5.60.

O   Feb-Nov, daily, 10.00-17.00. Dec-Jan, please phone for times.

P   Opposite

C   Worksheets based on national curriculum. Family quiz. Many working exhibits.

T   Yes

D   Wheelchair access to ground floor, remainder difficult due to stairs.

•   100 years of toys. Winner of 1995 National Heritage Shoestring Award for achieving the best results with limited resources. Many working exhibits.

The Printing House Museum

102 Main Street, Cockermouth CA13 9LX. Tel 01900 824984.

£   A £2. OAP £1.25 C£1. Fam £4.50.

O   Mon-Sat 10.00-16.00

P   Wakefield Road and Fairfield car parks.

C   Hands-on facilities

T   Opposite

D   Wheelchair access

•   Museum is set in 16th century building. Varied and interesting displays of historical presses and equipment; the earliest, a Cogger press, dates back to 1820.

ESKDALE

Eskdale Mill

Boot Village, Eskdale CA19 1TG. Tel 019467 23335.

£   A £1.25. OAP £1. C 50p. Fam £3.

O   Apl-Sep, Tue-Sun (incl BHs) 11.00-17.00.

P   In village or Ravenglass & Eskdale min railway, 400 metres

C   A guided tour is provided for everyone and children help in the milling process and are questioned on various aspects!!

R   Yes, also picnic area.

T   At railway station

D   Wheelchair access is difficult as mill is on a hillside.

•   Believed to be the oldest working mill in England (1587), situated in foothills of Scafell in beautiful scenery. The stones are driven by 12' overshot waterwheels, operated daily.

GRASMERE

The Wordsworth Museum
Dove Cottage, Grassmere LA22 9SH. Tel 015394 35544.

£ A £2.25 C£1.15.
O Daily,09.30-17.30. Cl for 3 days over Xmas & 4 weeks in Jan/Feb.
P Yes, also for coaches
C Education resource pack, children's guides.
R Yes
T Yes
D Partially wheelchair accessible.
• Museum offers a programme of special events and changing exhibitions on elements of romantic life, art and literature. Wordsworth's home 1799-1808. Situated in the heart of the English Lake District.

KESWICK

Cars of the Stars Motor Museum
Standish Street, Keswick CA12 5LS. Tel 017687 72090.

£ A £2.50 C £1.50. Fam £7.
O Easter-New Year, 10.00-17.00. Also Feb half-term. W/E in Dec.
P Nearby
R Nearby
T Nearby
D Good access
• Large collection of original T.V. and film vehicles incl Chitty, Chitty, Bang, Bang - Batmobile - Back to the Future - FAB 1 - De-Lorean - Flintstones - Herbie - K.I.T.T. etc.

Keswick Museum & Gallery
Station Road, Keswick CA12 4NF. 017687 73263.

£ A £1. Con 50p.
O Gd Fri-end Oct, daily, 10.00-16.00.
P 2 hr limit on road outside. Also on road 5 mins away, no limit. Pay & display in town.
C Traditional interactives, drawered cabinets, things in chests, musical stones.
T 5 mins away or in park opposite.
D Wheelchair access, guide/hearing dogs admitted
• Victorian museum full of character with local and natural history, curios and curiosities, a stone xylophone, 500 year old mummified cat and an important collection of original Lake poet manuscripts.

Pencil Museum
Carding Mill Lane, Greta Bridge, Keswick CA12 5NG. Tel 017687 73626.

£ A £2. Con £1. (u 5's free). Fam £4.50.
O Daily from 09.30 (last admission 16.00). Cl Xmas,Boxing & NY days.
P Yes
C Questionnaires and pencils.
R Machine in entrance
T Yes
D Facilities for disabled.
• The story of pencils from early beginnings (cottage industries) to present day production of the world famous Derwent pencils. World's largest pencils, war-time pencils,

technique video/watercolour or pastel, shop and children's area.

MARYPORT

Maritime Museum
1 Senhouse Street, Maryport CA15 6AB. Tel 01900 813738.
£   Free, donations welcomed
O   Easter-Oct, Mon-Thur, 10.00-17.00. Fri-Sat 10.00-13.00, 14.00-17.00. Sun 14.00-17.00.
    Nov-Easter, Mon-Sat 10.00-13.00. 14.00-16.30.
P   Within 5 mins walk.
C   Family quiz
T   Yes, upstairs.
D   Wheelchair access to ground floor only.
•   Many objects illustrating Maryport's maritime traditions, from a whale's tooth to a
    blunderbuss, sailmakers tools to telescopes, from a mutineer-Fletcher Christian-to great
    shipowner, Thomas Henry Ismay of White Star Line-owners of the Titanic.

Maryport Steamship Museum
Elizabeth Dock, South Quary, Maryport CA15 8AB. Tel 01900 815954.
£   A £1.90. Con £1.30. Fam £4.85.
O   Easter-Oct, daily, 10.00-16.00. Nov-Easter, weekends or by appt.
P   Yes
C   Hands-on facilities, activity sheets(small charge)
R   Soft drinks, sweets, crisps.
T   Nearby
D   Wheelchair access to ships is not possible. Toilets nearby.
•   Steam tug 'Flying Buzzard' portrays a 'lived-in' ship. Steam lighter 'Vic 96', shows forms
    of power used for propulsion and working of ships,i.e. muscle, wind and steam power.

Senhouse Roman Museum
The Battery, Sea Brows, Maryport CA15 6JD. Tel 01900 816168.
£   A £1.50 C 75p.
O   Apl-Ju. Oct & BHs, Tue. & Thur-Sun 10.00-17.00. Ju-Sep, daily 10.00-17.00. Nov-Mar,
    Fri-Sun 10.30-16.00.
P   Yes
C   Activity sheet
R   Ice cream, chocs, canned drinks
T   Yes
D   Ramp to north gallery. Help available with wheelchair access. Toilet.
•   Sculptures & inscriptions from Roman Fort at Maryport, next to museum; Roman altars;
    religious sculptures; reconstructed shrine; interpretative panels describing the fort,
    Roman coastal defences and the Senhouse family.

MILNETHORPE

Heron Corn Mill & Museum of Papermaking
Waterhouse Mills, Beetham, Milnthorpe LA7 7AR. Tel 015395 63363.
£   A £1.50. Con £1. Fam £4.50. 10% discount for 20+
O   Easter/1 Apl-Sep, Tue-Sun & BHs 11.00-17.00. School groups also Oct.
P   Yes, also for coaches
C   Milling demos. Demos of hand making of paper. Participation encouraged. Printed

material available on corn mill and papermaking.
R   Hotel in village, 400 metres
T   Yes
D   Very limited access due to nature of site and mill. No disabled toilet.
•   Working lowder type watermill. All gearing observable. 18th century building with later restoration. 14' high breast shot wheel. Displays of ancient and modern papermaking, artefacts and exhibitions.

PENRITH

Cumbria Police Museum
Police Headquarters, Carleton Hall, Penrith CA10 2AU. Tel 01768 891999. Ext. 7060.
£   Free
O   By appt only due to limited staff and security.
P   Yes
T   Yes
•   The museum displays history of police in Cumbria. Certain aspects of current operations can also be seen.

RAVENGLASS

Ravenglass & Eskdale Railway Museum
Ravenglass CA18 1SW. Tel 01229 717171.
£   A 50p C 20p, honesty box
O   End Mar-beginning Nov.
P   Yes
R   Yes
T   Yes
D   Facilities for disabled
•   Tells the story of the railway with videos, models and exhibitions.

ULVERSTON

Gleaston Water Mill
Gleaston, Ulverston, LA12 0QH. Tel 01229 869244.
£   A £1.50. OAP £1 C 75p.
O   Easter-end Oct. Tue-Sun 11.00-17.00. Winter Wed-Sun 11.00-16.00. Open BHs.
P   Yes
C   Special tours of the mill and/or our archaeological sites by educational groups by appt. Background info for group leaders, material handling etc.
R   Fully licensed cafe/restaurant. All food freshly prepared and coded - no packets!! Access to restaurant.
T   Yes
D   Disabled very welcome. Access to all site except first floor of watermill. Radar key. Access to restaurant.
•   Historic cornmill. Machinery working most days. 5.4m watermill. Impressive wooden cogs. Displays include social history, technical info, milling and farming artefacts, discoveries from our recent and ongoing archaeological digs.

Laurel and Hardy Museum
40 Upper Brook Street, Ulverston LA12 7BH. 01229 582292.
£   A £2. Con £1. Fam £4.
O   Daily, exc Jan, 10.00-16.30.
P   Public parking in nearby town centre.
R   Ice cream
T   Yes
D   Full access. Toilet.
*   Everything you want to know about Laurel and Hardy is here, incl personal items, letters
    photos and furniture, also a small cinema shows films and documentaries all day(no
    charge).

WINDEMERE

Windemere Steamboat Museum
Rayrigg Road, Windemere LA23 1BN. Tel 015394 45565.
£   A £2.90. Con £1.90. C £1.50. Fam £7.60.
O   Easter-end Oct, daily 10.00-17.00.
P   Yes, also for coaches
C   School visits welcomed, worksheets available.
R   Cafe
T   Yes incl baby changing facilities.
D   Almost all the facilities are accessible to wheelchair users.
*   A unique and historic collection of steam and motor boats, models, engines and
    nauticalia. Boat trips on the lake. Shop, cafe, model pond, picnic area. Attractive
    undercover wet dock.

WORKINGTON

Helena Thompson Museum
Park End Road, Workington CA14 4DE. Tel 01900 625998
£   Free
O   Apl-Oct, Mon-Sat 10.30-16.00. Nov-Mar,Mon-Sat 11.00-15.00.
P   Yes
T   Yes
D   Wheelchair access to ground floor only. Toilets.
*   The museum is a listed-Georgian building. Displays on the social and industrial history
    of Workington, a ship building port, also displays of fine and decorative art and costume.

DERBYSHIRE

ASHBOURNE

Museum of Childhood
Sudbury Hall. Sudbury, Ashbourne DE6 5HT Tel 01283 585305
£   A £3 C £1.50 Fam £7 combined tickets with Hall available
O   Apl-Oct Wed-Sun 13.00-17.30 Nov-Dec 21 Weekends 12.00-16.00
P   Yes
C   Yes, activity sheets for sale, historic toys and games to play with, Victorian schoolroom
    activity-occ weekends and summer school holiday activities - please phone for details.
R   Coach house tea room
T   Yes
D   Yes wheelchair available for indoor use
•   Discover aspects of childhood during last 150 years, contrast the experiences of
    childhood at work, home and school. Admire the toys on display and play some street
    games.

BAKEWELL

The Old Museum
Cunningham Place, Bakewell DE45 IFH Tel 01629 813165
£   A £2 C£1
O   Gd Fri-Oct Daily 13.30-16.00 July-Aug Daily 11.00-16.00
P   Public car park in town
C   Yes
R   Yes beverages and biscuits
T   Yes
•   An early Tudor house. Exhibitions of lace, costumes, children's samplers, toys, crafts,
    furniture and ceramics.

CHESTERFIELD

Chesterfield Museum

St Mary's Gate, Chesterfield S41 7TY Tel 01246 345727

£   Free
O   Mon-Sat Cl Wed 10.00-16.00
P   Some road parking, public car parks within walking distance
C   Childrens Guide 60p Hands on exhibition for 2 months each year.
T   Yes
D   Yes
*   Chesterfield museum tells the story of the town from Roman times to the present. Our most important exhibit is the medieval windlass used to build the famous Crooked Spire Church.

DERBY

Constabulary Memorabilia Museum

16 St Marys Gate Police Station, Derby DE1 3JN

£   Free
O   Mon-Thur 09.30-13.30 Open BH except Xmas and Boxing days
P   Public car park, Bow Lane
C   Yes Police motorcycle, handcuffs etc, quiz for school parties
T   Yes
D   Yes. Full facilities
*   19th Century uniforms, old handcuffs, truncheon, badges and much more.

Derby Industrial Museum

Full Street, Derby DE1 3AR Tel 01332 255308

£   Free
O   Mon 11.00-17.00 Tue-Sat 10.00-17.00 Sun 14.00-17.00 BH 14.00-17.00
P   Public car park
D   Yes access to all floors by passenger lift plus parking facilities by prior arrangement.
*   A museum of industry specialising in aero engines, railways, textiles and other aspects of Derby's industrial heritage.

Derby Museum and Art Gallery

The Strand, Derby DE1 1BS Tel 01332 255586

£   Free
O   Mon 11.00-17.00 Tue-Sat 10.00-17.00 Sun & BH 14.00-17.00 Cl Xmas & NY
P   None on site, multi-storey car park 50 metres in Bold Lane
C   Hol activities and workshops, quizzes, competitions and worksheets
T   Yes
D   Yes Wheelchair access and toilet facilities
*   Displays of natural history, archaeology, local history and regiments. Derby porcelain and paintings by Joseph Wright. Temporary art exhibitions.

Pickfords House Museum

41 Friar Gate, Derby DE1 1DA Tel 01332 255363

£   Free
O   Mon 11.00-17.00 Tue-Sat 10.00-17.00 Sun & BH 14.00-17.00 Cl Xmas.
P   At rear of museum, access via Agard Street

C Yes, quiz sheets, holiday competitions, dressing up box and old fashioned toys
T Yes
D Wheelchair access to ground and lower ground floor only. Tape guide for visually impaired.
• Georgian House with period room settings. Also Georgian garden, costumes, toys theatre and social history exhibitions.

Royal Crown Derby Museum

194 Osmaston Road, Derby DE32 8J" Tel 01332 712800
£ Free
O Mon-Fri 10.00-12.30 14.00-16.00 Cl weekends and BH
P Limited parking available
T Yes
D Limited access
• Unique opportunity to view superb collection of porcelain and china tracing the history and development of company from 1748 to present; also magnificent Ronald Raven collection in Victorian room setting.

9th/12th Royal Lancers Regimental Museum

The Strand, Derby DE1 !BS Tel 01332 716657
£ Free
O Mon 11.00-17.00 Tue-Sat 10.00-17.00 Sun 14.00-17.00 Cl Xmas & Boxing Days
P Public car park 20 metres
T Yes
D Wheelchair access via lift and chair lift. Toilet facilities.
• Information panels (including audio system) and items relating to the history of the regiment from 1715 to the present day. Displays include a reconstruction stable and W.W.1 trench scene.

EYAM

Eyam Museum

Hawkhill Road, Eyham S30 1RE Tel 01433 631371
£ A £1.50 C and OAP £1 Fam £4.25 Reductions for group bookings
O 25th March-2nd Nov Tue-Sun & BH 10.00-16.30
P Public car park opposite museum
R Available in village
T In public car park opposite, includes disabled
D Wheelchair access and chairlift to first floor
• The museum contains a detailed description of the Bubonic Plague in Eyam, illustrated by vivid paintings and sets. A presentation of the Eyam Heritage story and the geology of the district.

GLOSSOP

Glossop Heritage Centre

Bank House, Henry Street, Norfolk Square, Glossop SK13 8BW Tel 01457 869176
£ A 50p C, OAP, Student 25p
O Mon-Sat 10.30-16.00 All year
P 300 metres
C On request

R   Drinks
T   Yes
•   Victorian kitchen, Art Gallery, old newspaper from 1895 and Roman exhibits.

ILKESTON

Erewash Museum
High Street, Ilkeston DE7 5JA Tel 0115 944 0440 ext 331
£   Free
O   Tue-Thur, Fri, Sat 10.00-16.00 Cl Jan
P   Small visitor car park
C   Yes, replica traditional toys and games available
T   Yes
D   Wheelchair access to ground floor and toilets
•   Local and social history material relating to the Erewash area, housed in a Grade 2 listed Georgian/Victorian town house. Temporary exhibitions.

KEGWORTH

Kegworth Museum
52 High Street, Kegworth, DE74 2DA Tel contact only 01509 214460
£   A 50p C and OAP 25p
O   Easter-Sept Sun-Wed incl BH Mon 14.00-17.00
P   Street parking only
C   Yes, hands on and fun sheets
T   Yes
D   Access to ground floor and toilet
•   Main exhibits include various knitting machines, saddlers shop, tools etc, Kegworth school, Victorian Parlour, Royal British Legion section. All devoted to Kegworth and its people.

MATLOCK

The Working Carriage Museum
Red House Stables, Old Road, Darley Dale, Matlock DE4 2ER Tel 01629 733583
£   A £2.50 C £1 OAP £2
O   Daily 10.00-17.00 except Xmas Day
P   Small area close to museum. Overspill 200 metres
C   Yes, I Spy sheet, Horse and pony riding available, prebooking advisable
R   Drinks and confectionery
T   Yes including disabled
D   Wheelchair access
•   Bring history to life, see the horses and carriages used in the recent films 'Pride and Predjudice', 'Jane Eyre' and 'Sense and Sensibilty' plus many more.

Peak District Mining Museum
Matlock Bath DE4 3NR Tel 01629 58384
£   A £2 Child and OAP £1.50 Fam £4
O   Summer 10.00-17.00 Winter 11.00-16.00 Cl Xmas Day
P   Public car park next door.
C   Yes, hands on and work sheets, panning for gold

R   Drinks and snacks
T   Yes
D   Wheelchair access to ground floor and shop
•   Special party rates. Guided tours available. disaster shafts and pumps to work in museum. A good family day out.

MEASHAM

Measham Museum
56 High Street, Measham DE12 7HZ Tel 01530 273956
£   Free
O   All year-Tue 10.00-12.00 14.00-17.00 Sat 10.00-12.00
P   200 metres
C   Yes, questionnaires and worksheets
T   Yes
•   Central to the museum is the Dr Hart collection, a treasury of artefacts, pictures, letters and documents recording the history of a Midland village through the eyes of two local doctors-father and son-over nearly a century. Also items relating to the coal mining, terracotta and pottery industries of the area.

PINXTON

John King Museum
Victoria Road, Pinxton
£   Free Donation Box
O   Apl-Oct Sun 14.00-16.30 other times by arrangement
P   Yes
C   Yes
T   Yes
D   Yes
•   Museum houses mining memorabilia, engineering and railway artefacts, domestic equipment and a cobblers section.

SWADLINCOTE

The Moira Furnace Museum,
Furnace Lane, Moira, Swadlincote DE12 6AJ Tel 01283 224667
£   A £1 C 50p Price increases in 1998 due to refurbishment
O   June-Oct Tue-Sun 10.00-17.00 March-Apl Sat-Sun 14.00-18.00
P   50 metres
C   Yes, quiz sheet, 1998 will see mass of interactive units
R   Drinks and cakes etc
T   Yes
D   Level canal side area. Toilet available at craft workshops 50 metres
•   The furnace interior contains the museum which illustrates the early development of the iron industry and lives of those involved with it.

DEVON

APPLEDORE

North Devon Martitime Museum

Odun House, Oden Road, Appledore, Ex39 1PT Tel 01237 474852

- £ A £1 C and Con 50p OAP 70p
- O Easter-Oct 14.00-17.00 May-Sept 11.00-13.00 14.00-17.00
- P Free parking opposite with museum admission
- C Yes, hands on, questionnaires, activity sheets and Victorian school room for groups
- T Yes
- D Ground floor only and toilet facilities
- • Housed in a fine listed building the museum displays items from the local seafaring past. World War 11 display. Video shows most afternoons. Shop.

ASHBURTON

Ashburton Museum

1 West Street, Ashburton, TQ13 7AB

- £ Free
- O May-Sept Tue, Thur, Fri, Sat 14.30-17.00
- P Public car park 50 metres
- T Public Toilets 30 metres
- • Dartmoor artefacts, North American Indian Collection and local history.

BARNSTAPLE

Museum of North Devon

The Square, Barnstaple, EX32 8LN Tel 01271 46747

- £ A £1 C 50p OAP Con 50p Schools can register for £20 per annum
- O Tue-Sat 10.00-16.30
- P Limited, car parks nearby

C   Worksheets for schools
R   Vending machine
T   Yes
D   Yes, ground floor
•   Tarka centre. Undersea interpretation. Royal Devon Yeomanry. Changing exhibitions

BIDEFORD

Hartland Quay Museum
Hartland Quay, Bideford EX39 6DU
£   A 50p C 20p
O   Easter, Whitsun-Sept 11.00-17.00
P   Yes
C   Yes, quiz sheet, colouring posters, may touch items from shipwrecks
R   Opposite museum
T   No (toilets outside museum)
D   No wheelchair access, Hands on items for visually impaired
•   A small well designed museum in two rooms, interpreting the local coastline, its history, past industries, maritime services, geology, flora and fauna. Large collection of local shipwreck material

BRAUNTON

Braunton and District Museum
Bakehouse Centre, Caen Street, Braunton EX33 1AA Tel 01271 816688
£   A 1.25 C 50p (5-16) OAP/Student 75p Fam £3.50
O   Easter-Sept Mon-Sat 10.00-17.00 Sun 10.00-14.00 (Aug) Oct-Easter Mon-Sat 10.00-17.00
P   Free public car park next door
R   None on site but plenty nearby
T   Public toilets next door
D   Wheelchair access and toilets
•   Museum moved to new site- 'state of art' technology. Suitable for general interest and further study. Detailed study of fishing, shipping and agricultural history, wide range of exhibits for all ages.

BRIXHAM

Brixham Museum & History Society
Bolton Cross, Brixham TQ5 8LZ Tel 01803 856267
£   A £1.20 C & OAP 80p Fam £3.50
O   Easter -Oct Mon-Fri 10.00-17.00 Sat 10.00-13.00
P   Public car park
C   Yes
T   Yes
D   First floor access only, no toilet facilities
•   Located in the Old Police Station, displays portray Brixham's history including fishing, boatbuilding, smuggling, war-time defences, from Napoleonic through Victorian periods to present day.

COMBE MARTIN

Combe Martin Museum
4 Kingsley Terrace, Combe Martin EX34 OEW Tel 01271 882636
£   A 50p C and OAP 25p
O   Spring BH-Mid Sept 13.30-16.00 School Hol 11.00-16.00
P   Public car park
C   Hands on, questionnaires, colouring sheets
R   Cafes nearby
T   Toilets in public car park
D   Wheel chair access to upper floor only
•   Displays of old village industries, silver-lead mining, lime quarrying and burning, horticulture. agriculture, maritime and social history. Marine Life Interpretation Centre with guided exploration of sea-shore and rock pools.

DARTMOUTH

The Engine House
Mayors Avenue, Dartmouth, TQ6 9YY Tel 01803 834224
£   50p
O   Easter-Oct Mon-Sat 09.30-17.50 Sun 10.00-16.00 Nov-Easter Mon-Sat 10.00-16.00
P   Public car park next door
D   Wheelchair access
•   An original Necomes engine, now powered by electricity.

DAWLISH

Dawlish Museum
Barton Terrace, Dawlish EX7 9QH
£   A £1 C 50p
O   May-Sept Mon-Sat 10.30-17.00 Sun 14.00-17.00
P   Limited, Public car park adjacent
C   Yes, please telephone for details
T   Yes
D   Yes access to ground floor
•   Large collection of Victorian on three floors - Victorian kitchen, parlour, shop, bedroom. Railway memorabilia, toys, china, photos, prints etc.

EXETER

Connections Discovery Centre
Rougemont House, Castle Street EX4 3PU Tel 01392 265360
£   C £1.50 each, accompanying teachers and adults free
O   Open to prebooked school parties during term time
P   Public car parks near by
C   Handling collections
T   Yes
D   Wheelchair access to ground floor only and toilet
•   All displays linked to National Curriculum. Sessions run by Education staff prebooked parties - Toys and childhood, Ancient Greece, The Romans, The Victorians, The home front in W.W 11, Africa.

Royal Albert Memorial Museum
Queen Street, EX4 3RX Tel 01392 265858
£   Free
O   Mon-Sat 10.00-17.00
P   Public car parks in city centre
C   Quiz sheets and special activities during holiday periods
R   Cafe
T   Yes
D   Wheelchair access and toilets, parking for badge holders at rear
•   Large museum in central Exeter with important collections - artefacts from around the world, natural history (Local and foreign), West country silver, Romans, local history and archaeology, fine art, clocks, geology etc.

Underground Passages
Romangate Passsage off High St Exeter EX4 3PZ Tel 01392 265887
£   Sept-June A £2.50. C £1.50 Fam £6. Jul &Aug A £3.50 C £2.25 Fam £9
O   July, Aug, Sept & School Hol Mon-Sat 10.00-17.00 other times Tue-Fri 14.00-17.00 All Sat
P   Car parks in city centre
C   Low passages passable to children only
•   Dating from 14th Century these passages under Exeter High Street were built to supply fresh water to the city. Visitors pass through an exhibition and video presentation before their guided tour

EXMOUTH

Exmouth Museum
Sheppards Row, Exeter Road, Exmouth EX8 1PW Tel 01395 263785
£   A 50p OAP 30p C & Student Free
O   Apl-Oct Mon-Sat 10.30-12.30 Tue, Wed, Thur 14.30-16.30
P   Public car park. The Estuary Car Park
D   Wheelchair access downstairs only (two thirds of display area)
•   A local museum with displays of historic interest including a Victorian kitchen, a 1930's dining room, the Joan Clarke Memorial Lace Exhibition. Railwayana, china and glass etc.

HOLSWORTHY

Holsworthy Museum
Manor Offices, Holsworthy EX22 6DJ
£   A 30p C Free
O   Apl-Oct Wed 10.00-16.00(other times by arrangement)
P   Public car park in town
T   Public toilets nearby
•   Many artefacts of local interest, agricultural implements, domestic equipment, local crafts and archives

HONITON

Allhallows Museum of Lace and Local History
High Street, Honiton EX14 8PE Tel 01404 42996
£   A £1 C 30p OAP 80p

O   Easter-Sept 10.00-17.00 Oct 10.00-16.00
P   Public car park 200 metres
C   Yes, quiz, brass rubbing
T   No (emergency only)
D   Limited wheelchair access to two lace areas
•   The most comprehensive collection of Honiton lace housed in a listed building. Story of a Rotten Borough.

ILFRACOMBE

Ilfracombe Museum
Wilder Road, Ilfracombe EX34 8AF Tel 01271 86354
£   A £1 C and Students 30p OAP 50p
O   Apl-Oct Mon-Sun 10.00-17.30 Nov-March Mon-Fri 10.00-12.30
P   Car park at sea front
C   Yes, brass rubbing
T   Yes
D   Yes
•   A fascinating collection of over 20,000 items of natural history, Victorian, maritime, minerals, archaeology, maps, paintings, photos, militaria, costume and local history.

LYNTON

Lynton and Exmoor Museum
St Vincent Cottage, Market Street EX35 6AF
£   A £1 C 20p OAP and students 70p
O   Easter-Oct Mon-Fri and Sun pm
P   Public car park next to museum
T   In public car park
•   Exhibits portray range of social history - craft, agriculture, maritime and natural history. Of special interest. Exmoor kitchen. Model and photographs of Lynton/Barnstaple narrow gauge railway

MERTON

Barometer World and Museum
Quicksilver Barn, Merton EX20 3DS Tel 01805 603443
£   A £2 C 25p
O   Feb-Dec Mon-Sat 10.00-16.00
P   Yes but limited to twelve vehicles
C   Yes, small activity sheet for 2 age groups with colouring competition
T   Yes
D   Wheelchair access for standard size wheelchairs, limited access to toilet
•   A unique exhibition of approximately 300 English domestic barometers from 1680 to the present day. Showroom collection of new and antique barometers, barographs, books and weather related items

OKEHAMPTON

Museum of Dartmoor Life
3 West Street, Okehampton EX20 1HG Tel 01837 52295
£ A £1.60 Student 80p OAP £1.30 Fam ticket £4.50 Parties -POA
O All year Mon-Fri 10.00-17.00 & Easter-Sept -weekends
P Yes on site car park and public car park 3 minutes walk
C Questionnaire for school visits, hands on (at own risk)
R Tea Rooms
T Yes
D Museum no wheelchair access, but shop has access. Toilets
• This lively museum tells the story of how people have lived, worked and played on and around Dartmoor through the centuries.

SALCOMBE

Salcombe Maritime and Local History Museum
Town Hall Basement,
Market Street, Salcombe TQ8 8DE
£ A £1 C 50p up to 12 years
O Easter-Oct 10.30-12.30 14.30-16.30
P Public car parks in town
C Yes, please telephone for details
D Limited
• Maritime items relating to Salcombe district.

SIDMOUTH

Norman Lockyer Observatory
Salcombe Hill, Sidmouth EX10 ONY Tel 01395 579 941
£ A £2 C£1
O Public open afternoons Wed & Sun in July & Aug. Evenings monthly in winter
  Please telephone for more details.
P Yes
C Telescope for public viewing
T Yes plus disabled
D Yes
• Centre for science education, practical astronomy, amateur radio, and meteorology.

SOUTH MOLTON

South Molton Museum
The Square, Town Hall, South Molton EX36 3AB
£ Free
O March-Nov
P Public car park nearby free except Thursday
T Yes
D Yes
• Displays offer a most coherent story line of the life and times of the town with items and photographs depicting domestic activities, trades, industry and farming - all fascinating glimpses of the past.

TEIGNMOUTH

Teignmouth Museum
29 French Street, Teignmouth TQ14 8ST Tel 01626 777041
£   A £1 C free
O   Mon-Sat 10.00-16.30 Sun 14.00-16.30
P   Public car park nearby
C   Hands on and activity sheets
T   At railway station opposite
D   Limited
•   Discover Teignmouth's ancient maritime past. Articles from Teignmouth's own Armada period wrecks. Exhibits from the lace school.

TIVERTON

Tiverton Museum
St Andrew Street, Tiverton EX16 6PH Tel 01884 256295
£   A £1 C 50p OAP 75p
O   Feb-Dec including BH Mon-Sat 10.30-16.30 Cl Xmas and Jan
P   Public car park 100 metres at Beck Square
T   Yes
D   Access to ground floor
•   A comprehensive local museum of unusual scope, embodying wagon gallery, wartime history, grand western canal, local industries, agricultural hall, 200 year old Smithy, costume gallery, railway locomotive and relics, lace machinery gallery.

TOPSHAM

Topsham Museum
25 The Strand, Topsham EX3 0AP Tel 01392 873244 (Answerphone)
£   A £1.50 C Free if accompanied OAP and Student £1
O   March-Sept Mon, Wed, Sat 14.00-17.00 Some Sun June-Sept
P   Public car park 300 metres
C   Yes, questionnaires and some hands on
R   Yes
T   Yes
D   Wheelchair access to ground floor and first floor of Sail Loft only. Toilet facilities
•   17th Century furnished house plus large sail loft showing Topsham history (including model of town in 1900), maritime trade and shipbuilding. wildlife of Exe estuary on ground floor of sail loft.

TORQUAY

Bygones
Fore St, Torquay TQ1 4PR Tel 01803 326108
£   A £2.95 C £1.95 OAP £2.50 Fam £8.50
O   June-Aug 10.00-22.00, March, Apl, May 10.00-18.00 Nov-Feb 10.00-14.00
    Winter weekends and school hol 10.00-17.00
P   Public car park nearby
C   Questionnaires and activity sheets
R   Station Tea Rooms

T Yes
 Wander back in time and see a real old world street including a pub and period display rooms. Railway exhibits. Collection of militaria and W.W.1 Trench Experience. Torquay Museum

Torquay Museum

529 Babbacombe Road, Torquay TQ1 1HG. Tel 01803 293975
£ A £2. Cons £1.25. under 5s free. Season tickets available.
O Mon-Fri 10.00-16.45. Easter-Oct, Sat 10.00-16.45. Sun 13.30-16.45
P Limited on forecourt. Public car park Museum Road
C Quiz sheets on request. Annual Agatha Christie competition.
R Dispensing machine
T Yes
• Eight galleries including Agatha Christie, archaeology and finds from Kents Cavern, local history, geology and natural history, Victoriana, Devon regiments, autograph collection and an Egyptian mummy. Regular temporary exhibitions.

TOTNES

Totnes Costume Museum

Bogan House, 43 High Street, Totnes TQ9 5NP Tel 01803 862827
£ A £1.20 C 40p OAP 80p Fam £1.20
O Spring BH-Sept Mon-Fri 10.00-17.00
P Public car park next door
T Public toilets next door
• Collection holds male and female dress from mid 18th Century to the present day.

DORSET

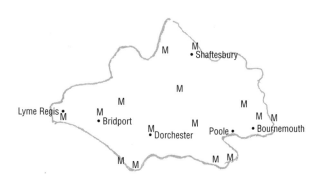

BLANDFORD FORUM

Blandford Forum Museum Trust

Bere's Yard, Market Place, Blandford Forum DT11 7HU. Tel 0125450388

- £   A £1 C Free. O.A.P. No Con.
- O   Apl-Sept Mon-Sat 10.00-16.00
- P   Several car parks nearby
- R   Cafes nearby
- T   Yes
- D   Yes - downstairs only
- •   The museum houses a selection of fossils. Items relating to Blandford's 19th Century painter and sculptor Alfred Stevens. Rural, military and schoolroom bygones and Fire Room depicting the Great Fire of Blandford in 1731.

Royal Signals Museum

Balndford Camp, Blandford DT11 8RH. Tel 01258 482248

- £   A £3 C£1.50 Fam £8. O.A.P. £2.
- O   All year Mon-Fri 10.00-17.00 June-Sept Mon-Fri 10.00-17.00 Sat-Sun 10.00-16.00 Cl 10 day at Xmas
- P   Yes. Free
- C   Some hands on Exhibits
- R   Yes
- T   Yes
- D   Wheelchair access and toilets.
- •   Displays history of military communications since the Crimea War and the history of Royal Signals; containing signalling equipment, uniforms, medals, vehicles and motorcycles. some interactive displays.

BOURNEMOUTH

The Bournemouth Bears
Old Christchurch Lane, Bournemouth BH1 1NE
- £ A £2.95 C £1.95 OAP £2.50 Fam £8.50
- O Apl-Sept 09.30-17.30 Oct-March 10.00-16.00
- P Car Park Richmond Hill Gardens - 100 metres
- C Fun Sheet
- R Refreshments nearby
- • There are old bears, new bears, tiny bears, famous bears, dressed bears, artist bears and limited editions at Dorset's only Teddy Bear Museum.

Dinosaur Safari
Expocentre, Old Christchurch Lane, Bournemouth BH1 1NE Tel 01202 293544
- £ A £2.95 C £ 1.95 Fam £8.50 OAP £2.50
- O 09.30-17.30 All year daily (phone for winter opening)
- P Car Park Richmond Hill Gardens - 100 metres
- C Hands on displays, fun sheets
- R Refreshments nearby
- • Everything you have ever wanted to know about the fascinating world of dinosaurs. Computer and hands on displays help to unravel the mysteries of the dinosaurs.

Mummies
Old Christchurch Lane, Bournemouth BH1 1NE Tel 01202 293544
- £ A £2.95 C £1.95 Fam £8.50 OAP £2.50
- O Apl-Sept 09.30-17.30 Oct-March 10.00-16.00
- P Richmond Hill Car Park -100 metres
- C Fun sheet
- R Refreshments nearby
- • The secrets of the Pyramids are revealed. Unlock the mysteries of Ancient Egypt and enter a world of hidden tombs, preserved bodies and strange and magical rituals.

BRIDPORT

Bridport Museum
South Street, Bridport DT6 3NR Tel 01308 422116
- £ A £1 C 50p OAP 75p Discount ticket available for entry into Bridport Museum and Harbour Museum-A £1.50 C 75p OAP £1.25
- O Apl-Oct Mon-Sat 10.00-17.00
- P Long and short stay car parks within a short level walk of museum
- R Refreshments available throughtout Bridport
- T Public toilets 100 metre level walk from museum
- D Ground floor access only
- • Costume, fine art, natural history, local history and rural life. Centre for genealogical and local history research. Guided tours of Bridport by arrangement.

Harbour Museum
West Bay, Bridport DT6 45A Tel 01308 420997
- £ A £1 C 50p OAP 75p. Discount ticket available as for Bridport Museum.
- O Apl-Oct Mon-Sun 10.00-18.00 (20.00 in Aug)
- P Long and short stay car parks within short level walk of museum

R   Refreshments available throughout Bridport
T   Public toilets next door to museum
D   Ramp to entrance of museum on one level only. Radar toilet next door ro museum, key held by museum.
•   The history of Bridport's rope and net-making industry, and the story of West Bay. Guided tours of West Bay by arrangement.

CHRISTCHURCH

Redhouse Museum and Gardens
Quay Road. Christchurch BH23 1BU Tel 01202 482860
£   A1 C 60p Con 60p
O   Tue-Sat 10.00-17.00 Sun 14.00-17.00
P   Public car parks 100 metres
C   Fun sheets, questionnaires to fill in
R   Yes Beverages and biscuits
T   Yes
D   Limited access to ground level only
•   Local history, costume, geology, natural history and archaeology. Formal garden with culinary and medicinal herbs, secluded informal garden with old fashioned roses, and less common shrubs and trees.

CORFE CASTLE

Town Hall Museum
West Street, Corfe Castle
£   Free
O   Apl-Oct Mon-Sun 09.30-18.00 Nov-March Sat-Sun 10.00-17.00
P   Public car park in West Street (charge)
D   Wheelchair access
•   Dinosaur footprints. Early implements from clay workings, farms and houses. Wall displays on the local clay and stone industry. A copy of the 16th Century town mace.

DORCHESTER

Teddy Bear House
Antelope Walk, Dorchester DT1 1BE Tel 01305 263200
£   A £2 C £1 Fam £5.50
O   All year Mon-Sat 09.30-17.00 Sun 10.00-14.30
P   Town centre car parks 250 metres away
C   Story sheet
R   Refreshments available in town
•   Visit Edward Bear and his large family of human sized teddy bears as they relax at home and work in the old Dorset Teddy Bear Factory.

Mill House Cider Museum. A Dorset Collection of Clocks
33 Moreton Road Owermoigne Dorchester DT2 8HZ Tel 01305 852220 Fax 01305 854760
£   A £1.50 C Free (under 18) Cider museum
    A £2.00 C £1 (over 8) Clock museum Composite museum ticket £3
O   Mon-Sun 09.00-17.00 Cl Xmas, Boxing & NY Days
P   Yes

C   Guide sheets available. Please do not touch
R   Sweetshop and Off-licence with Ciders etc
T   Yes
D   Wheelchairs can enter the museum
•   A large collection of cider equipment with 10 minute video of cider being made. Some 30-45 longcase and turrets clocks. Longcase all Dorset clocks. clocks working to show pendulums. Tours by arrangement.

Dorset County Museum
High West Street, Dorchester DT1 1XA Tel 01305 262735
£   A2.80 Child under 5 Free Con and Fam tickets available
O   June-Sept Mon-Sat 10.00-17.00 July-Aug Sun 10.00-17.00
P   None on site. Public car park in town
C   Questionnaires
T   Yes
D   Ground floor only. Toilets not accessible by wheelchair
•   Major collection of local history, natural history, geology, literary manuscripts and archaeology. New gallery on Thomas Hardy and Dorset.

The Keep Military Museum
The Keep, Bridport Road, Dorchester DT1 !RN Tel 01305 264066 Fax 01305 250373
£   A £2 C £1 OAP £1 Group rates on application
O   All year Mon-Sat 09.30-17.00 Cl Xmas & NY
P   Car park 50 metres
C   Yes, questionnaires, trail in Gallery during July
T   Yes
D   Access to ground floor only, toilets not accessible
•   The museum is housed in an interesting listed building which has been newly renovated. Medals, weapons and uniforms reside alongside interactive computerised displays and video.

Tolpuddle Martyrs Museum
Tolpuddle, Dorchester DT2 7EH Tel 01305 848237
£   Free
O   Apl-Oct Tue-Sat 10.00-17.30 Sun 11.00-17.30 Nov-March Tue-Sat 10.00-16.00 Sun 11.00-16.00 Cl 24th Dec-2nd Jan
P   Parking in Lay-by on A35
C   Activity packs available at £1.95
T   Yes
D   Wheelchair access and toilets
•   The museum and cottages were built in 1934 by the Trades Union Congress in memory of six agricultural workers transported to Australia in 1934 after forming a trade union. The museum tells their story and also introduces other historical sites in the village.

GILLINGHAM

Gillingham Museum
Chantry Fields, Gillingham SP8 Tel 01747 823176
£   Free Donations invited
O   Tue, Thur, Fri 10.00-17.00 Sat 09.30-12.30
P   Yes free

R   No Refreshments available in town
T   Yes
D   Yes
•   Exhibitions in the form of illustrated panels ranging from the Iron age through to the Saxon era. The railway and the industry it brought to Gillingham. A large amount of Victoriana and a display of John Constable's Gillingham paintings and sketches.

LYME REGIS

Lyme Regis Philpot Museum
Lyme Regis DT7 3QA Tel 01297 443370
£   A £1 C 40p OAP and Groups 80p
O   Apl-Nov Mon-Sat 10.00-17.00 Sun 10.00-12.00 14.30-17.00 Winter Sat-Sun 10.00-12.00 14.30-17.00
P   Public car parks nearby
C   Questionnaires and activity sheets
•   A large part of the subject matter is local history, geology (particularly Mary Anning) and local literary associations. The museum was refurbished spring 97. There is also a shop.

PORTLAND

Portland Museum
217 Wakeham, Portland DT5 1HS Tel 01305 821804
£   A £1.60 C and Student Free OAP 80p
O   Apl-Sept 5 days a week Oct-March Cl
P   Opposite museum
C   Hands on facilities and questionnaires
T   Yes
D   Access limited. Talking Museum for the blind
•   Set in two thatched cottages, a purpose built gallery and extensive gardens, the Museum is a treasure trove of Island history from dinosaurs to geological wonders.

SHAFTESBURY

Shaftesbury Town Museum
1 Gold Hill, Shaftesbury Tel 01747 852157
£   A 75p C 10p
O   Gd Fri-Oct 11.00-17.00 daily
P   No but public car parks nearby
C   Questionnaires
R   Refreshments nearby
T   No (emergency only)
•   The museum is being kept as close as possible to the way it looked when it started 50 years ago.

SHERBORNE

Sherborne Museum
Abbey Gate House, Sherborne DT9 3BP Tel 01935 812252
£   A £1 C and students free
O   Easter-Oct Tue-Sat 10.30-16.30 Sun 14.30-16.30 Cl Mon

P   No (Nearest public car park at Culverhayes, Long street)
D   Wheelchair access
•   Major themed exhibition each year and permanent exhibitions of Victorian Dolls'House,
    the history of Sherbourne Silk Mills, models and drawings of Sherborne Old and New
    Castles.

STURMINSTER NEWTON

The Museum and Mill
Bath Road, Sturminster Newton Tel 01258 472347
£   Free
O   Apl-Sept Sunday 14.00-16.30 (Museum) Easter-Sept Sat, Sun, Mon, Thur 11.00-17.00
    (Mill)
P   Yes on site
T   In Mill
•   Displays many aspects of local history (and surrounding villages) and including famous
    local personalities. Wander through the Mill or join one of the frequent tours.

SWANAGE

The Coach House Museum
'Barton' The Hyde, Langton Matravers, Swanage BH19 3HE Tel 01929 423168
£   A 60p C and Student 25p
O   Apl-Oct Mon-Sat 10.00-12.00 14.00-16.00.
P   Small free car park on site
C   Questionnaires and hands on facilities
D   Wheelchair access, special facilities for blind visitors
•   Small museum with audio-visual introduction, rock specimens, fossils, stonemason's
    tools, carvings, documents, photographs, capstan, reconstruction of section of quarry-
    mine, shop-books, souvenirs, including stone.

WAREHAM

The Blue Pool Museum
The Blue Pool, Furzebrook, Wareham BH20 5AT Tel 01929 551408
£   A £2.40 C £1.20 OAP £1.80 Special rates for groups
O   Easter to early Oct
P   Yes
R   Yes in Tea House
T   Yes plus disabled toilet
D   Wheelchair access to tea house, museum and shops.
•   The museum shows how the local clay industry was affected by the arrival of tobacco in
    the 16th Century and tea in the 17th Century. Examples of clay tobacco pipes and
    teaware are on display.

WEYMOUTH

Nothe Fort
Barrack Road, Weymouth DT4 8UF Tel 01305 787243
£   A £2.50 C (accompanied)free Con £1.50 Groups by appointment
O   Mid May-late Sept daily 10.30-17.30 Sun & BHs all year from 14.00

- P Yes
- C Yes, for school parties
- R Yes
- T Yes
- D Yes
- • Restored Victorian defence work with displays of that period. Second World War and other military episodes of local significance brought to life with contemporary weaponry and vehicles.

Brewers Quay

Hope Square, Weymouth DT4 8TR Tel 01305 777622 Fax 01305 761680
- £ Weymouth Museum Exhibition Free Admiission charge for other attractions.
- O All year Mon-Sun 09.30-17.30
- P On On site
- C Yes
- R Yes
- T Yes
- D Access for wheelchairs not possible within The Timewalk. Disabled toilet facilities
- • 'The Time Walk Journey' - 600 years of Weymouth's history. 'Discovery' -Hands-On mullti-media attraction.

WIMBORNE MINSTER

The Priest's House Museum and Garden

23-27 High Street, Wimborne Minster BH21 1HR Tel 01202882533
- £ A £2 C 80p OAP and students £1.60 Fam £5 Season ticket £5
- O Apl-Oct Mon-Sat 10.30-17.00 cl 16th July June-Sept Sun & BH Weekends 14.00-17.00
- C Yes, hands on in Childhood Gallery, feely box, replica toys
- T Yes
- D Yes, wheelchair access to ground floor and garden
- • A friendly local museum, bigger than it looks, with a wonderful garden. Victorian kitchen and Ironmonger's Shop. Georgian Parlour, Rural Life Gallery and Archaeology. New Childhood Gallery.

COUNTY DURHAM

BISHOP AUKLAND

The Weardale Museum of High House Chapel

Ireshopeburn, Bishop Auckland DL13 1EY Tel 01388 537417

£   A £1 C 30p Child in school party 25p
O   May-July & Sept Wed-Sun 14.00-17.00, daily during Aug
P   200 metres away at the Ranch Inn
C   Hands on facilities
R   At the Ranch Inn
T   Yes
D   Very limited access
•   Displays of local landscape, rocks and minerals. Kitchen reflects the domestic life of a working Weardale family around 1890. The Wesley Room tells the story of John Wesley, founder of Methodism.

DARLINGTON

Darlington Museum

Tubwell Row, Darlington DL1 1PD Tel 01325 463795

£   Free
O   Mon, Tue, Thur, Fri, Sat 10.00-13.00 14.00-16.30 Cl Xmas, Boxing & NY Days
    Gd Fri and May BH
P   Public car park Crown Street
C   Yes, some open exhibits, free worksheet
D   Wheelchair access ground floor only
•   A small friendly local museum with lots for the family. Rocks, fossils, birds, minerals, a giant's glove, polar bear. Souvenir and gift counter.

County Durham

DURHAM

Durham Cathedral Treasury
Durham DH1 3EQ Tel 0191 384 4854
£   A £1 C 20p OAP 80p
O   Mon-Sat 10.00-16.30. Sun 14.30-16.30.
P   Parking at Freeman's Place
C   Questionnaire
R   Yes
T   Yes
D   Yes
•   Relics-vestments, coffin, cross and comb associated with St Cuthbert of Holy Island (died 687 A.D). together with pre-conquest and medieval manuscripts.

Museum of Archaeology
The Old Fulling Mill, The Banks, Durham DH1 3EB Tel 0191 374 3623
£   A 80p C 20p. Con 40p
O   Apl-Oct 11.00-16.00 Nov-March 12.30-15.00
P   Multi -storey car park in city centre
C   Activity sheets for different age groups. School groups catered for. Special childrens activity days at holiday times please telephone in advance to check days.
T   Yes
•   The museum is ideally placed to combine with a riverside walk or visit to the cathedral-only 5 minutes walk away.

Durham University Oriental Museum
Elvet Hill, Durham DH1 3TH Tel 0191 374 7911
£   A £1.50 Con. 75p Groups 50p
O   Mon-Fri 09.30-13.00 14.00-17.00 Sat-Sun 14.00-17.00 Cl Xmas-NY
P   Parking on site
C   Hands on facilities during teaching periods when schools visit
T   Yes
D   Wheelchair access to 25% of exhibits, no adapted toliet.
•   The Oriental Museum has fascinating displays of objects from Ancient Egypt, the Near East, Indian sub-continent, China and Japan. Also a regularly changing exhibition programme.

Durham Museum and Art Gallery
Aybley Heads Durham DH1 5TU Tel 0191 384 2214
£   A £1 Con 50p
O   Tue-Sat 10.00-17.00 Sun 14.00-17.00
P   Yes
C   Yes, please telephone for details
R   Drinks and biscuits
T   Yes
D   Yes
•   Continuously changing displays and exhibitions. Lunchtime concerts. Sat afternoon talks. Please phone for further details.

SHILDON

The Timothy Hackworth Victorian & Railway Museum
Soho Cottages, Hackworth Close, Shildon DL14 1PQ Tel: 01388 777999 (fax same)

£   A £1.50 C & OAP £1 Fam £4 School groups 80p
O   Gd Fri-last Sun in Oct
P   Free
C   Hands on and activity sheets
R   Tea, coffee, juice. Large grassed picnic area
T   Yes
D   Access to ground floor and one of engine sheds, toilet facilities
•   This museum is based in the home of the pioneer locomotive engineer, Timothy Hackworth. Displays and relics which cover railway and locomotive development with other facets of Victorian era including period rooms. Special event days, please telephone for details. Shop.

ESSEX

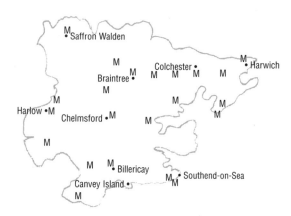

BILLERICAY

Barleylands Farm Museum and Visitor Centre
Barleylands Farm, Barleylands Road, Billericay CM11 2UD Tel 01268 282090
£   A £3. Cons £1.50. 10% discount for groups of over 10
O   Easter-Oct Mon-Sun 10.00-17.00 Oct-March Tue-Sun 10.00-17.00 Cl Xmas and Boxing Days
P   Yes plus disabled parking
C   Yes for pre-booked childrens groups
R   Tearooms and restaurant
T   Yes
D   Wheelchair access and disabled toilet. Wheelchairs available
•   Unique visitor centre comprising of farm museum with excellent collection. Animal centre, working crafts studio, glass blowing studio with viewing gallery.

BRAINTREE

Braintree District Museum
Manor Street, Braintree CM7 7YG tel 01376 325266
£   A £2 and £1 Con £1 and 50p children free during school holidays
O   Easter-Xmas Tue-Sat 10.00-17.00 Sun 14.00-17.00
P   100 metres
C   Yes
R   Vending machine for drinks
T   Yes plus disabled
D   Yes
•   The Gallery exhibits illustrate the districts national importance in the area of textiles and metal window design. Natural history gallery on the life and works of John Ray.

BRIGHTLINSEA

Brightlingsea Museum
1 Duke Street, Brightlingsea CO7 OEA Tel 01206 303185
£   A 50p. Con 25p
O   Mon- & Thur 14.00-17.00. Sat 10.00-16.00
P   In Duke Street
T   Opposite museum
• 60 years of senior education in Brightlingsea' and 'Roman Brighlingsea'

CANVEY ISLAND

Castle Point Transport Mueum
105 Pont Road, Canvey Island SS8 7TP Tel 01268 684272
£   Free, but charge for special open day in October
O   Apl-Oct Sun 10.00-17.00
P   Yes
T   Yes
• This historic 1930s' bus depot houses a collection of over 30 buses and commercial
  vehicles spanning the years 1929-1972 with origins from Maidstone-Glasgow. A
  working museum with vehicles in active restoration.

CHELMSFORD

The Chelmsford & Essex Museum and The Essex Regiment Museum
Oaklands Park, Moulsham Street, Chelmsford CM2 9AO Tel 01245 353066
£   Free
O   Mon-Sat. 10.00-17.00. Sun 14.00-17.00. Cl Gd Fri. Xmas & Boxing days
P   Car parking on left when entering the park
C   Yes plus special activity weeks
R   No but plenty in Moulsham Street
T   Yes plus disabled
D   Wheelchair access for ground floor only with ramp at back door
• Working beehive, story of Chelmsford archaeology and geology rooms, social history,
  costume, glass, ceramics, Victorian living room and kitchen. Craft showcase, exhibitions
  room, evening talks

COGGESHALL

Coggeshall Heritage Centre
St Peters Hall, Stoneham Street, Coggeshall Tel 01376 563003
£   Free, donation appreciated
O   Easter-mid Oct. Suns. BHs, Sats & Mons 14.15-16.45
P   Public car park nearby
R   Tearooms in Stoneham Street
T   Public toilets on Market Hill
D   Limited
• Different themes each year, emphasis on Coggashall's past as a wool town, seed
  growing, lace making, Coggeshall Abbey and fine buildings. Parties of 5+ and guided
  town walks by appointment.

COLCHESTER

Hollytrees Museum
Museum Resource Centre, 14 Ryegate Road, Colchester CO1 1YG. Tel 01206 282940
£   Free
O   Tue-Sat 10.00-12.00. 13.00-17.00
P   Central car park
T   Nearby
•   A Georgian town house featuring costume and toys -find out what your grandparents played with when they were children.

Mersea Island Museum
High Street, West Mersea, Colchester CO5 8QD Tel 01206 385191
£   A 50p. Con 25p
O   May-Sept. Wed-Sun & BH Mons 14.00-17.00.14.00-17.00.
P   Limited on site. Public car park nearby
C   Yes
T   Yes
D   Wheelchair access
•   Small independent museum illustrating local history and wildlife. Full scale replica of weather-boarded fiisherman's cottage with kitchen interior. Gun punt as used for wildfowling. Temporary exhibitions.

Natural History Museum
All Saints Church, High Street, Colchester
£   Free
O   Tue-Sat. 10.00-13.00 14.00-17.00
P   In town centre
C   Yes
D   Wheelchair access but no adapted toilet.
•   With its many hands on displays and events this museum gives you an interesting perspective on the local natural environment from the Ice Age to the present day.

Tymperleys Clock Museum
Trinity Street, Colchester
£   Free
O   Apl-Oct. Tue-Sat. 10.00-13.00 14.00-17.00
P   In town centre
•   Enjoy the architectural splendour of the 15th century timber framed house, home to a fine collection of Colchester made clocks.

DAGGENHAM

Valence House
Becontree Avenue, Dagenham RM8 3HT Tel 0181 595 8404
£   Free
O   Mon-Fri 09.30-13.00 14.00-16.30. Sat 10.00-16.00.
P   Yes
C   Yes
R   Cafe open Saturdays only
T   Yes plus disabled and baby changing facilities

D   Wheelchair access to ground floor only
•   17th century manor house showing local history collection and fine portraits of the Fanshawe family. Herb garden and moat in the grounds.

DUNMOW

John Webb's Windmill
Mill Row, Thaxted, Nr Dunmow
£   A 50p. C 25p
O   May-Sept. weekends & BHs 14.00-18.00.
P   Public car park in town
T   Nearest in town
•   The Mill consists of five floors and the bulk of the machinery is intact. On two floors there is a museum of rural and domestic bygones. Picnic area.

EARLS COLNE

Rebel Air Museum
Earls Colne Airfield, Earls Colne SS3 OHB Tel 01702 217288
£   A £1.50. Con 75p
O   Easter-Oct, weekends & BHs 10.00-18.00
P   Yes
C   Yes
T   Nearby
D   Access but no toilet facilities
•   A more personal collection of aviation history; many items show the human side of the 1939-45 war as it went on around the Essex war time airfields.

EPPING

North Weald Airfield Museum
Ad Astra House, Hurricane Way, North Weald Airfield, Epping CM16 6AA Tel 01992 560 690
£   A £1. Con 50p
O   Weekends & BHs 12.00-16.00
P   Yes
T   Yes
D   Limited
•   Displaying the history of RAF North Weald from 1916 to the present with photographs and models.

GREAT BARDFIELD

The Cottage Museum
Dunmow Road, Great Bardfield, Tel 01371 810689
£   Free
O   Easter-Sept, Sat. Sun & BHs 14.00-18.00
P   Parking in road next to museum
•   The cottage museum houses the Historical Society's collection of local domestic and agricultural artefacts in the setting of two roomed 17th century thatched home. Elsewhere in the village the society also runs a Victorian lock-up known as 'The Cage'

The East Anglian Gallery
Crown Street, Great Bardfield
£   Free
O   Sun 14.00-17.30 during exhibitions (please phone for details)
R   Wine is served on private view days
T   Yes
D   Wheelchair access
- The gallery houses works of art donated to the village by Edward Bawden, Eric Ravilious, Shiela Robinson and John Aldridge.

HARLOW

Mark Hall Cycle Museum & Gardens
Muskham Road, Harlow CM20 2LF Tel 01279 439680
£   A £1.50. Con 75p.
O   Tue. Wed 10.00-16.30. 1st & 3rd Sun each month 11.00-16.00
P   Yes
C   Yes
T   Yes
D   Yes
- Cycles and accessories illustrating the history of the bicycle from 1818 to the 1980s.

HARWICH

Harwich Lifeboat Museum
Timberfields, Wellington Road, Harwich
£   A 50p Child free if accompanied
P   Yes adjacent
- Contains 37ft lifeboat with opportunity to go on board. Plus full history of lifeboats in Harwich.

Harwich Maritime Museum
Harbour Crescent, Harwich
£   A 50p Child free if accompanied
O   May-Aug, daily 10.00-17.00
P   Yes
- Displays on Royal and Merchant Navy housed in a disused lighthouse with fine views of shipping movements within harbour.

Harwich Redoubt Fort
Rear of 29 Main Road, Harwich
£   A £1 Child free if accompanied
O   May-Aug 10.00-17.00. Sept-Apl. Suns 10.00-12.00. 14.00-17.00.
P   Parking in Harbour Crescent 200 metres
R   Light drinks
- 200 foot diameter circular fort built 1810. 10 guns on battlements. WW1 and WW2 memorabilia displays.

Harwich Maritime Museum
Harwich Green, Harwich Tel 01255 507594
£   A 50p child free if accompanied

O   May-Sept, daily 10.00-17.00
P   Park in street or nearest public car park 150 metres
R   Cafe 50 metres
T   Yes
D   Access to ground floor only
•   Ground floor displays naval history of Harwich and HMS Ganges. Middle floor - Merchant Navy Top floor has observation dome with marvellous 360' viewing. Outside gallery walkway.

The National Vintage Wireless and Television Museum

The High Lighhtouse, West Street, Harwich CO12 3DQ Tel 01206 322606
£   A £1. Con 50p.
O   Gd Fri-Sept, daily 12.30-16.30
P   Park on road outside
C   Yes
T   Yes
•   Housed in 90ft lighthouse, the museum traces the history of broadcasting from Marconi and Baird's early experiments to the present day. Large collection of vintage equipment and radio Caroline exhibition

KELVEDON

Kelvedon Museum

Old School, Maldon Road, Kelvedon Tel 01376 570307
£   Free
O   Mar-Oct. Mon 14.00-17.00. Sat 9.30-12.30. Cl BHs.
P   Yes
D   Yes
•   The museum relates the manorial history of Kelvedon and Feering. The main exhibits contain mostly domestic, horticultural and agricultural bygones.

MALDON

Maldon District Museum Association

The Promenade Lodge, 47 Mill Road, Maldon CM9 5HX Tel 016231 842688
£   A 50p. Con 25p.
O   Mar-Nov. Wed 14.00-16.00. Sat 10.00-16.00. Sun & BHs 11.00-16.00
P   Car park adjacent
C   Yes
R   Nearby
T   Nearby
D   Ground floor access. Toilet nearby.

MANNINGTREE

Manningtree & District Local History Museum

The Public Library, High Street, Manningtree CO11 1AD
£   Free, donations appreciated
O   Fri. 10.00-12.00. 14.00-16.00. Sat 10.00-12.00
P   Parking at Co-op Superstore
C   Low level childrens displays

R   Available in High Street
T   Adjacent.
D   Wheelchair access. Toilet
•   Miscellany of photographs and objects relating to local sports, trade and industry, domestic life etc. Thematic exhibitions.

SAFFRON WALDON

Saffron Waldon Museum
Museum Street, Saffron Waldon CB10 1BJ Tel 01799 510333
£   A £1. C Free. Con 50p.
O   Mar-Oct. Mon-Sat 10.00-17.00. Sun 14.30-16.30. Nov-Feb. Mon-Sat 10.00-16.00. Sun 14.30-16.30
P   Yes
C   Yes
T   Yes including disabled facilities and baby changing room
D   Yes
•   The museum built in 1835, houses wide-ranging collections including archaeology, natural history, ancient Egyptians, ancient Greeks, costume, ceramics, ethnographic collections and local history. A family sized friendly museum.

SOUTHEND ON SEA

Central Museum
Victoria Avenue, Southend on Sea SS2 6EW Tel 01702 215130/215131
£   Free to museum but charge for planetarium
O   Mon-Sat 10.00-17.-00
P   At library, adjacent to museum
T   Yes
D   Access to ground floor only via ramp at side door. No adapted toilet
•   Displays of archaeology, natural, social and local history-telling the story of man in his environment within the south east area. There is also a programme of temporary exhibitions.

Southchurch Hall Museum
Southchurch Hall Park. Tel 01702 467671.
£   Free
O   Tue-Sat 10.00-13.00. 14.00-17.00
T   Yes
D   Access restricted to certain areas on ground floor
•   Moated late 13th century timber framed building with Tudor extensions. Rooms furnished in Medieval, Tudor and Victorian styles.

Prittlewell Priory
Priory Park Southend. Tel 01702 342878
£   Free but maybe charge to special exhibitions.
O   Tue-Sat 10.00-13.00. 14.00-17.00t plus Aug BH Sun and Mon
P   Yes
T   Yes, down 5 steps.
D   Wheel chair access to ground floor. No adapted toilet
•   12th Century Cluniac Priory set in a park. Contains displays of the Priory's history, Essex

wildlife, printing presses, plus a nationally important collection of radios and televisions.

Southend Pier Museum

Southend Pier, Western Esplanade, Southend on Sea SS1 2EL Tel 01702 611214

£   A 50p. Accompanied children u/12 free. Special rates for groups

O   May-Oct. Fri-Mon 11.00-17.00 (18.00 in school hols)

P   Parking available on sea front and top of Pier Hill Public car park close by

C   Various hands-on items

T   Nearby on pier

D   Access available with prior notice through adjacent playground

•   Major exhibits include pier rolling stock 1890-1949, pier signal box with operational signal levers, extensive illustrated informative displays of pier's history from 1830, sales kiosk, postcards, books, videos, souvenirs etc.

Southend Planetarium

Central Museum, Victoria Avenue, Southend SS2 6EW. Tel 01702 215131.

£   A £2.10. Con £1.55. Fam £5.75. Children under 5 not admitted to Planetarium. Group booking rates available.

O   Wed-Sat, performances 10.00a.m. 11.00a.m. 12noon. 2.00p.m. 3.00p.m. 4.00p.m.

P   Public parking next to library which is adjacent to museum.

T   Yes

D   Entry to museum only via ramp at side door. No wheelchair/disabled assess to Planetarium. No disabled toilet.

•   The projector provides a clear illusion of the night sky with stars and the milky way. Investigate the scale of space, the sun and myths and legends of the skies.

STANSTEAD

House on the Hill Toy Museum

Stanstead, CM24 8SP. Tel 01279 813237.

£   A £3. C £2.20. OAP/Student £2.60.

O   Cl mid Dec-mid Jan, otherwise open daily, summer 10.00-16.00. winter 10.00-15.00.

P   Yes

C   Hands-on, activity sheets

T   Yes

•   Largest privately owned toy museum in Europe covering 7000 sq.ft with 25,000 exhibits. Collectors shop within the museum which buys and sells old toys.

ST OSYTH

East Essex Aviation Soc & Museum

Martello Tower, Orchards Holiday Park, Point Clear, St Osyth CO16 8NG. Correspondence to Mrs E Barrell, 37 Brooklands Road, Brantham, Essex CO11 1RP.Tel) 01255 428028/01206 391012.

£   Free

O   Sun 10.00-14.00. Mon 19.00-22.00. Wed & Thur in Jun-Sep 10.00-14.00. Also BH weekends 10.00-16.00.

P   At pub next door.

C   Activity sheet as part of quide book.

R   At pub next door.

T   Access to toilets at holiday camp.

D   Due to nature of the tower wheelchair access to 2nd floor is not possible. Toilet at holiday camp.
*   We cover civil and military history from both world wars and our collection is housed in a historic Martello Tower - the only one open to the public in Essex.

UPMINSTER

Upminster Mill
St Mary's Lane, Upminster.
£   Free
O   Please phone 01708 772394 for open weekends
P   Yes
T   Yes
*   Smock windmill built in 1802 with guided tours.

Upminster Tithe Barn, Agricultural & Folk Museum
Hall Lane, Upminster (next to golf club).
£   Free
O   Please phone 01708 772394 for open weekends.
P   Yes
C   Questionnaire
T   Yes
D   Accessible for disabled
*   15th century barn.

WALTHAM ABBEY

Epping Forest District Museum
39-41 Sun Street, Waltham Abbey EN9 1EL. Tel 01992 716882.
£   Free during public opening hours but charge for events/tours at other times. Please phone for details.
O   All year, Fri-Mon 14.00-17.00. Tue 12.00-17.00. Groups by appt Wed & Thur.
P   Pay and display within 5 mins walk.
C   Victorian handling objects. Tudor dressing up and more hands on items in some of the temporary exhibitions.
R   Coffee sold in the shop.
T   Yes
D   Ramps to downstairs galleries, garden and shop. Toilet is wheelchair accessible. Stairs only to upstairs galleries.
*   Museum situated in two timber framed buildings dating from 1520 and 1760. Permanent displays represent the Tudors and Victorians. Temporary exhibitions range from historical subjects to contemporary arts and crafts.

WALTON-ON-THE-NAZE

Walton Maritime Museum
East Terrace, Walton on the Naze CO14 8PZ.
£   A 50p. Fam. £1.
O   July-Sep and BH weekends (ex Xmas & NY) 14.00-17.00.
P   Immediately outside on edge of beach.
C   GCSE curriculum interests - Nase cliffs and their erosion, fossils.

R   Kiosk on adjacent beach.

    Yes

D   Fully accessible to wheelchairs. Toilet.

•   Housed in the old lifeboat house, this collection reflects Walton's relationship with the sea, it's lifeboats, piers, steamers, mills, boating lake, backwaters, the Nase cliffs and their erosion etc.

GLOUCESTERSHIRE

Tewkesbury • M

M
• Moreton in Marsh

M
• Gloucester

M   M
• Cheltenham

M

M
• Cinderford

M

Cirencester •   M

M

M

BIBURY

Arlington Museum
Bibury GL7 5NL. Tel 01285.740368.
£   A £2. Con £1.40. Fam £5.
O   Daily 10.00-15.30 Cl Xmas
P   In village
C   Facilities available
R   Licensed restaurant & Millstream Terrace
T   Yes
D   Access to ground floor and tearoom
•   Current mill dates back to 17th century. Trace the history through pictures, photos and documents. Examples of milling and Victorian life. See 200yr old working machinery, etc.

BOURTON-ON-THE-WATER

Cotswold Motor Museum & Toy Collection
The Old Mill, Bourton on the Water. GL54 2BY. Tel 01451 821255.
£   A £1.60 C 80p .
O   Feb-Nov. daily 10.00-18.00.
P   In village.
C   Hands-on, questionnaire activity sheets
R   In village
T   In village.
D   Wheelchair access. Toilets nearby.
•   Home of BBC TV's character Brum, together with the beautiful cars and motor cycles, there is Britain's largest display of vintage advertising signs. Also toys and vintage caravans, all dressed to the period.

CHELTENHAM

The Bugatti Trust

Prescott Hill, Gotherington, Cheltenham GL52 4RD. Tel 01242 677201.

£   Free, donations welcomed.
O   Mon-Fri 10.30-15.30. Cl weekends & BHs but open Suns when there is a hill climb event at Prescott.
P   Yes
T   Yes, also for disabled.
•   Bugatti artefacts. Usually 2 cars on display. Many albums of photos. Basically a study centre for Bugatti enthusiasts. Curator here Thur & Fri.

Cheltenham Art Gallery & Museum

Clarence Street, Cheltenham GL50 3JT. Tel 01242 237431.

£   Free, donations welcome.
O   Mon-Sat 10.00-17.20 Cl BHs
P   Yes
C   Handling tables, activity sheets.
R   Yes
T   Yes, also baby changing facilities.
D   Fully accessible for wheelchair users; lift, ramps. Toilet.
•   World-renowned Arts and Crafts Movement collection inspired by Willliam Morris. Rare Chinese and English ceramics. 300 years of Dutch and British paintings. Cheltenham's social history. Exhibitions

Holst Birthplace Museum

4 Clarence Road, Cheltenham GL52 2AY. Tel 01242 524846.

£   A £1.50. Con 50p.
O   Tue-Sat 10.00-16.20. Cl BHs.
P   Portland Street, 2 mins walk.
C   Activity sheets.
T   Yes
D   Access difficult for ambulant disabled persons due to nature of building(stairs & steps).
•   Regency terrace house where the composer of 'The Planets' was born shows the 'upstairs-downstairs' way of life of Victorian and Edwardian times.

Pittville Pump Room Museum

Pittville Park, Cheltenham GL52 3JE. Tel 01242 523852.

£   A £1.50. Con 50p. Groups of 10= 50p.
O   May-Sep 10.00-16.30. Oct-Apl 11.00-16.00.
P   Yes
C   Quiz sheet, reproduction hats to try on (adults may also try!!)
R   Tea, coffee, soft drinks
T   Yes
D   Parking and toilet on ground floor but no wheelchair access to museum due to 43 steps.
•   'Gallery of Fashion' housed in library/reading room/billiard room of Grade 1 listed building, originally used for taking the spa waters-still available. Original costumes from 1760 to present day. Temporary exhibits.

CINDERFORD

Dean Heritage Centre
Camp Mill, Soudley, Cinderford, Forest of Dean GL14 2UB. 01594 822170.
£   A £2.95. Con £2.50. C £1.60. Fam £8.50.
O   Feb-Oct 10.00-18.00. (17.00 Feb. Mar. Oct).
P   Yes, also for coaches
C   Hands-on, museum trails and quizzes
R   Yes
T   Yes
D   Wheelchair ramp. Toilet. Info leaflet.
•   The Dean Heritage Centre tells the story of the unique Forest of Dean set in the heart of the forest with cafe, craft shops, picnic sites and adventure playground.

CIRENCESTER

Corinium Museum
Park Street, Cirencester GL7 2BX. Tel 01285 655611.
£   A £1.75. OAP & parties £1.50. Student £1. C 80p. Fam £4.30. Season tickets available.
O   Nov-Mar, Tue-Sat 10.00-17.00. Sun 14.00-17.00. Apl-Oct, Mon-Sat 10.00-17.00. Sun 14.00-17.00.
P   Public parking nearby in centre of Cirencester.
C   Quiz sheets. Magnetic mosaic pieces and Roman pottery to handle. Activities arranged throughout the year.
R   Black Jack Coffee House adjacent.
T   Yes
D   Wheelchair access throughout.
•   Splendid displays of Roman mosaics and reconstructions of Roman life in Cirencester. Also displays on medieval life through to Civil war in the Cotswolds. Events programme available on request.

GLOUCESTER

Gloucester Folk Museum
99-103 Westgate Street, Gloucester GL1 2PG. Tel 01452 526467.
£   Free
O   Mon-Sat, 10.00-17.00. Also Suns July-Sep 10.00-16.00.
P   NCPs nearby.
C   Various quiz/activity sheets, hands on facilities, talks on toys and games with prior arrangement. Holiday activities and events organised.
R   Nearby in Westgate Street.
T   Yes
D   Wheelchair access to ground floor only, ramps provided.
•   Fine Tudor timber-framed buildings wheelwright, carpenter and ironmongers shops. Family museum with something for everyone, from 15th century to present day. Regular exhibitions, activities, events and demos, please phone for details.

Gloucester Transport Museum
The Old Fire Station, Bearland, Gloucester. Tel 01452 526467(branch of Glos Folk Museum)
£   Free
O   Exhibits are on permanent public display and can be viewed from outside at any time.

P NCP nearby.

C Exhibitions and events with a transport theme are held from time to time at the Folk Museum.

R Cafes nearby.

• Transport collection housed in former fire station, includes horse-drawn fire engine, horse-drawn tram, vintage motor cycles, baby carriages, various cycles.

The Robert Opie Collection at the Museum of Advertising & Packaging

The Albert Warehouse, Gloucester Docks. GL1 2EH. Tel 01452 302309.

£ A £2.95. Con £1.95. C 95p. Fam £6.95. Party rates for 10+

O Mar-Sep, daily 10.00-18.00. Oct-Feb, Tue-Sun 10.00-17.00. Open BHs except Xmas & Boxing Days. Groups on winter Mons by arrangement.

P Pay and display.

C Free worksheets, hands-on etc.

R Light refreshments.

T Close-by on docks site.

D Museum is on ground floor, can open fire door if necessary. Toilet on docks site.

• Looking through at shop window from the 1800's to present day.

LYDNEY

Dean Forest Railway Museum

Dean Forest Railway, Norchard Steam Centre, Forest Road, Lydney GL15 4ET. Tel. 01594 845840/843423 for talking timetable.

£ Admission to museum free but Dean Forest Railway make a charge when trains are running.

O Jan-Easter Wed. Sat & Suns, then daily 10.30-17.00.

P Adjacent to steam centre.

R Cafe open only on days when trains are running.

T Yes

D Wheelchair access to museum, shop and toilet and on trains by prior arrangement.

• Museum contains artefacts from former Severn and Wye railway, the 4 pre-nationalisation companies and British Rail. The railway operates train rides on dates as advertised(or please phone for details). Gift shop.

Lydney Park Museums

Lydney Park House, Old Park, Lydney GL15 6BV. Tel 01594 842844.

£ £2.20 Sun & BHs. £1.20 Wed. Accompanied children free. Includes car park, entrance to gardens, Roman temple site and museums. School party rates negotiable.

O Easter Sun-early June. Sun, BHs & Wed 10.00-18.00.

P Yes also for coaches when parties are booked in advance.

R On open days

T Yes

D Museum entrance not suitable. Gardens and refreshments possible.

• The Roman and N.2 museums are open to the public on open days. Parties of 25+ may be booked in advance during period Mar-July(for museums and temple site only from mid June-July).

Gloucestershire

MORTON-IN-MARSH

Wellington Aviation Museum,
Morton in Marsh, GL56 0BG. 01608 650323.
£   A £1. Under 10's 50p.
O   Daily 10.00-12.30. 14.00-17.30.
P   Yes
T   Yes
D   Wheelchair facilities around museum only.
•   Wellington and other aircraft artefacts, strong collection of R.A.F. Morton in Marsh 1941-1959 and also village information coupled with general R.A.F. items.

NORTHLEACH

Cotswold Countryside Collection
The Fosseway, Northleach GL54 3JH. Tel 01451 860715.
£   A £1.60. Con £1.40. C 80p Fam £4. Season tickets available.
O   Easter-Nov, Mon-Sat 10.00-17.00. Sun 14.00-17.00, except BH Sun, 10.00-17.00. Nov-Xmas, open Sats, please phone for times.
P   Yes
C   Activities available, please ask for further info.
R   Yes
T   Yes
D   Wheelchair access to ground floor/outdoor displays and cafe. Toilet.
•   Housed in an 18th century prison the museum shows the rural crafts and life of the Cotswolds. Displays on social progress in a rural community reflecting the advanced ideas of prison reform of the age.

STROUD

Oakridge Museum
c/o D E Battison, Hilcrest, Oakridge Lynch, Stroud GL6 7NR. Tel 01285 760490.
£   Donation
O   Apl-Oct, last Sat in month or at other times by telephoned appt.
P   At village hall, 75 metres.
C   Hands-on. Activity sheet available.
T   Yes
D   Access is up stairs.
•   Local arts and crafts movement, William Simmonds, Village history/events/memorabilia. Photos/records.

TETBURY

Tetbury Police Museum
Old Court House, 63 Long Street, Tetbury GL8 8HX. Tel 01666 503552.
£   Free, donations welcome.
O   Easter-Oct, 09.45-16.15.
P   Public car parks in town.
T   In town
•   Uniforms and various artefacts from Gloucester police force housed in the old police cells.

TEWKESBURY

Tewkesbury Museum
64 Barton Street, Tewkesbury GL20 5PPX. Tel 01684 292185.
£   A 50p. Con 25p. School parties free.
O   Daily, Mar-Oct.
P   Public parking nearby also street parking with spaces for disabled.
C   Limited material but special arrangements are made for school parties.
R   Available nearby.
D   Access poor as museum is in 14th century building.
•   Displays of local materials, collection of woodworking tools and scale model fairground.

WINCHCOMBE

Winchcombe Fold & Police Museum
Town Hall, High Street, Winchcombe GL54 5LJ. Tel 01242 602925.
£   A 80p. OAP 60p. C & students 40p. Fam £2.
O   Apl-Oct, Mon-Sat 10.00-17.00.
P   Within 5 mins walk.
C   Questionnaires, activity sheets.
R   Cafes within 2 mins walk.
T   Yes
D   Wheelchair access not possible as museum is upstairs in old Town Hall.
•   The story of British police including collection of uniforms and equipment. History of Winchcombe from Neolithic times to present day. Shop. Picnic area.

WOTTON-UNDER-EDGE

Wotton-under-Edge Heritage Centre
The Chipping, Wotton-under-Edge GL12 7NR. Tel 01453 521541.
£   Free. Use of research room £1 per day.
O   Tue-Sat, 10.00-13.00. 14.00-17.00 (16.00 in winter).
P   Adjacent.
C   Some hands-on exhibits. Quizzes.
R   Available nearby.
T   Yes
D   Wheelchair access. Toilet.
•   Displays illustrate local life and history, local and family history research resources. Tourist info point. Small shop.

HAMPSHIRE

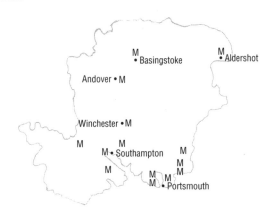

ALDERSHOT

Aldershot Military Museum
Queens Avenue, Aldershot GU11 2LG Tel 01252 314598
£   A £2 Con £1
O   Please phone for opening times
P   Yes
C   Question sheets
R   Canned drinks
T   Yes
D   Wheelchair access to museum
•   History of the 'Home of British Army' as well as Farnborough birthplace of British Aviation. Large vehicle gallery showing Chieftan tank, jeeps and artillery items.

Queen Alexandra's Royal Army Nursing Corps (QARANC) Museum
Keogh Barracks, Ash Vale, Aldershot GU12 5RQ Tel 01252 34029/340320
£   Free
O   All year except BHs, Mon-Fri 09.00-15.30 Groups by arrangement
P   50 metres away
C   Questionnaires
R   Restaurant nearby
T   Yes
D   Full facilities incl toilets
•   The museum tells the story of the Army Medical Services from 1660 to present day, includes ambulances and a hospital train ward coach.

ANDOVER

Andover Museum

6 Church Close, Andover SP10 1DP Tel 01264 366283

£   Free

O   Tue-Sat 10.00-17.00

P   Yes

C   Hands on for pre-booked school parties

R   Coffee shop

T   Yes

D   Ramps available. Stair lift to first floor

•   The museum features include natural history and aquarium, local archaeology, religion and superstition. Victorian Andover incl workhouse scandal and displays up to 1960s.

Museum of the Iron Age

6 Church Close, Andover SP10 1DP Tel 01264 366283

£   A £1.50 Con 75p Fam £4 Pre-booked school parties free

O   Tue-Sat 10.00-17.00

P   Yes

C   School work sheet may be bought

R   Coffee shop

T   Yes

D   Ramp to front door. No wheelchair access to first floor

•   Displays give a vivid impression of what life was like for our prehistoric ancestors who farmed, fought, worshipped and died in Wessex, 70 generations ago.

BASINGSTOKE

Willis Museum

Basingstoke RG21 7QD Tel 01256 465902

£   Free

O   Mon-Fri 10.00-17.00 Sat 10.00-16.00 Cl BHs

P   Nearby in town centre

C   Hands on, activity sheets, questionnaires

R   Yes, home made cakes and biscuits

T   In adjacent building

D   Wheelchair access. Lift

•   First floor displays shows Basingstoke history incl archaeology of local sites. Interactives for people to participate in. Temporary exhibitions. Second floor exhibits maps and horology.

EASTLEIGH

Eastleigh Museum,

25 High Street, Eastleigh SO50 5LF Tel 01703 643026

£   Free

O   Tue-Fri 10.00-17.00 Sat 10.00-16.00

P   Nearby at Swan Centre

C   Hands on facilities provided on request. Quizzes and activity sheets provided from time to time

T   Nearby at Swan Centre

D   Wheelchair access. Toilet
- Displays and videos showing history and growth of Eastleigh with emphasis on local and social history based around life in the 1930s with diramic displays. Temporary exhibitions in rear art gallery. Local interest exhibitions.

EMSWORTH

Emsworth Museum
10b North Street, Emsworth PO10 7DD. Correspondence to Secretary, 24 Hollybank Lane, Emsworth PO10 7UE Tel 01243 373780
£   25p Under 16s free if accompanied
O   Easter Sat-Oct Sat & BHs 10.30-16.30 Sun 14.30-16.30 Fri in Aug 10.30-16.30
P   Yes
C   Competition for children with prize for spotting objects specially hidden amongst exhibits
- Much admired local history museum staffed entirely by volunteers. Packed with exhibits, some nautical incl model of famous Emsworth ship 'Echo'. Special exhibition on P G Woodhouse who lived locally for ten years.

GOSPORT

Gosport Museum
Walpole Road, Gosport PO12 1NS Tel 01705 588035
£   Free
O   May-Sept Tue-Sat 10.00-17.00 Sun 13.00-17.00
P   Nearby
C   Activity sheets
R   Coffee shop
D   Full access for wheelchairs. Audio tape guide for blind persons. No toilet
- Collection features history of Gosport incl geology and local history.

FAREHAM

Westbury Manor Museum
84 West Street, Fareham PO16 0JJ Tel 01329 824895
£   Free
O   Mon-Fri 10.00-17.00 Sat 10.00-16.00
P   Nearby
C   Activities for local children during some school holidays
R   Small coffee lounge overlooking Victorian style Garden
T   Yes
D   Wheelchair access to ground floor only (listed building difficulties) Toilet
- Westbury Manor Museum is a small community museum which serves the borough of Fareham. Its displays tell the story of the borough using a range of display techniques.

HAVANT

Havant Museum
56 East Street, Havant PO6 1BS Tel 01705 451155
£   Free
O   Tue-Sat 10.00-17.00

P   Short stay adjacent
R   In adjoining arts centre complex
T   In adjoining arts centre complex
D   Two dedicated parking spaces. Wheelchair access to all ground floor displays incl temporary exhibition gallery

LYNDHURST

New Forest Museum

High Street, Lyndhurst SO43 7NY Tel 01703 282269
£   A £2.50 OAP £2 C £1.50 Fam £6.50
O   Daily Apl-Oct 10.00-18.00 Nov-Mar 10.00-17.00 cl Xmas day
P   Adjacent
T   Adjacent
D   Full access
•   Museum is situated in the main car park in Lyndhurst. Using a multi projector audio visual show and exhibition it tells the story of the New Forest, its history, characters, traditions and wildlife.

PETERSFIELD

The Bear Museum

38 Dragon Street, Petersfield GU31 4JY Tel 01730 265108
£   Free
O   Tue-Sat 10.00-17.00
P   Nearby in town centre
C   Hands on teddy bear trail, teddy bears picnic
R   Nearby, in town
T   In emergency
D   Regret no access for wheelchairs as 16th century building on different levels
•   The world's first teddy bear museum founded in 1984 by Judy Sparrow. Bears dating from 1905 to present day. Bears house and teddy bears picnic. Bring your own teddy and we will tell you something of its history.

PORTSMOUTH

City Museum & Records Office

Museum Road, Portsmouth PO1 2LJ Tel 0175 827261
£   Free
O   Daily 10.00-17.30 Cl 24th-26th Dec
P   Yes
C   Museum trail
R   Yes
T   Yes
D   Wheelchair access. Wheelchair available. Lift
•   Local history and decorative fine art. Room settings show life in Portsmouth from 17th Century using audio-visual techniques. 'Portsmouth at Play' exhibition shows leisure persuits from Victorian period to 1970s. Temporary exhibition gallery.

Royal Naval Museum

H M Naval Base, Portsmouth PO1 3NH Tel 01705 733060

£   A £3 OAP £2.50 C £2
O   Mar-Oct 10.00-17.00 Nov-Feb 10.00-16.30 Cl Xmas & Boxing days
P   In Queen /street outside Naval base, no parking allowed in naval base
C   Limited hands on facilities in 20th Century gallery. More available in 1999
R   On site in Heritage area
T   Yes
D   Certain areas closed whilst development being undertaken, which when completed will allow full wheelchair access.
•   800 years of naval history, incl the finest collection of Nelson commemorative items. A famous artefact, the Wyllie Panorama shows the Battle of Trafalgar. Also state barge of Charles 11 used to carry Nelson's body for his state funeral.

ROCKBOURNE

Rockbourne Roman Villa & Museum

Rockbourne SP6 3PG Tel 01725 518541

£   A £1.50 Con 75p Fam £4
O   Apl-June & Sep weekdays 12.00-18.00 Weekends & BHs 10.30-18.00 Jul & Aug daily 10.30-18.00
P   Yes, also for coaches
C   Yes
T   Yes
•   Outside exhibits of mosaic floors, bath suites and hypocaust etc. Museum shows artefacts found on site, way of life, food, education, bathing, religion and death.

SOUTHAMPTON

Foresters Heritage Trust

Ancient Order of Foresters, College Place, Southampton SO15 2FE Tel 01703 229665

£   Free
O   Mon-Fri
P   Some parking meters in front of office
C   Not really of interest to children
T   Yes
•   Collection illustrates the 160 year history of a mutual self-help friendly society. suitable for adults.

Museum of Archaeology

God's House Tower, Winkle Street, Southampton SO14 2NY Tel 01703 635904

£   Free
O   Tue-Fri 10.00-12.00 13.00-17.00 Sat 10.00-12.00 13.00-16.00 Sun 14.00-17.00
P   Meter parking on street nearby
C   Activity sheets
D   Two dedicated parking bays at entrance. No wheelchair access as exhibition areas are up 3 flights of stairs.
•   God's House Tower is part of the old town walls. Main exhibitions show what life was like in Roman, Saxon and Medieval Southampton.

Southampton City Art Gallery

North Guild, Civic Centre, Southampton SG14 7LP Tel 01703 632601

Free

Tue, Wed & Fri 10.00-17.00 Thur 10.00-20.00 Sat 10.00-16.00 Sun 14.00-17.00

Metered parking Mon-Sat and nearby multi-story in West Park Road

Sketching encouraged, stools provided in the gallery

Fountains Cafe located in foyer provides wide range of affordable foods.

Yes

Wheelchair access, lift and toilet

Collection spans six centuries of European art incl 17th Century Dutch landscapes and a particularly well presented British 20th Century collection of paintings, sculptures and installations.

Southampton Hall of Aviation

Albert Road South, Southampton SO14 3FR Tel 01703 635830

A £3 OAP £2 C over 5s £1.50 Part rates for 10+ on request

Tue-Sat 10.00-17.00 Sun 12.00-17.00 School Holiday Mons 10.00-17.00

Meters outside or Ocean Village

Sea Vixon cockpit

Yes

Lift to all floors. Toilets

History of Aviation in the Solent area and Hampshire, telling the story of 26 aircraft companies incl Supermarine where Spitfire was developed and built. Also story of Flying Boat operation which visitors may board and have conducted tour of flight deck.

Southampton Maritime Museum

The Wool House, Town Quay, Southampton SO14 2AR Tel 01703 223941

Free

Tue-Fri 10.00-13.00 14.00-17.00 Sat 10.00-13.00 14.00-16.00 Sun 14.00-17.00

Meter parking nearby

Maritime interactive exhibition

One dedicated parking space opposite museum. Wheelchair access to ground floor

Housed in the historic Wool House, the museum tells the story of Southampton docks from 1838 and the great ocean liners which sailed from the port.

Tudor House Museum & Garden

Bugle Street, Southampton SO14 2AD Tel 01703 332513

Free

Tue-Fri 10.00-12.00 13.00-17.00 Sat 10.00-12.00 13.00-16.00 Sun 14.00-17.00

On street meter parking

Hands on elements in exhibitions

Yes

One dedicated parking bay opposite museum. Wheelchair access to ground floor and garden. Toilet

The beautiful old house was built in 1495 and is now the social history museum with exhibitions of life in Tudor, Georgian and Victorian Southampton.

SOUTHSEA

Natural History Museum
Cumberland House, Eastern Parade, Southsea PO4 8RF Tel 01705 827261
£   A £1.60 C & Student £1.15 OAP £1.30 Fam £4.35 Apl-Sept
     A £1.60 C & Student 65p Child under 13 free OAP 80p fam £2.85 Oct-March
O   Apl-Oct 10.00-17.30 Nov-March 10.00-16.30
P   Street parking or public car park 600 metres
C   Yes
•   Containing wildlife dioramas and geology of the Portsmouth area, full siz
    reconstruction of dinosaur 'gaundon' and other fossil remains. Riverbank and freshwate
    aquarium. woodland and local marsh life.

WINCHESTER

The Gurka Museum
Penisula Barracks, Romsey Road, Winchester SO23 8TS Tel 01926 842832
£   A £1.50 C and OAP 75p group rates available
O   Tue-Sat 10.00 - 17.00 BHs 12.00-17.00
P   Yes
C   Yes plus Easter competitions, curry tasting in Oct
R   Confectionery and vending machines. Cafe ten minutes walk away
T   Yes
D   Yes and toilet facilities
•   Tableaux, dioramas, visual and video descriptions telling the story of the Ghurkas servic
    to the Crown and Nepal, all set in historic surroundings.

The King's Royal Hussars Museum
Peninsula Barracks, Romsey Road, Winchester SO23 8TS Tel 01962 828541
£   Free
O   All year Tue-Fri 10.00-16.00 Weekends and BHs 12.00-16.00 Cl 23 Dec-2 Jan
P   Yes
T   Yes
D   Yes and toilet facilities
•   Museum relates the history of three famous regiments including 'Charge of the Ligh
    Brigade', service in the Boer War, both World Wars and todays Army. also cupboard i
    which Trooper Fowler hid from the Germans for three years during WW1.

Light Infantry Museum
Peninsula Barracks, Romsey Road, Winchester SO23 8TS Tel 01962 828550
£   Free
O   Mon-Sat 10.00-16.30 Sun 12.00-16.00 Cl for 10 days over Xmas
P   Limited on site, public car park within easy reach of museum
C   Yes activity sheet
R   Vending machines
T   In adjoining museum
D   Yes plus toilet facilities
•   This museum shows glimpses of the distant past but concentrates on a moder
    regiment and more recent events. Fall of the Berlin Wall, Gulf War and Bosnia.

e Royal Green Jackets Museum

eninsula Barracks, Romsey Road, Winchester SO23 8TS Tel 01962 863846

A £2 C & OAP £1 Fam £6 Groups+ £1.25 each, H M Forces free

Mon-Sat 10.00-13.00 14.00-17.00 Sun 12.00-16.00 Cl for 14 days over Xmas

Yes free

By arrangement for school groups etc

Yes

Yes plus chair lifts

A Regimental museum telling the story of the regiment, covering five continents. Displays include a Waterloo diorama measuring 22' x 9' with a sound and light commentary.

e Royal Hampshire Regiment Museum And Memorial Garden

eale's House, Southgate Street, Winchester SO23 9EG Tel 01962 863658

Free, donations welcome

Nov-Easter Mon-Fri 10.12.30 14.00-16.00

Easter-Oct Mon-Fri 10.00-12.30 14.00-16.00 Weekends & BHs 12.00-16.00

Town centre car parks

Available for school parties only

Yes

Wheelchair access to most displays

Museum of Royal Hampshire Regiment from 1702 to 1992, when it amalgamated with Queens Regiment. Uniforms, medals, portraits and many other artefacts.

'inchester City Museum

ie Square, Winchester Tel 01926 848269

orrespondence to 75 Hyde Street, Winchester SO23 7DW

Free

Summer Mon-Sat 10.00-17.00 Sun 14.00-17.00 Winter Tue-Sat 10.00-17.00 Sun 14.00-17.00

10 minutes walk away

Hands on facilities

Access to ground floor

History of the city of Winchester and archaeology. New Roman gallery.

HEREFORDSHIRE

M •Kington M •Leominster
M •Weobley
M •Hereford
M •Ross-on-Wye

HEREFORD

Churchill House Museum
Venns Lane, Aylestone Hill, Hereford HR1 1DE. Tel 01432 267409
£ A £1. Con 40p.
O Oct-Mar, Tu-Sat, 14.00-17.00. Apl-Sep, Tu-Sun 14.00-17.00. Cl Mon except BHs
T Yes
D Wheelchair access to ground floor only.
• Victorian room settings, nursery, parlour, housekeepers room, kitchen.

Cider Museum
21 Ryelands Street, Hereford HR4 0LW. Tel 01432 354207.
£ A £2.20. Con £1.20. Group rates for 15+ available.
O Easter-Oct, daily 10.00-17.30. Nov-Easter, Mon-Sat 13.00-17.00. Will open outside these times for pre-booked parties.
P Yes, also for coaches.
C Quiz sheet.
T Yes
D Wheelchair access to ground floor.
• The cider museum, housed in a former cider works, explores the history of cidermaking since it's earliest origins through to mass production. Working distillery. Programme of events and tempory exhibitions.

Waterworks Museum
Broomy Hill, Hereford HR4 0AY. Tel 01342 361147.
£ A £2. Con £1.
O Open in steam every Easter, Spring & Aug BH Sun & Mon. Also last Sun in every month Apl-Sept and 2nd Sun in Jul.Aug.Sept. Private parties by arrangement.
P Yes
C Questionnaires,hand pumps etc.

R   Yes
I   Yes
D   Wheelchair access. Toilet.
•   Majestic water pumping engines in action. Discover the story of drinking water. Horse-drawn fire engine. 1895 Lancashire boiler. Picnic in the grounds or by the river Wye.

KINGTON

Kington Museum
Mill Stree, Kington HR5 3AL Tel contact 01544 231486
£   Free, Donation welcomed
D   Easter-Oct Mon, Wed & Fri 10.30-16.00 May-Sept Mon, Fri and Sat 10.30-16.00
P   Public car park opposite museum
T   Public toilets plus disabled 20 metres
D   Wheelchair access
•   Mixed collection of local items/history. Family history research (locally) a speciality. Guided town walk available Wednesday afternoons 14.30 May-Sept. Other times by arrangement.

LEOMINSTER

Leominster Folk Museum
Etnam Street, Leominster HR6 8AQ Tel 01568 615186
£   Free, Donations welcome
D   March-Oct Mon-Fri 10.30-17.00 Sat if staff available
P   Public car park near by
D   Limited to down stairs access only. No toilet
•   We are a small independent museum specialising in the local history of Leominster and surrounding area.

ROSS-ON-WYE

The Button Museum
13 Kyrle Street, Ross-on-Wye HR9 7DB Tel 01989 566089
£   A £1.50 Child Free if accompanied OAP and students £1.25
D   Apl-Oct daily 10.00-17.00 Cl Nov-March
P   Public car park near by
I   Yes
D   Wheelchair access but no toilet
•   A unique award winning museum displaying two hundred years of buttons from high fashion and everyday use to working clothes, uniforms and leisure pursuits. Something of interest for all the family.

WEOBLEY

Weobley Museum
Back Lane, Weobley HR4 8S9.
£   Free, donations welcome.
D   Easter/Apl,May,June, Mon & Wed 10.30-13.00. Jul.Aug.Sep, Mon-Thu10.30-13.00. BH weekends 14.30-17.00.
P   Small car park adjacent and ample parking in village.

C   Puzzle corner. Model building joints to dismantle and re-assemble.
R   In village
T   Adjacent to museum
D   Steps up to main room of museum but wheelchair access to lower room. Toilet adjacent
•   A small independent museum with local emphasis, concentrating mainly on our heritage
    of superb timber framed buildings; second room contains themed tableau incorporating
    costume and artefacts.

HERTFORDSHIRE

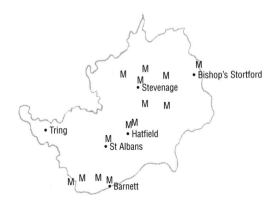

BARNET

Barnet Museum
31 Wood Street, Barnet EN3 4BE Tel 0181 440 8066
£   Free
O   Tue-Thur 14.30-16.30 Sat 10.00-12.00 14.30-16.30 Allyear Cl public hols
P   Public car parks and meter
C   Educational hand outs
T   Yes
•   Costumes, battle of Barnet display, photographic collection, domestic items and memorablilia of Barnet Life.

BISHOP'S STORTFORD

Bishop's Stortford Local History Museum
Cemetery Lodge, Apton Road, CM23 3SU
£   Free, Donations welcome
O   May-Sept every first Fri & Sat 14.00-17.00 of each month
P   Public car parks in town
T   Next door
•   The museum collection includes crafttools, bygones, archaeology, a Chemist's shop and the history of the construction of water pumps made in Bishop's Stortford.

Rhodes Memorial Museum
South Road, Bishop's Stortford CM23 3JG Tel 01279 651746
£   A £1, C Free if accompanied Con 50p
O   Tue-Sat 10.00-16.00 All year, check re opening if coming long distance
P   Yes
C   Quizzes
T   Yes

D   Access to Commonwealth Centre not museum. Toilets
- Birthplace of Cecil John Rhodes (1853-1902), founder of Rhodesia, Prime Minister c
Cape Province, Chairman of the British South Africa Company and Chairman of D
Beers. The museum records his life.

BROXBOURNE

Nazeing Glass Works

Nazeing New Road, Broxbourne EN10 6SW Tel 01992 464485
£   A £1 Con & OAP 75p 10+ 75p
P   Yes
R   Cafe 200 metres
T   Yes
D   Access to ground floor and toilet facilities
- The last surviving glass factory in South East England dating back to 1612. All glas
ware handmade, watch crafts and skills dating back to Ancient Egypt.

BUSHEY

Bushey Museum & Art Gallery

Rudolph Road, Bushey WD2 3DU Tel 0181 420 4057
£   Free
O   Thur-Sun 11.00-16.00 Tel re BH's
P   Small car park at museum, public car park at Kemp Place 100 metres
C   Some activity sheets. School parties catered for
T   Yes
D   Wheelchair access to ground floor via ramp
- Permanent displays on the history of Bushey plus changing exhibitions of fine art from
the Monro Circle and also the Herkomer school of art and its successors.

DATCHWORTH

Datchworth Museum

9 Datchworth Green, Datchworth SG3 6TL Tel 01438 813477
£   Free Donations welcome
O   3rd Sun each month. Also by private arrangement -private visits for small groups from
History Socs. etc
P   Parking on road or by arrangement with pub
C   Quiz
D   Access to one floor only
- Housed in Blacksmith's Shop which was last used in 1953, the leather bellows are stil
intact and form main feature of museum. The bulk of the collection donated by village
residents is from the earliest part of this century up to and including W.W.1.

HATFIELD

Mill Green Museum & Mill

Mill Green, Hatfield AL9 5PD. Tel 01707 271362.
£   Free
O   Tue-Fri 10.00-17.00. Sat. Sun. BHs 14.00-17.00. Milling takes place, subject to demand
on Tue. Wed. Sun.

᛫ Yes
᛫ Handling trays, quiz sheets.
᛫ Yes
᛫ Wheelchair access to museum and ground floor of mill. Toilet not wheelchair accessible.
᛫ This mill was in regular use until 1911, now fully restored and milling again in the traditional way. Local history museum for Welwyn is based in the Mill House, former home for generations of millers and their families.

HERTFORD

Hertford Museum
18 Bull Plain, Hertford SG14 1DT. Tel 01992 582686.
᛫ Free
᛫ Tue-Sat 10.00-17.00.
᛫ Multi-storey car parks within 5 mins walk.
᛫ Holiday activities.
᛫ Nearby in town.
᛫ Yes
᛫ Wheelchair access to ground floor and Jacobean garden. Toilets.
᛫ Local history museum in 17th century town house with attractive Jacobean knot garden. Varied programme of temporary exhibitions and holiday activities for children. Museum shop. Friendly welcome for all our visitors.

HITCHIN

Hitchin Museum & Art Gallery
Paynes Park, Hitchin SG5 1EQ. Tel 01462 434476.
᛫ Free
᛫ Mon-Sat 10.00-17.00. Sun 14.00-16.30.
᛫ Yes
᛫ Interactive activities.
᛫ One dedicated parking space. Ramp for wheelchair to front door.
᛫ Displays include social history of Hitchin, Victorian chemist shop and medicinal herb garden, 200 years of fashion plus a changing programme of special exhibitions.

LETCHWORTH

First Garden City Heritage Museum
296 Norton Way South, Letchworth SG6 1SU. Tel 01462 482710.
᛫ Free
᛫ Mon-Sat 10.00-17.00. Open BHs but closed Xmas & Boxing days.
᛫ Howard Hall car park, town centre car park off German Road.
᛫ 2 touch screen computers.
᛫ Yes
᛫ Parking by prior arrangement. Access to two-thirds of museum displays. No toilet facilities.
᛫ The development of the world's first garden city, Letchworth. Also regular special exhibitions and events relating to different aspects of the town's history. Talks and guided tours of town also provided.

Letchworth Museum & Art Gallery
Broadway, Letchworth SG6 3PF Tel 01462 685647
£ Free
O All year Mon-Sat 10.00-17.00 Cl Sun & BHs
P Pay & Display Car Park nearby
C Fun quiz during school hols, some exhibitions have 'hands on'. Frequent workshops
R Cafes in town centre
T Yes on upper floor
D Ground floor access only
• Attractive Gallery showing displays of local wildlife; extensive local archaeological collections, varied monthly changing exhibitions, regular programme of workshops. Well stocked shop-pocket money prices.

MUCH HADHAM

The Forge Museum & Victorian Cottage Garden
High Street, Much Hadham SG10 6BS. Tel 01279 843301. Out of opening hours please phone museum manager 01462 431133.
£ A 80p. Con 40p. Groups/school parties welcome by appt.
O Sat 11.00-17.00. Sun 12.00-17.00 (dusk in winter)
P Opposite at village hall.
C Hands-on facilities. Demonstrations by appt.
R Tea. coffee during summer months.
T Yes
D Wheelchair access difficult. Ideal 'smelly' garden for sight impaired.
• Victorian cottage garden and 19th century bee shelter. Varied collection of bygone tools. Exhibitions and craft demos. Working blacksmith operates most days exc Sun. Gift shop.

RICKMANSWORTH

Three Rivers Museum Trust
Basing House, Rickmansworth. Correspondence to Mrs J Thatcher, 202 High Street, Rickmansworth WD3 1BD. Tel 01923 446779.
£ Free, donation appreciated.
O Mon-Fri 14.00-16.00. Sat 10.00-16.00.
P 2 hour free park at Northway.
C Questions on local history welcomed.
T At Watersmeet.
D Two small steps to negotiate.
• Artefacts and photos from Three Rivers district incl archaeological finds, Victorian and WWII items, local booklets and view postcards for sale.

ST ALBANS

Museum of St Albans
Hatfield Road, St Albans. AL1 3RR. Tel 01727 819340.
£ Free
O Mon-Sat 10.00-17.00. Sun 14.00-17.00.
P Ye
T Yes

D   Access to ground floor.
•   Discover the fascinating story of this historic cathedral city, with lively displays and collections. Also the home of the Salaman Collection of trade and craft tools. Wildlife garden and picnic area. Shop.

St Albans Organ Museum
320 Camp Road, St Albans AL1 5PE. Tel 0171 851557/0171 869693.
£   A £2. C 60p. Fam £5.
O   Every Sun 14.00-16.30. Other times/party visits by arrangement.
P   Ample off and on -street parking.
R   Light refreshments
T   Yes
D   All on ground floor level with wide doors.
•   A playing collection incl mechanical dance organs by Mortier, DeCap and Bursens, music boxes, player pianos. Theatre pipe organs by Wurlitzer and Sporden-Rutt. Violano-Virtuoso mechanical violin and piano. Regular theatre pipe organ concerts.

Verulamium Museum
St Michaels Street, St Albans AL3 4SW. Tel 01727 819339.
£   A £2.60. Con £1.50. Fam £7.
O   Mon-Sat 10.00-17.30. Sun 14.00-17.30(last admission 17.00).
P   Yes
C   Hands-on discovery areas. Touch screen databases. Accessible collections. 'Touch the Past' sessions for schools.
T   In adjacent park.
D   Wheelchair access. Toilet in adjacent park.
•   Discover life and times of Roman St Albans. Recreated Roman rooms. Some of the best Roman mosaics and wall plasters outside the mediterranean. Shop.

STEVENAGE

Stevenage Museum
St George's Way, Stevenage SG1 1XX. Tel 01438 354292.
£   Free but charge for special events
O   Mon-Sat 10.00-17.00. Cl Sun & BHs.
P   In town centre.
C   Interactive exhibitions. Free colouring and quizzes.
T   Yes, also baby changing facility.
D   Wheelchair access, Toilet.
•   Discover the story of Stevenage through hands-on displays, videos and computer quizzes. For details of special exhibitions and events please phone for free 'whats on' leaflet.

TRING

The Walter Rothschild Zoological Museum
Akeman Street, Tring HP23 6AP. Tel 01442 824181.
£   A £2.50. Con £1.25. Fam £6.
O   Mon-Sat 10.00-17.00. Sun 14.00-17.00.
P   Yes
C   Activity sheets

T   Yes
D   Wheelchair access to ground floor only. Toilet nearby.
•   From whales to fleas, sharks to butterflies, over 4000 animal species on display in a unique Victorian setting. Picnic area.

WATFORD

Watford Museum
194 High St, Watford WD1 2HG Tel 01923 232297
£   Free
O   Mon-Sat 10.00-17.00
D   Disabled parking only, other parking in town centre
C   Yes
T   Yes including disabled
D   Yes
•   Local history, brewing, printing, WW 11, Earl of Essex, Victorian room setting, good art collection including Epstien sculptures. Changing temporary exhibitions.

WELWYN

Welwyn Roman Baths
Welwyn By Pass, Welwyn AL9 5PD Tel 01707 271362
£   A £1 C under 16 free
O   Thur-Sun 14.00-17.00 open BHs
P   Yes on site
C   Yes, quiz sheets, wordsearch etc
T   Public toilets in village
D   Wheelchair access to all the site. No toilet facilities
•   The remains of a third century AD bath house, the one visible feature of a villa complex, preserved in a specially constructed vault under the A1 (M)

ISLE OF WIGHT

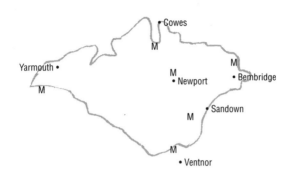

BEMBRIDGE

Bembridge Maritime Museum
Sherbourne Street, Bembridge PO35 5SB Tel 01983 872223/873125
£ A £2.25 C £1.35 OAP/Student £1.60 Family rates available
O Apl-Oct daily 10.00-17.00
P Limited on site, more parking available in village
C Worksheeets, 'hands on' limited owing to nature of exhibits
R Licensed restaurant opposite museum
T Public toilets 100 metres
D Limited to ground floor access only
• The museum is full of maritime relics spanning many centuries- pirate gold and silver, artefacts from local shipwrecks, audio-visual display of diving and lifeboat rescues, diving equipment and unique collection of model ships.

COWES

Cowes Maritime Museum
Beckford Road, Cowes PO31 7SG Tel 01983 293341
£ Free
O All year Mon,Tue-Wed, Fri 09.30-18.00 Sat 09.30-16.30
P On street parking or pay and display on St Mary's Street
C Children and adults can operarte the Norwegian patent foghorn, 'hands on' sessions by appointment
T Yes
D Wheelchair access to grounf floor, no disabled toilet facilities
• An attractive small museum displaying paintings, photographs, boats, models and other artefacts relating to the maritime history of Cowes; particularly its yachting and shipbuilding heritage. Included on display is Prince Philip's Flying Fifteen 'Coweslip'.

NEWPORT

Guildhall Museum
High Street, Newport PO30 1TY Tel 01983 823366
£   A £2 C £1 OAP £1.80 Family £5
O   Mon-Sat 10.00-16.00 Sun 11.00-16.00
P   Pay and display in Sea Street
C   Yes 'hands on', interactive databases, microscopes, quizzes and games
R   None on site but several near by
T   Yes
D   Yes full access, induction loop system, toilet facilities
•   An exciting new museum which looks at the Isle of Wight from the time of dinosaurs to present day; using the latest in 'touch screen' technology, hands on exhibits, videos, quizzes and games-this is an experience that should not be missed.

SANDOWN

Museum of Isle of Wight Geology
High Street, Sandown PO36 8AF Tel 01983 1404344
£   Free
O   All year Mon-Fri 09.30-17.30 Sat 0.9.30-16.30
P   On street parking
C   Worksheet 60p
•   Relates the geological story of the Isle of Wight - features the dinosaur and other fossil remains found on the island. Reconstructed life size dinosaurs.

VENTNOR

Ventnor Heritage Museum
11 Spring Hill, Ventnor PO30 1PE Tel 01983 855407
£   A 50p C and OAP 20p
O   Mid May-Oct Mon-Sat 10.00-12.30 14.00-16.00 Cl Wed & Sat pm
P   Public car park 100 metres
•   The museum theme-old postcards also items on shipwrecks, railways, 2nd World War. Extensive archives on history of town and surrounding area.

YARMOUTH

Maritime Heritage Exhibition
Fort Victoria., Westhill Lane, Norton, Yarmouth PO41 ORR Tel 01983 761214
£   A £1 C 50p OAP 75p Schools 20p
O   Easter-Sept 10.00-17.00
P   Free parking on site
C   Yes worksheets
R   None on site but cafe near by
T   Yes
D   Yes
•   An introduction to underwater archaeology, based on the Solent plus the history of Fort Victoria. 2D and 3D exhibits plus artefacts from shipwrecks.

KENT

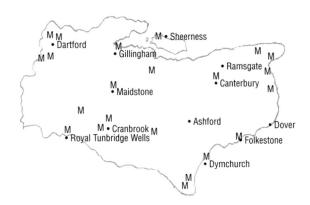

M M
• Dartford
M M

M
• Sheerness

M
• Gillingham

M
• Ramsgate M
M
• Canterbury

M

M
• Maidstone

M

M
M • Cranbrook M
M
• Royal Tunbridge Wells

• Ashford

• Dover
M Folkestone

M
• Dymchurch

M
M

BEXLEY

Hall Place

Bourne Road, Bexley DA5 1PQ Tel 01322 526574

£ Free
O Mon-Sat 10.00-17.00 (16.15 in winter) Sun 14.00-18.00 during Summer BHs 14.00-18.00 Cl Xmas & NY
P On site Free
C Sometimes available depends on current exhibition
R Yes
T Public toilets next to Cafe
D Access to ground floor only
• Historic house (c.1540) set in prize winning formal gardens. Houses local museum, art galleries and local studies library.

BROADSTAIRS

Crampton Tower Museum,

The Broadway, Broadstairs, CT10 2AB. Tel 01843 864446

£ A 80p. C 40p
O Gd Fri-early Oct, daily 14.30-17.00
P Rear of railway stn, 5 mins walk. Vere Rd, off High St. 10 mins walk
C Questionnaires for school parties only.
• Museum dedicated to the life of T R Crampton, a Victorian civil engineer, native of Broadstairs. Museum housed in Crampton Tower built 1859 as part of towns first waterworks. Original drawings and patents of Cramptons. Designs of locomotives and other items. Also mechanics workshop containing history of local transport.

Kent

Dickens House Museum
Victoria Parade, Broadstairs, CT10 1QS. Tel 01843 862853
£   A £1. C 50p
O   Apl-mid Oct, daily 14.00-17.00
P   Limited on road, 150 metres. Car park 500 metres
D   Limited access
*   The house, on main seafront, has been adapted to commemorate Charles Dickens association with Broadstairs and contains his own letters and personal belongings. Victoriana and costume.

CANTERBURY

Canterbury Heritage Museum
Stour Street, Canterbury CT1 2JE 01227 452747
£   A £1.90 C 95p Con £1.25 Fam £4.35 Groups of 10 - 10%
O   Mon-Sat All year 10.30-17.00 June-Oct Suns 13.30-17.00 Cl Gd Fri & Xmas week
P   Public parking nearby
C   Activity sheets
T   Public toilets nearby
D   Wheelchair access to ground floor
*   A fascinating time-walk of Canterbury's 2000 year story. From the building of the Roman town to the delights of the Rupert Bear Gallery. Housed in a magnificent medieval building.

Canterbury Royal Museum & Art Gallery
High Street, Canterbury, CT1 2JE. Tel 01227 452747
£   Free
O   All year, Mon-Sat. 10.00-17.00. Cl Gd Fri & Xmas week
P   Parking nearby
C   Activity sheets for some exhibitions
R   No
T   Public toilets nearby
D   No
*   Museum housed in Victorian building with decorative arts and picture collection incl the Cooper gallery, also the museum of Royal East Kent Regiment, the Buffs.

CRANBROOK

Cranbrook Museum
Carriers Road, Cranbrook TN17 3JX. Tel 01580 712368
£   A £1.50. C 50p. School parties half-price by arrangement.
O   Apl-Sep, Tue-Sat 14.00-16.30. Mar, Oct & Nov, Wed, Thur, Sat 14.00-16.30
P   Nearest car park in Jockey Lane
C   Not as yet
T   Yes
D   Wheelchair access to ground floor only but also to toilet and gardens.
*   15th century building housing display of exhibits and archives telling the story of this Wealden town through the centuries.

CRAYFORD

World of Silk

David Evans & Co. Bourne Road Ind Est, Bourne Road, Crayford, DA1 4BP Tel 01322 559401

£   Full guided tour(book in advance) A £2.50. C over 5 & con £2. Fam of 4 ticket £8.

O   All year except Sun & BHs

P   Yes

C   Plenty to touch and see

R   Light lunches with home-made cakes and wine

T   Yes

D   Ramps and toilets

•   Discover the hidden world of silk for yourselves.

DARTFORD

Dartford Borough Museum

Market Street, Dartford, DA1 1EU. Tel 01322 343555

£   Free

O   Open all year, weekdays except Weds 12.30-17.30. Sat 09.00-13.00 & 14.00-17.00

P   Short stay nearby

C   Actives are organised in conjunction with temporary exhibits

T   30 metres

•   Archaeological and historical objects from Dartford. Reconstruction of drapers shop with "cash railway" Regular exhibitions.

DYMCHURCH

New Hall Museum

New Hall Close, Dymchurch, TN29 0LD. Tel 01303 872142

£   Free but donations welcomed

O   Tue, Wed, Thur 14.15-16.15

P   Limited free parking

•   Exhibits pertaining to Romney Marsh housed in old court room and jury room

EDONBRIDGE

Haxters Mill Riverside Brassiere & Bar

Haxted Road, Edonbridge, TN8 6PU. Tel 01732 862914.

£   A £1. C 75p

O   Open Easter then weekdays only to 1st May, then open every day(except Mon) to end Sept

P   Yes

R   Full bar licence, Alfresco dining by millstream

T   For brassiere customers only

•   Unique combination of working watermill with museum of mill machinery and telling history and multiple uses of water power.

Kent

FAVERSHAM

Farming World
Nash Court, Boughton, Faversham ME13 9SW. Tel 01227 751144
£ A £2.50. C1.50. Con & Disabled £2.
O 1st Mar-1st Nov, daily 09.30-17.30
P Parking for 300 cars and 20 coaches
C Field and pond study area. Educational Packs, FUN.
R Tea room and fast food
T Yes
D Tarmac path around Open Farm, wheelchair access throughout. Toilets.
• The Open Farm is part of our rural heritage and houses small museum of agricultural memorabilia.

Fleur De Lis Heritage Centre
13 Preston Street, Faversham ME13 8NS Tel 01795 534542
£ A £1.50 C 50p OAP £1
O Apl-Sept Mon-Sun 10.00-16.00 Oct-March Mon-Sat 10.00-16.00
P Public car park 500 metres (40p an hour)
R None on site but cafes nearby
T In car park
D Ground floor accessible only as listed building
• Reconstruction of Barber's shop and post office, working telephone exchange, displays detailing the history of Faversham

FOLKESTONE

Folkestone Museum
2 Grace Hill, Folkestone, CT20 1HD. Tel 01303 850123
£ Free
O Mon-Sat 09.30-17.00
P Pay car park 2 mins walk
C Activity sheets
T Yes
D Stairs to 1st floor(being refurbished 1997 to allow full wheelchair access). No toilet.
• New displays being introduced to include interactive.

Kent Battle of Britain Museum
Aerodrome Road, Hawkinge, Nr Folkstone CT18 7AG
£ A £3 C £1.50 OAP £2.50 Group dis. available
P On site, free
R Drinks and snacks available from the shop
T Yes
D Wheelchair ramps to all buildings. No toilet facilities
• The Museum's original 1940 buildings situated on historic airfield contain the world's largest collection of authentic Battle of Britain relics and related memorabilia.

GILLINGHAM

Royal Engineers Museum

Prince Arthur Road, Gillingham, ME4 4UG. Tel 01634 406397.

£ A £3. Cons £1.50. Fam ticket £6.50. Group dis avail. Guided tours £4 per head.

O All year, Mon-Thur 10.11-17.00. Sat & Sun 11.30-17.00. Fri by appt only.

P Free parking for 60 cars

C Working models, questionnaires, children's guide

R Yes

T Yes

D Easy wheelchair access throughout. Disabled toilet suite.

• Work of Britain's soldier-engineers incl. bomb disposal, bridging, demolition's, diving, flying. Mulberry Harbour. Superb media display with 24 Victoria Crosses and regalia of Field Marshal Lord Kitchener.

LYDD

Lydd Town Museum

Old Fire Station, Queens Road, Lydd TN29. Correspondence to Friends of Lydd, 11 Seaview Road, Greatstone, New Romney TN28 8RH. Tel 01797 366566.

£ Free, donation appreciated

O Easter, May day & Sp BH weekend 14.30-17.00. Mid July-mid Sept, daily 14.30-17.00. Weekends in Sep & Oct 14.30-17.00.

P Yes. Coaches nearby.

C Hands-on and questionnaire.

T Nearby

• Various exhibits. Vehicles on show incl 1890 Merryweather fire engine, horse-drawn bus, landau, beach cart. Conducted tours of town on request, £1 per person.

MAIDSTONE

Maidstone Museum & Art Gallery

St Faith's Street, Maidstone. ME14 1NY. Tel 01622 754497.

£ Free

O Mon-Sat 10.00-.17.00. Sun 11.00-16.00

P Pay & display opposite

C Activities chest, variety of object for children to find/explore/play instruments/dress up.

R Yes

T Yes but no special facilities for disabled

D Wheelchair access to ground floor galleries

• Fine regional museum housed in Chillington Manor, boats a rich and impressive variety of historical objects, fine art and natural history.

MARGATE

East Kent Maritime Trust

Old Town Hall Museum, Market Place, Margate, CT9 1ER. Tel 01843 231213.

£ A £1. C & Cons 50p. Student 75p.

O Apl-Sep every day 10.00-17.00. Oct-Mar Mon-Fri 09.30-16.30.

P Car park 2 mins, also time zoned street parking

C Work Sheets

R   Nearby
T   Nearby
D   Restricted
•   Maritime museum. Exhibitions from May.

ORPINGTON

Bromley Museum
The Priory, Church Hill, Orpington BR6 0HH. Tel 01689 873826.
£   Free
O   Apl-Oct, Sun-Fri, 13.00-17.00. Sat 10.00-17.00. BHs 13.00-17.00. Nov-Mar, closed Sun & BHs.
P   Yes
C   Museum trail. Sometimes worksheets to go with temporary exhibitions.
T   In Priory gardens
D   Access to ground floor.
•   Housed in part of Medieval building. Archaeology and history of Bromley, ethnographic collection of Lord Avebury who gave us bank holidays. Temporary exhibitions.Tours by appointment.

RAMSGATE

Minster Agricultural & Rural Life Museum,
Bedlam Court Lane, Minster, Ramsgate, CT12 4HE. Tel 01843 823271.
£   A £2.50. Snr Citizens £1.50. C£1. Fam ticket £6.
O   Easter Sat-30 Sept.
P   Limited on site
C   Yes
R   Yes
T   Yes
D   Access to ground floor only.
•   Craft workshops, agricultural machinery, implements, rural life exhibits. Owls and birds of prey, fowl & animals. Pond walk & picnic area.

East Kent Maritime Trust, Maritime Museum
Pier Yard, Royal Harbour, Ramsgate CT11 8LS. Tel 01843 587765.
£   A £1.50. C/Cons 75p. Fam.ticket £4.
O   Apl-Sept every day 10.00-17.00. Oct-Mar Mon-Fri 9.30-16.30
P   Nearby plus time zoned street parking
C   Work sheets, hands-on especially on vessel (combined museum/steam tug admission fee)
R   Nearby
T   Nearby
D   Very restricted

Ramsgate Museum
Guildford Lawn, Ramsgate CT11 9AY. Tel 01843 593532.
£   Free
O   Mon-Thur 09.30-18.00. Fri 9.30-19.00. Sat 09.30-17.00.
D   Wheelchair access.
•   The museum tells the story of Ramsgate in days gone by with paintings and photos of

Royal Harbour, churches, breweries, shops, personalities, W.W.I and II and holiday souvenirs.

ROMNEY

Romney Toy & Model Museum

New Romney Station, New Romney, TN28 8PL. Tel 01797 362353.

£   A £1. C 50p (incl entry to platform on Romney, Hythe & Dimchurch Railway)
O   Weekends in Mar & Oct. Daily from Gd Fri till last Sun in Sept.
P   On site, 25p
R   Cafe on station
T   On station
D   Stairlift fitted. Toilets. Ramps to station areas.
•   Collection of toys and models and 2 large operating model railways.

Brenzett Aeronautical Museum Trust

Ivychurch Road, Brenzett, Romney Marsh, TN29 0EE. Tel 01797 344747

£   A £2. C 50p. Con £1.
O   Easter weekend, Sat & Sun till end of Oct. 11.00-17.30. Cl Xmas
P   Free
C   Hands-on under supervision
R   Nearby
T   Yes
D   Yes
•   Large new extension being constructed during 1997.

ROYAL TUNBRIDGE WELLS

Tunbridge Wells Museum & Art Gallery

Civic Centre, Mount Pleasant, Royal Tunbridge Wells,TN1 1JN Tel 01892 526121/547221

£   Free
O   Mon-Sat 09.30-17.00. Cl Sun, BHs & Easter Sat.
P   Nearby
D   Wheelchair access
•   Displays of local history, Tunbridge ware, dolls & toys, archaeology, agricultural & domestic bygones, natural history and exhibitions of art and craft

SANDWICH

The White Mill Folk Museum

The Causeway, Ash Road, Sandwich. Tel 013204 612076

£   A £1. C £ Con 50p
O   Easter Sun- mid Sept 14.30-17.00 Sun & BHs. Also Fri & Sun mornings through the year 10.00-12.30. Also open for special events.
C   Hands-on facilities for various sections and activity sheets
R   Gifts and ice-creams
T   Yes
D   Access to part of site and to all auxiliary buildings except windmill. Toilet available
•   The only windmill in Kent with entire mill complex complete also a working forge and wheelwrights. Furnished cottage for hands on bread making etc. Picnic area.

The Precinct Toy Collection

38 Harriet Street, Sandwich CT13 9ES. Tel 01304 8621114.

£   A £1. C under 14 & Cons 50p. C under 4 free.
O   Weekend before Easter till end Sept. Mon-Sat 10.30-16.30. Sun 14.00-16.30. Oct-2nd weekend in Dec. Sat & Sun 14.00-16.00
P   On quayside - rear of Guildhall - municipal 5 mins.
C   'Find the exhibit' question sheets
R   Cafes nearby
T   Yes
D   Wheelchair access. toilet on quayside
•   Toys from 1860's, furnished dolls house, Noah's Ark, teddies and much more. Dogs permitted if on a lead.

SEVENOAKS

Shoreham Aircraft Museum

13 High Street, Shoreham TN14 7TB Tel 01959 524416

£   £1. C Free
O   First Sun in May to last Sun in Sept 10.00-17.00
P   Yes
C   Fun sheets
R   Home-made cakes and teas.
T   Yes
D   regretfully only by special arrangement
•   Outstanding collection of memorabilia from Battle of Britain and air war over southern England W.W.II. flying helmets, uniforms and insignia. Exhibition of Home Front ephemera. Prints for sale.

SHEERNESS

Minster Abbey Gatehouse Museum

Union Road, Minster-in-Sheppey, Sheerness ME12 2HW. Tel 01795 872303

£   A 60p. C 5-15 30p. Con 50p. Reductions for pre-booked parties
O   Easter, May, Sp BH Sat & Sun June, Daily excl Thur mid July-Sept 14.00-17.00. Other time by appt
P   Next door, free
C   Old typewriters and adding machines. Ancient spiral staircase to (safe) flat roof, huge view. Crystal radio.
R   Takeaway in village, cafes on coast 1/2 mile away
T   Yes
D   Listed building on 4 levels therefore access restricted to ground floor, shop and toilet.
•   Mediaeval gatehouse, circa 1450. local fossils, early phones and radios, early 20th century toys and school items. Costumes. Unforgettable roof top view.

SITTINGBOURNE

Court Hall Museum

High Street, Milton Regis, Sittingbourne. Postal enquiries to Dr R Baxter, Tudor Cottage, Cellor Hill, Lynsted, Sittingbourne ME9 9QY. Tel 01795 5215151DY.

£   50p Con 20p. Group discounts
O   Apl-Sept Sats 14.00-17.00 Groups accepted at other times by appt.

P   Nearby
C   Interpretation panels. Viewable 'prisoner' in life-size cell
•   Museum housed in rare custom built half-timbered public building dating from 1450 AD. collection of manorial equipment and items of local history.

Dolphin Sailing Barge Museum
Crown Quay Lane, Sittingbourne ME10 3SN. Tel 01795 424132
£   A £1.50. C & Cons 75p
O   Easter - end Oct, Suns & BHs
P   Yes
R   nearby pub
T   Yes also for disabled
•   Shipwright's shop, sail loft and forge contain the story of the Thames Spritsail barge. Sailing barges in basin undergoing repair.

STAPLEHURST

Brattle Farm Museum
Staplehurst TN12 0HE. Tel 01580 891222.
£   A £1.50. Con £1.
O   Easter-Oct, Sun & BHs.09.30-18.30. Groups welcome by appointment.
P   Yes, also for coaches
C   Hands on with supervision
R   Tea, coffee or apple juice for groups
T   Yes
D   80% wheelchair access. Toilet
•   Vast collection incl vintage cars, bikes, engines, horse-drawn wagon and machinery. Blacksmiths, wheelwrights, dairy, laundry, kitchen and comestic bygones. Pair of working oxen.

TENTERDEN

Tenterden & District Museum
Station Road, Tenterden TN30 6HN Tel 01580 764310
£   A 75p. C 25p. Con 50p. Reduction for parties
O   Mar Sat & Sun 14.00-16.30 (or Easter) till end Oct daily exc Fri 14.00-16.45, also mornings late July & Aug.
P   Public car park adjacent
C   School parties catered for by arrangement
T   Nearby
D   Not easy for physically disabled
•   Displays covering 1,000 years of local history and exhibits relating to hop picking, farming, the Cinque Ports, the Weald and Victorian domestic life.

WHITSTABLE

Whitstable Museum & Gallery
Oxford Street, Whitstable CT5 1DB. Tel 01227 276998
£   Free
O   Mon, Tue Thur, Fri, Sat 10.30-13.00 14.00-16.00 Cl Wed, Sun Gd Fri and Easter week
P   Nearby

R   Cafes close by
T   2 mins walk
D   Full wheelchair access but no toilet on site
•   Lively museum exploring Whitstable's unique coastal community and seafaring traditions. Special features on oysters, diving, shipping and wrecks. Regularly changing special exhibitions.

Chuffa Trains Museum
82 High Street, Whitstable CT5 1AZ Tel 01227 277339
£   A £1.50. C 75p. Con £1. Fam ticket £3.75
O   Weekdays 10.00-15.00 (17.00 during school hols). Sats 10.00-17.30. Cl Weds Suns & BH Mons
P   Yes 70p all day
C   Activity area providing hands-on facilities
R   Cafes and fish shop nearby
T   Yes
•   Fascinating exhibition of railway artefacts, memorabilia, model trains. Recall nostalgic memories of steam trains and discover the history of Whitstable's 'Crab & Winkle Railway'

LANCASHIRE

Lancaster M M
M
Blackpool
M Preston M
M Burnley M M
M M M
M Blackburn
M
M
Bolton M
M Oldham
M M
M Manchester
Stockport

ASHTON-UNDER-LYNE

Museum of the Manchesters
Town Hall, Market Place, Ashton-under-Lyne OL6 7SF Tel 0161 342 3078
£   Free
O Mon-Sat 10.00-16.00
P Town centre parking
C Reconstructed WW1 trench with sounds and smells, oral history and worksheets
R Available nearby
T Yes
D Wheelchair access
• Reconstructed WW1 trench, Anderson shelter, V.C's, medals and uniforms, oral history
and archive film.

BLACKBURN

Blackburn Museum and Art Gallery
Museum Street, Blackburn BB1 7AJ. Tel 01254 667130
£   Free
O Tue-Fri 12.00-16.45. Sat 9.45-16.45 (please check as changes are possible)
P Town centre
C Activity sheets, occasional workshops
R Nearby in town centre
T Yes also for disabled
D Fully accessible
• Museum and art galley sited in grade II building. Displays include local history,
paintings, manuscripts, coins, rare books, icons, history of the East Lancs Regiment and
culture of western India and Pakistan. Displays of textile machinery.

BURNLEY

Burnley Museum
Towneley Hall, Art Gallery & Museums, Burnley. BB11 3RQ. Tel 01282 424213
£   Free. Guided tours £2 on Wed afternoons or booked in advance for groups
O   All year exc over Xmas-Fri 10.00-17.00. Sun 12.00-17.00
P   Nearby
C   Activities for schools, work sheets, play areas, discovery centre in natural history centre, hands-on computers
R   Yes
T   Yes
D   Toilets and rest room. Wheelchair access to ground floor through rear door. Access to natural history centre and museum of local crafts and industries.
•   Country house in beautiful grounds with separate museum of crafts and industries and natural history centre with aquarium and discovery centre. Exhibitions and displays. Summer demonstrations and activities(please phone for details)

The Weavers' Triangle Visitor Centre
85 Manchester Road, Burnley BB11 1JZ. Tel 01282 452403
£   Free, donations appreciated
O   Easter-Sept Sat-Wed 14.00-16.00 Oct-Suns
P   Adjacent inn car park or nearby public parking
C   Questionnaires
R   Yes
T   Yes
D   Access involves some steps. Level access to basement and canal towpath. Help given where necessary.
•   Museum in Wharfmaster's house and canal toll office at Burnley wharf. Cotton industry and canal displays. Weavers dwelling. Victorian parlour. Schoolroom. Working model fairground. Towpath walk through Victorian industrial area.

BURY

Bury Art Gallery & Museum
Moss Street, Bury BL9 0DR Tel 0161 2535878
£   Free
O   Tue-Sat 10.00-17.00
P   1 hr limited street parking. adjacent
C   Only available on request for school visits
T   Yes incl for disabled
D   Limited access for wheelchairs, ramp to library, goods lift to basement and 1st floors by arrangement
•   Home to the Wrigley collection of Victorian oil and water colour paintings incl works by Turner, Constable and Landseer. Lively programme of temporary exhibitions of contemporary art. Bury as it was in the 1950's. working model railway.

CARNFORTH

Wolf House Gallery
Gibralter, Silvergate, via Carnforth LA5 0TY. Tel 01524 701405
£   Free

O Summer, everyday exc Mon 10.30-13.00, 14.00-17.30. Winter, Sat & Sun only 10.30-17.30
P Yes
C Play area only
R Home made scones and biscuits. Teas and coffee. Log fire in winter
T Yes
D Some difficulty - we always can cope with individuals but difficult with large groups

CLITHEROE

Clitheroe Museum
Castle Hill, Clitheroe BB7 1BA Tel 01200 424635
£ A £1. C 25p. Con 50p
O Easter - end Sept 7 days. Feb, Mar, Oct, Nov, Dec, Sat-Wed. Cl Jan.
P Disabled parking at museum. Car parks in town.
C Activity sheets and full education room for school use
T Yes but none for disabled
D Wheelchair access to ground floor only.
• History and geology of the area with many features, clog shop, print shop, Edwardian kitchen, lead mine, well stocked gift shop. Please phone for details of special open days.

COLNE

The British in India Museum
Newtown Street, Colne BB8 0JJ. Tel 01282 613129/870215
£ A £2. C 50p
O Please phone for opening times
P Street parking
D Few steps to negotiate
• Fascinating collection of model soldiers, dioramas, postage stamps, picture postcards, paintings and uniforms

FLEETWOOD

Fleetwood Museum
Queen's Terrace, Fleetwood FY7 6BT. Tel 01253 876621
£ A £1.10. Con 55p. Fam £2.75
O Easter to end of Blackpool illuminations, Sat. Sun .Mon. Thur 14.00-17.00. Tue. Fri 11.00-17.00. Also Wed & Sat- July-Sept 11.00-17.00
P Free parking on road. Pay & display also available
C Hands-on displays. Work sheets and occasional quizzes for temporary exhibitions
R Cafes nearby
T Yes
D Difficult at present but lifts and ramps in plans for major extension
• Museum in former customs house and town hall. Displays on history of Fleetwood, inshore and deep sea fishing, salt mine tunnel, dolls house. Future extension will house reconstructed dock scene incl 2 historic boats

Lancashire

LANCASTER

King's Own Regimental Museum
Market Square, Lancaster LA1 1HT. Tel 01524 64637
£ Free
O Mon-Sat 10.00-17.00 Cl Xmas-NY
P Nearby in city centre
C No special facilities
R Nearby
T Nearby
D Ramp access to front of building

City Museum
Market Square, Lancaster LA1 1HT. Tel 01524 64637
£ Free
O Mon-Sat 10.00-17.00 Cl Xmas-NY
P Mitre House, 5 mins walk
C Various work sheets. Museum education officer
R Nearby in city centre
T Nearby in city centre
D Ramp access to ground floor. Further improvements in progress.
• History and archaeology of Lancaster and area.

Maritime Museum
Custom House, St George's Quay, Lancaster LA1 1RB. Tel 01524 64637.
£ A £2. Con £1. Lancaster residents free
O Easter-Oct daily 11.00-17.00 Nov-Easter 14.00-17.00 daily exc Xmas-NY (winter opening under review please telephone prior to visit)
C Hands-on displays incl full size reconstructions. Activity work sheets.
R Yes
T Yes also suitable for disabled
D Wheelchair access to virtually all the galleries, partly by lift.
• Waterfront museum occupying historic port buildings. Modern colourful displays incl reconstructions and a/v show dealing with 18th century slave trade, inshore fishing, Morcombe bay and Lancashire canal.

LYTHAM

Lifeboat Museum
East Beach, Lytham. Enquiries to 35 Ripon Road, Ansdell, Lytham FY8 4DS. Tel 01253 730155
£ Free, donations to RNLI appreciated
O End of May-end Sept, Sat. Sun. Tue. Thur 10.30-16.30. Also Weds in Jul, Aug 13.30-16.30.
P Pay & display 400 metres
C Lifeboat ride 20p. Life jackets to try on
T 40 metres away
D Wheelchair access good. Toilet 40 metres away
• Museum housed in original lifeboat house of 1860, shows history of Lytham and St Anns lifeboats since 1851 to present day with particular reference to wreck of 'Mexico' in 1886, the RNLI's worst disaster.

LEYLAND

South Ribble Museum & Exhibition Centre
The Old Grammar School, Leyland, PR5 1EJ. Tel 01772 422041
£ Free
O Tue 10.00-16.00. Thur 13.00-16.00. Fri 10.00-16.00. Sat 10.00-13.00. Cl Xmas - NY Easter Fri & Sat
P Small car park side of building, 200 metres to town car parks
• Timber framed Tudor Grammar School circa 1580. Local history displays (permanent) and monthly programme of exhibitions by local artists.

MANCHESTER

Museum of Transport
Boyle Street, Cheetham, Manchester M8 8UW. Tel 0161 2052122
£ A £2.50. Con £1.50. Fam £7
O All year, Wed, Sat, Sun & BHs 12.00-17.00
P On street
C Several buses open for inspection. Education packs available
R Yes
T Yes
D Full access and help available
• The museum tells the story of road public transport in Greater Manchester. From house bus to metrolink. Over 80 vehicles. Annual special events and rallies. Souvenir shop. Archives and small exhibits

The Pump House: People's History Museum
Left Bank, Bridge Street, Manchester 3ER. Tel 0161 8396061
£ A £1.00. Con Free. Free to everyone on Fridays
O All year Tue-Sun, 11.00-16.30. Cl Mon except BHs
P Gartside Street next to museum, metered parking on street
C Plenty of hands-on exhibits and activity sheets
R Licensed cafe/bar
T Yes
D Full access to all areas. Toilet.
• Discover the extraordinary story of ordinary people from Victorian cotton mill workers to professional footballers. Unique collection of colourful banners provides backdrop to the displays and reconstruction's.

Manchester Transport Museum
Middleton Road, Manchester. Tel. 0161 7401919. Enquires to Mr Runnett, 121 Park Road, Littlelever, Bolton. Lancs 01204 577349.
£ A 50p. Con. 20p. Fam £1.20. Multi-ride Fam £1. C 50p.
O Trams operate Suns & BHS Apl-Oct 12.00-17.00 Weds mid June July 10.30-15.00
P Heaton Park or Smithy Lodge
• Heaton Park vintage tramway. Displays of artefacts and photos showing development of tramcars in Manchester. Souvenir shop.

Greater Manchester Police Museum
Newton Street, Manchester M1 1ES. Tel.016 8563287.
£ Free

O   Tue 10.30-15.30. other weekdays by appointment
P   Nearby
C   Quiz sheets
D   Access to ground floor only. No toilet
•   Museum housed in the 1879 Newton Street Police Station containing the original charge office and station cells with Victorian beds and wooden 'pillows'. History of policing in Manchester region, forensic science, uniforms, equipment and transport. Extensive archive and photo collections ,viewed by prior arrangement

National Museum of Labour History
103 Princess Street, Manchester M1 6DD
£   £1.00 C and Con free (Friday - Free Admission)
O   All year Tue-Sun 11.00-16.30 Open BH Mons
P   None on site
C   Yes
R   Cafe
T   Yes
D   Access throughout the museum
•   Working class life and institutions. Banners, photographs, badges, ephemera, tools, regalia and paintings. Textile Conservation Studio. Labour Party and Communist Party Archives.

The Pankhurst Centre
60-62 Nelson Street, Manchester M13 9WP. Tel 0161 2735673.
£   Free
O   Mon-Fri 10.00-15.00. Cl Xmas, Easter & BHs
P   Yes
R   Cafe
T   Yes
D   Wheelchair access. Toilet.
•   Exhibitions on the suffragette movement. Changing contemporary programmes. Art gallery. Edwardian parlour. Shop.

Manchester United Football Club - Museum and Tour Centre
Sir Matt Busby Way, Old Trafford, Manchester M16 0RA. Tel 0161 8774002mily
£   Tour & museum, A £5.50. Con £3.50. Fam £12 Museum only, A £2.95. Con £1.95. Fam £6.95
O   All year Tue-Sun. BH. Mon
P   Yes
R   Yes
T   Yes
D   Wheelchair access. Toilet
•   A must for all football fans to see behind the scenes at the Theatre of Dreams. Due to demand we advise visitors to pre-book tours

The Manchester Museum
University of Manchester, Oxford Road, Manchester M13 9PL Tel 0161 275 2634
£   Free
O   All year Mon-Sat 10.00-17.00 Cl Xmas and NY
P   On University car park charge of £3
C   Yes

T   Yes
D   Wheelchair access with assistance, toilet facilities
•   Fifteen Galleries on four floors, displays from archaeology to zoology. Award winning Egyptian gallery. Temporary exhibitions.

NELSON

Pendle Heritage Centre
Park Hill, Barrowford, Nelson BB9 6JQ. Tel 01282 695366
£   House & display - A £1.75. C 80p. Con £1. Fam £4.50.
    Walled garden, Cruck Barn & animals - A £1.20. C 80p. Con £80p. Fam. £4.50
    Joint ticket - A £2.75. C £1.50. Con £1.50. Fam £6.
O   Daily all year 10.00-17.00 Cl Xmas Day
P   Yes, free
C   Questionnaires and activity sheets
R   Full catering 10.00-17.00
T   Yes incl disabled
D   Access to ground floor, gardens, barn and animals
•   Set in range of grade II listed buildings showing development from 16th century, history of the area, incl Pendle witches story on video, walled garden. Impressive Cruck barn now restored and showing farm life incl seasonal events of sheep shearing, hedge laying, hay making, dry stone walling, butter making, etc. Parlour shop with wide range of goods for sale.

OLDHAM

Saddleworth Moor Museum & Art Gallery
High Street, Uppermill, Oldham OL3 6HS. Tel 01457 874093.
£   A £1.20. Con 60p. Fam £3.
O   mid-Mar-Oct, Mon-Sat 10.00-17.00. Sun 12.00-17.00. Nov-mid-Mar, Mon-Sun 13.00-16.00. Cl Xmas day.
P   Yes
C   Unique and award winning family boxes - free with admission - full of things to do, touch and discover. Hands on activity area - 'Weave a message' - 'Create a picture' etc.
R   Cafes in village
T   Yes
D   Ramped access and stair lift to ground floor and art gallery. 5 steps to first floor. Guide sheets in Braille and large print. Toilet.
•   The story of Saddleworth - a Yorkshire community on the Lancashire side of the Pennines. Traditions, textile industry, transport and people, brought to life in an old canalside mill. Family friendly.

PRESTON

Museum of The Queen's Lancashire Regiment
Fulwood Barracks, Preston. PR2 8AA. Tel 01772 260362.
£   Free, donations appreciated
O   Tue-Thur 09.30-16.00, or by appointment
P   Yes (vehicles may be liable to search)
C   Original objects for handling. Shop
R   Soft drinks machine

T   Yes
• Largest military heritage collection in the north-west situated in the finest listed barracks of its type in England.

Ribchester Roman Museum
Riverside, Ribchester, Preston PR3 3XS Tel 01254 878261
£   A £1.35 C 70p
O   All year Mon-Fri 09.00-17.00 June-Aug Sat-Sun 11.30-17.50 Sept-May Sat-Sun 12.00-17.00
P   Car park in village
D   Access for disabled
• Depicts Roman life in Ribchester. Many archaeological objects including a magnificent cavalry tombstone, a copy of the Ribchester cavalry parade helmet and complementary models, external remains of the fort.

ROSSENDALE

Rossendale Museum
Whitaker Park, Haslingden Road, Rawtenstall, Rossendale,. BB4 6RE. Tel 01706 217777/226509
£   Free
O   Mon-Fri 13.00-17.00. Sat Nov-Mar 10.00-16.00. Apl-Oct 10.00-17.00. Sun Nov-Mar 12.00-16.00. Apl-Oct 12.00-17.00
P   Yes
C   Questionnaires for arranged visits by school groups
R   Kiosk in park open weekends and school hols, afternoons, Easter - end Sept.
T   Next to kiosk. If locked ask at museum for key
D   Access through side door to ground floor only. Toilets as above.
• Former 19th century mill owner's house set in parkland. Collections include natural history, fine arts, recreation of Victorian drawing room, local history and costume, temporary exhibitions.

SALFORD

Lancashire Mining Museum
Buile Hill Park, Eccles Old Road, Salford M6 8GL Tel 0161 736 1832
£   Free
O   Mon-Fri 10.00-12.30 13.30-17.00 Sun 14.00-17.00
P   Free parking
C   Yes
R   Sweets and drinks at shop
T   Yes
D   No
• The museum of the former Lancashire coalmining industry. Three floors of displays including recreated mines and traditional displays. Temporary exhibitions through year. Archives and library open by appointment.

Ordsall Hall Museum
Ordsall Lane, Salford M5 3EX Tel 0161 872 0251
£   Free
O   Mon-Fri 10.00-12.30 13.30-17.00 Sun 14.00-17.00

Free on site
Quiz sheets to accompany temporary exhibitions
Yes plus baby changing facilities
Access limited to ground floor only
An Elizabethan black and white manor house containing period rooms. A varied temporary exhibition programme.

alford Museum and Art Gallery

eel Park Crescent, Salford, M5 4WU. Tel 0161 7362649
Free
Open all year Cl Xmas, Boxing Days, Gd Fri, Easter Sat & Mon
Yes
No hands-on or questionnaires Work sheets, various activities organised during school holidays
Yes
Yes
Wheelchair access, lift and toilet
Reconstructed Victorian Street, Victorian gallery, temporary exhibitions all year, ceramics and statues.

TALY BRIDGE

stley Cheetham Art Gallery

taly Bridge Public Library, Trent Street, Staly Bridge (Manchester)Tel 0161 338 2708
Free
Mon Tue, Wed, Fri 13.00-17.00 Sat 09.00-16.00
Town centre parking
Available nearby
Yes
A varied exhibition programme throughout the year with something for everyone.

TOCKPORT

tockport Museum

ernon Park, Turncroft Lane, Stockport SK1 4AR. Tel 0161 474 4460.
Free
Apl-Oct. daily 13.00-17.00. Nov-Mar. Sat. Sun 13.00-17.00.
Yes in small area outside gates
Snacks
Yes
Wheelchair access to ground floor only.
Local history, natural history, hidden treasures.

WIGAN

he History Shop

ibrary Street, Wigan WN1 1NU. 01942 828128.
Free
Mon 10.00-19.00. Tue-Fri 10.00-17.00. Sat 10.00-13.00.
Multi-storey nearby. On street parking.
Yes

D   Wheelchair access.
- 'Founded on Coal' - the story of our area. 'Charter 96' - celebrating Wigan's 750th anniversary. Art gallery - temporary exhibitions. Genealogical and local history centre.

WHITWORTH

Heritage Museum
North Street, Whitworth OL12 8RE Tel 01706 853049/852958
£   Annual membership fee £2.50 OAP £1.50
O   Tue 19.30-21.30 Sat 14.00-16.00
P   Yes
R   Tea/coffee biscuits
T   Yes
- The museum gives an insight into bygone days of Whitworth and comprises an interesting collection of local articles relating to the War years and Valley life through the ages.

LEICESTERSHIRE

ASHBY DE LA ZOUCH

Ashby de la Zouch Museum
North Street, Ashby de la Zouch, LE65 1HV. Tel 01530 560090
£ A 25p. Con 20p. C 15p
O Easter Sat- end Sept Mon-Fri 10.00-12.00, 14.00-16.00. Sat 10.00-16.00. Sun 14.00-16.00
P Adjacent
R Nearby in town
T Disabled only, others in nearby town
D Total wheelchair access
• Winner of County Heritage Award. Model of Ashby Castle under siege. General history of Ashby. Temporary exhibitions, history.

HINCKLEY

Hinckley & District Museum
Framework Knitters' Cottages, Lower Bond Street, Hinckley,. LE10 1QX. Tel 01455 251218
£ A 50p. Con 25p
O Easter Mon- end Oct, Sat & B.H. Mons 10.00-16.00 Sun 14.00-17.00
P Pay & display nearby. On-street Sun.
C 'Hinckley from Stone Age to Medieval Times' illustrated picture book to colour, 50p
R Yes
• Restored 17th century thatched cottages housing displays illustrating aspects of the history of Hinckley and district, incl 1740 stocking frame. Displays changed each season.

Leicestershire

LEICESTER

Newarke Houses Museum

The Newarke, Leicester LE2 7BY. Tel 0116 2473222
£   Free
O   Mon-Sat 10.00-17.30. Sun 14.00-17.30. Cl Xmas & Boxing Day Gd Fri
P   Newarke Street multi storey
C   Some facilities
T   Limited
D   Very limited
•   Toys, Victorian street scene, shops, clocks, furniture.

Guru Nanak Sikh Museum

c/o Mrs V Kaur, 9 Holybones, Leicester LE1 4LJ. Tel 0116 2628606.
£   Free, donations appreciated
O   Thur 13.00-16.00. Groups with pre-arranged appointment.
P   Yes
C   During exhibitions, normally in May
R   Free refreshments for groups only
T   Yes also suitable for disabled
•   Museum depicts history of Sikh nation illustrated by paintings, coins, rare manuscripts
    models of Sikh shrines, photo gallery

The Jewry Wall Museum and Site

St Nicholas Circle, Leicester LE1 4LB. Tel 0116 2473021
£   Free
O   All year - Mon-Sat 10.00-17.30. Sun 14.00-17.30. Cl Xmas & Boxing Days Gd Fri
P   Public parking 100 metres
C   Family activity sheets. Handling boxes and educational programme for pre-booked
    school parties
R   Nearby in High Street
T   Yes
D   Wheelchair access from Vaughan College car park in Holy Bones. Electronic door
    opening from wheelchair level. Gallery and shop on one level. Toilet
•   Museum of Leicestershire archaeology from earliest times to middle ages. Site on public
    baths of Roman Leicester, incl Jewry Wall, one of largest pieces of Roman masonry to
    survive in modern urban context

'Discovering Cricket at Grace Road'

Leicestershire County Cricket Club, County Ground, Grace Road, Leicester LE2 8AD Tel 0116
2832128
£   Free
O   By prior appointment
P   Yes
C   Quiz and treasure hunt
T   Yes
D   Wheelchair access and toilet
•   Extensive collection of cricket memorabilia situated within the Pavilion Suite of the
    Leicestershire County Cricket Club.

The Guildhall

Guildhall Lane, Leicester LE1 5FQ Tel 0116 2532569

£ Free

⊙ All year Mon-Sat 10.00-17.30. Sun 14.00-17.30

P Pay and display 100 and 200 metres

Questionnaires, treasure trail

Yes

Wheelchair access to ground floor. Toilet reasonably accessible to wheelchair users

The Guildhall is among the finest medieval buildings in use today as a living museum during the day. It also serves as a distinctive venue hosting a wide variety of theatre, story telling and music during the evenings.

William Carey Museum

Central Baptist Church, Charles Street, Leicester LE1 1LA

£ Free

⊙ On Suns at service times - 10.30-12.30. 17.30-19.00. Other times by arrangement by phoning 0116 2766862

P On streets around Church

✓ Yes

⊙ Facilities for disabled

Tableaux of Carey's ministry in Leicester and as a missionary, translator and social reformer in India. He founded a college at Serampore which still trains local students

Charles Moore Collection of Musical Instruments

Music Dept. University of Leicester, University Road, Leicester LE1 7RH. Tel 0116 2522781/01234 36027

£ Free

⊙ By arrangement

P University main site car park

⊙ All instruments can be handled

R Bar/restaurant in Charles Wilson Building

Yes

⊙ Access by ramp to lift

The collection is housed on the 18th floor of the Attenborough building. Collection ranges from 18th to early 20th century instruments, incl an early bassoon and two ophicleides.

The Leicester Gas Museum

c/o British Gas, P.O. Box 28, 195 Aylestone Road, Leicester LE2 7QH. Tel 0116 2503190

£ Free

⊙ Tue-Fri 12.30-16.30, except B.Hs

P Free on site

⊙ Hands-on items. Fun quiz. Education pack

Yes

D Wheelchair access ground floor only

From coal gas to natural gas; from gas lighting to modern appliances with many surprises. See the all gas 1920's kitchen, gas hairdryers and gas powered radio.

Raw Dykes Ancient Monument

Aylestone Road, Leicester. All correspondence to, The Curator, Jewry Wall Museum, St Nicholas Circle, Leicester LE1 4LB. Tel as for Jewry Wall Museum, 0116 2473021

£   Free
O   Viewing area open at all times
P   On street parking opposite monument (Saffron Lane)
•   Linear earthwork representing surviving portion of aqueduct delivering water to Roman Leicester (Ratae Corieltauvorum)

The Abbey Pumping Station

Corporation Road, Leicester Tel 0116 2661330

£   Free except for special events, then A £2.50. Con £1. Fam £5 Phone for dates of special events
O   Mon-Sat 10.00-17.30. Sun 14.00-17.30
P   On site parking
C   Hands-on facilities, activity sheets
R   Not at present but hopefully by 1998
T   Yes and baby changing facilities
D   Wheelchair access to galleries but not unfortunately to beam engines. Disabled toilets.
•   History, science and technology of public health in Leicestershire. 'Exhibition Flushed with Pride', country's large working steam beam engine built in 1891. Picturesque Victorian pumping station in own grounds. Narrow gauge railway on site. Programme of special events, please phone for details.

LOUGHBOROUGH

Loughborough War Memorial & Carillon Tower

Queen's Park, Loughborough, Tel 01509 634704

£   A 40p. Con free
O   Gd Fri-30 Sept, Mon,Tue, Wed, Frii, Sun 13.00-17.00. Thur, Sat 10.00-17.00
P   Granby Street. Small charge
R   Cafe in Queen's Park
T   In Queen's Park
•   The first and finest Carillon in Britain, giving regular recitals, please phone for dates. War memorial museum is within the Carillon Tower, three floors of militaria. Magnificent views from the viewing balcony.

Great Central Railway Museum

Great Central Station, Loughborough,. LE11 1RW. Tel 01509 230726

£   Platform ticket from booking office
O   Opening times vary with manning of station, in general the museum is open later when trains are running
P   On road parking
R   Available on station when trains are running
T   On station
D   Access to platform and railway
•   Collection of items relating to the Great Central line both before and after grouping. We have limited space but plenty of height so our displays are rather unusual.

The Old Rectory Museum

Rectory Place, Loughborough,. LE11 1UW. Tel 01509 232419

£ Free

⊃ Sats Apl-Oct. Groups day or evening by appointment

P On site for cars and mini buses. Coaches 200 metres

C Stone Age Quern(making flour). Other small objects

R Cafe 200 metres

T 200 metres

⊃ Bottom floor only. 2 ramps

LUTTERWORTH

British Aviation Heritage

Bruntingthorpe Aerodrome,Nr Lutterworth. LE17 5QS. Tel 0116 2478040

£ A £3. C (under 14) £1. Under 5's free

⊃ Sun all year, museum. Open days spring and autumn. 'Rolling Thunder' main event July. Please phone for details

P Free on site

C None on Sun but lots on open days

R Catering on open days. Visitors may picnic on Suns.

T Limited on Suns but good on open days

⊃ Good access and wide doorway

• Static exhibits of cold war jets incl Victor, Vulcan, Lightning, Buccaneer, Hunter, etc. Open days - taxy runs in above aircraft. 'Rolling Thunder' - aircraft display and family day, some flying displays. Other attractions incl classic cars, bikes, funfair, quad bikes, trade stands, hot air balloons, model flying.

Stanford Hall Motorcycle Museum

Lutterworth, Leicestershire LE17 6DH. Tel 01788 860250

£ A £3. C£1.35 (includes Stanford Hall grounds)

⊃ Easter Sat - end Sept, Sat, Sun, BH Mon & Tue 14.30-17.30 Special events days open 12.00, house open 14.30. Please phone for list of special events

P On site

R Yes

T Yes

⊃ Museum accessible for wheelchairs. Disabled toilet

• Outstanding collection of racing and vintage motorcycles with frequent changes of exhibit.

MARKET HARBOROUGH

Hallaton Village Museum

Hog Lane, Market Harborough. LE16 8UB. Tel c/o 01858 555602.

£ Free

⊃ May-Oct Weekends & BHs 14.30-17.00

• New exhibition every year plus photos and local farming and village artefacts

East Carlton Countryside Park

East Carlton, Nr Market Harborough LE16 8YF. Tel 01536 770977

£ Free

⊃ All year weekdays 9.30-16.45. Weekends 10.30-17.15

P   Free
R   Cafe
T   Yes
D   Wheelchair access to centre only. Disabled toilet

Harborough Museum

Council Offices, Adam & Eve Street, Market Harborough. LE16 7AG. Tel 01858 821085
£   Free
O   Mon-Sat 10.00-16.30. Sun 14.00-17.00 Cl Xmas & Boxing Days Gd Fri
P   Free adjoining museum
C   Brass rubbings, assemble wheel in wheelwrights section
T   In council offices, with disabled access
D   Access via lift in council offices Mon-Fri. Contact staff for Sat & Sun visits
•   Displays include the Symington Collection of Corsetry, reconstruction of local bootmaker workshop, Drayton villa mosaic. Local industries.

MELTON MOWBRAY

Melton Carnegie Museum

Thorpe End, Melton Mowbray,. LE13 1RB. Tel 01664 69946
£   Free
O   Oct-Easter Mon-Sat 10.00-17.00. Easter-end Sept Mon-Sat 10.00-17.00. Sun 14.00-17.00
P   Public parking nearby
T   Yes
D   Wheelchair access and disabled toilet. Museum on one level
•   Local history museum with exhibits of sporting paintings, fox hunting, crafts and industries incl stilton cheese and Melton pork pies, archaeology, geology and a two-headed calf. Regular temp exhibitions.

WIGSTON

Wigston Framework Knitters Museum

42/44 Bushloe End, Wigston, LE18 2BA. Tel 0116 2883396
£   A £1. C 50p
O   Every Sun, 1st Sat of each month, or anytime by arrangement
P   Free on street
C   Hands on
R   Tea and biscuits
T   Yes
D   Wheelchair access to ground floor only. No toilet
•   Late 17th century master hosier's house with two-storey Victorian frameshop in the garden, with hand frames, moulds and tools.

Wigston Magna Fold Museum
White Gate Farm, Newton Lane, Wigston Magna,. LE18 3SH. Tel 0116 2880917
£ Free
O Easter-Oct weekends 14.00-17.00 or by arrangement
P Yes
C Yes, in part
R Yes
T Yes
D Facilities
• Local memorabilia reflecting social history of district. 1500 artefacts. May close at end of 1997 season.

LINCOLNSHIRE

ALFORD

Alford Manor House
West Street, Alford LN13 9DJ Tel 01507 463073
£   A £1.25 Child as part of family group free. Groups special rates
O   Easter-Sept Mon-Sat 10.00-16.30 Sun 13.00-16.00
P   Yes in grounds Coaches need to notify first
C   Special day in August, competitions during Museum week in May
R   Light refreshments Tue, Fri and BHs
T   Yes
D   Limited, toilets not suitable
•   A living museum spanning 300 years, shops from the past, pharmacy, veterinary surgery, bootmaker and prison cell. Discover Alford's connection with America.

Mawthorpe Museum
Mawthorpe, Alford LN13 9LU. Tel 01507 462336.
£   A £2. Con £1.
O   Every Thur Jul-Sep, Some Suns in Jul & Aug, also Aug BH Mon - 10.30-17.00.
P   Yes
C   Hands-on
R   Yes
T   Yes
D   Wheelchair access to main buildings. Toilet does not have bars.
•   The museum displays all aspects of Lincolnshire life incl steam engines, tractors, blacksmiths, butchers, chemists, grocers, railway, barbers, cobblers, wartime memorabilia, bottle collection, kitchen equipment, sewing machine and much more. Picnic area. Coach parties welcome by appt.

BARTON UPON HUMBER

Baysgarth House Museum

Baysgarth Park, Caistor Road, Barton upon Humber DN18 6AH. Tel 01652 632318.

£ Free
O Thur & Fri 10.30-15.30. Sat & Sun 10.30-16.30. Stables & cottage closed 12.00-13.00.
P Yes
C Holiday activities often organised, please phone for details
T Yes
• Period rooms, displays of pottery & porcelain, local history & archaeology, rural crafts & industry.

BOSTON

Boston Guildhall Museum

South Street, Boston PE21 6HT. Tel 01205 365954.

£ A £1.20. OAP 80p. Adult admission includes use of audio guided tour. U/16s free. Admission free on Thur. Party rates available, also functions in banqueting hall. Please phone for details.
O Mon-Sat 10.00-17.00. Suns Apl-Sep 13.30-17.00
P Nearby in town
T Yes
D Parking opposite museum. Wheelchair access to ground floor incl entrance hall, cells and kitchens. Access to other areas under review, please phone for up-to-date info. Accessible toilet.
• Built in 1450, and where, in 1607, the Pilgrim Fathers were imprisoned. See entrance hall where monthly exhibitions are held, cells, kitchens, maritime room, council chamber, court room and banqueting hall.

GOOLE

Goole Museum & Art Gallery

Carlisle Street, Goole. Correspondence to Eryc Office, Church Street, Goole DB14 5BG. Tel 01405 722251.

£ Free
O Mon.Wed.Fri 10.00-19.00. Tue, Thur 10.00-17.00. Sat 10.00-12.00.
P Yes
C Facilities, incl town trail, available
T Adjacent
D In course of preparation, please phone.
• Collections of local history, superb ship models and paintings.

IMMINGHAM

Immingham Museum

Margaret Street, Immingham D40 1LE. Tel 01469 577066.

£ Free
O Mon-Fri 10.00-16.00
P Yes
C Quiz
R Yes

T   Yes
D   Full access for disabled
•   The museum reflects the great central railway and it's part in developing the docks and railways in the area. Natural history, archaeology and local history displays.

LINCOLN

Incredibly Fantastic Old Toy Show
26 Westgate, Lincoln LN1 3BD. Tel 01522 520534.
£   A £1.90. Con £1.50 C (5-16) £1.
O   Easter Sun-Sep, Tue-Sat 11.00-17.00. Sun & BH Mons 12.00-16.00. Oct-Dec Sat. 11.00-17.00. Sun 12.00-16.00. Other times by appointment.
P   Free 1 hr on Westgate. City car parks opposite. Others nearby.
C   Push-buttons, sensors, distorting mirrors, pier-end machines, story/info paddles, carry steps, toys and books box for young children. Worksheets and display table for school parties.
T   50 metres a way near coach/car park.
D   Wheelchair access vie ramp(please ask for assistance if required). Displays on one floor. Info paddles for close reading.
•   A colourful and comprehensive collection of toys dating from 1780's. Fun and entertaining for all ages, with videos, lights, music, posters and old photos.

Museum of Lincolnshire Life
Burton Road, Lincoln LN1 3LY. Tel 01522 528448.
£   A £1.20. C 60p. Party/school group rates available.
O   May-Sept, daily 10.00-17.30. Oct-Apl Mon-Sat 10.00-17.30. Sun 14.00-17.30.
P   Yes
C   Wide range of hands-on activities - term and school holidays - groups must book - individuals during holidays.
R   Home made cakes, etc. available most of the year.
T   Yes
D   Dedicated parking. 90% fully accessible. Upper floor 10%.
•   One of the largest social history museums in the region. 'From a teapot to a tank' - there's more to Lincolnshire life.

MABLETHORPE

Ye Olde Curiosity Museum
61 Victoria Road, Mablethorpe LN12 2AF. Tel 01507 472406.\plain
£   Free
O   Daily from 10.00.
P   Limited parking on road.
D   Wheelchair access.
•   Morris Minor Traveller still in working order. Large collection of glass lampshades-oil, gas and electric, plus hundreds of fittings. Extensive collection of Christmas lights and decorations.

NORTH HYKEHAM

Lincolnshire Vintage Vehicle Society
Whisby Road, North Hykeham. LN6 5QT. Tel 01522 500566/689497.
£ Free, donations appreciated.
O May-Oct, Mon-Fri 12.00-16.00. Sun. 10.00-16.00. Nov-Apl Sun 14.00-17.00.
P Yes
C Can be arranged.
R Usually on Sundays.
T Yes
D Fully accessible. Toilet.
• Over 40 vehicles, mostly restored, from 1920's to 1960's on show in newly opened exhibition hall. Buses, cars, lorries and a fire engine all on show.

SCUNTHORPE

Scunthorpe Museum & Art Gallery
Oswald Road, Scunthorpe, DN15 7BD. Tel 01724 843533.
£ Free
O Tue-Sat. BHs 10.00-16.00. Sun 14.00-17.00.
P Yes
C Computer game, range of activity sheets often available in holiday periods, and range of workshops and other activities.
T Yes
D Wheelchair access to ground floor only.
• Collections of archaeology, history, geology and wildlife of Sth Humberside region. Temporary exhibitions.

SKEGNESS

Church Farm Museum
Church Road South, Skegness PE25 2HF. Tel 01754 766658.
£ A £1. C 50p.
O Apl-Oct, daily.
P Yes
C Family events throughout the year.
T Tearoom when available.
T Yes
• 19th century furnished farmhouse and farm implements, mud and stud thatched cottage, gardens, orchard, farm livestock, regular events, Sunday demos. Temporary exhibitions.

SPALDING

Ayscoughfee Hall Museum & Gardens
Churchgate, Spalding PE11 2RA. Tel 01775 725468.
£ Free
O Mon-Thur 10.00-17.00. Fri 10.00-16.30. Sat 10.00-17.00. Sun 11.00-17.00. Nov-Feb closed at weekends.
P Yes
C Quiz sheets.

R   Cafe in gardens, open Apl-Sept.
T   Yes
D   Wheelchair access to ground floor of hall only. Toilet.
•   Medieval wool merchant's house in 5 acres of gardens, houses museum of South Holland life, incl galleries on drainage, agriculture and horticulture. Large bird collection. Play area in gardens.

WAINFLEET

Magdalen Museum

St John Street, Wainfleet, Skegness. Tel (contact) 01754 881261.

£   70p.
O . Easter-Sept. Tue-Sun & BHs 13.30-16.30.
P   Yes
C   Plenty of items of interest
R   Yes
T   Yes
D   Main museum not really suitable but Victorian kitchen is accessible.
•   This is a local history museum run by volunteers in a fine Medieval building. The ever changing displays show the social history, environment and hobbies of this area.

WOODHALL SPA

Woodhall Spa Cottage Museum

Iddesleigh Road, Woodhall Spa LN10 6SH. Tel 01526 353775.

£   A £1. Accompanied children free. Rates for parties of 10+.
O   Apl-Oct Mon-Sat 10.00-17.00 Sun 11.00-17.00
P   Public car parks near by
D   Wheelchair access
•   The nucleus of the Museum's exhibits is a collection of photographs and memorabilia collected by the Wield family which illustrates the story of Woodhall Spa from beginning to present day, not forgetting the connection with the 617 Squadron (The Dambusters).

LONDON

• Hendon
• Harrow
• Wembley
• Walthamstow
• Ealing
• Paddington
• CITY
• Southwick • Woolwich
• Chelsea
• Greenwich
Thames
• Wandsworth
• Wimbledon
• Croydon

CENTRAL LONDON

Crossness Engines

Thames Water Crossness Works, Belvedere Road, Abbey Wood SE2 9AQ. Tel (Tue & Sun 09.00-16.00 only) 0181 3113711.

£ A £2. Con £1.50. Fam £4.

O By appointment, one Tue and one Sun per month. Visits start at 14.00 and last about 90 mins.

P Yes, free

C Children in care of adult welcome. Activity sheet. School parties welcome.

T Yes

D Wheelchair access. No adapted toilet.

• The worlds largest rotative beam engines being restored in original Victorian engine house, now Grade I listed building. Outstanding ironwork and brickwork. museum of sanitation engineering.

Grant Museum of Zoology and Comparative Anatomy

Dept of Biology, Darwin Building, Gower Street, University College, Camden WC1E 6BT. Tel 0171 3877050 ext 2647.

£ Free

O By appointment only, weekdays 09.00-17.30. Cl BHs

P No on-site parking

C Hands-on facilities

R Within grounds of college

T Yes

D Wheelchair access limited. Toilet in college grounds.

• Unique Victorian-esque natural history collection covering the whole animal kingdom. Several rare and extinct specimens and impressive collection of skeletal, taxidermy and spirit specimens.

Kirkaldy Testing Museum
99 Southwark Street, Southwark SE1. Tel 01322 332195.
£   A £2.
O   First Sun of each month 10.30-15.00, or by appointment
P   No on-site parking
C   Children only admitted if accompanied by adult
T   Yes
D   Very restricted access
•   The unique machine and integrity of one of the worlds first independent testing concerns. An historical look at materials testing.

National Army Museum
Royal Hospital Road, Chelsea, SW3 4HT Tel 0171 730 0717
£   Free
O   All year 10.00-17.30 Cl Xmas, NY, Gd Fri & May BH
P   Street parking only - meter
C   Children can try on armour
R   Cafe
T   Yes
D   Yes
•   The story of the soldier in peace and war from Agincourt to Bosnia. Fascinating exhibits include paintings, weapons, models, photographs and one of the world's finest collection of uniforms.

Percival David Foundation of Chinese Art
University of London, 53 Gordon Square, Camden WC1H 0PD. Tel 0171 3873909
£   Free, donations appreciated
O   Mon-Fri 10.30-17.00. Cl BHs and Xmas-N.Y.
P   No on-site parking
T   Yes
D   Limited access, advised to telephone prior to visit
•   Finest collection of Chinese ceramics outside China. A number have previously been in the possession of Chinese emperors.

Pollock's Toy Museum
1 Scala Street, W1 0171 636 3452
£   A £2.50 C under 18 £1
O   Mon-Sat 10.00-17.00 Cl BHs
P   None on site. Underground Goodge Street. Buses 10, 24, 29, 73 to Goodge Strreet
C   Yes please telephone for details
•   The museum housed on three floors of two small houses, displays include - board games, mechanical toys, teddies, dolls, folk toys from Baltic countries, toy theatres and Pollock's Toyshop is situated on the ground floor.

Thames Division Museum
Wapping Police Station, 98 Wapping High Street, Wapping E1 9NE. Tel 0171 2754422
£   Free
O   By appointment only
P   On-street pay and display
•   Items of uniform and equipment and models covering formation to present day. Also books and archive material plus records of all police officers serving on the division.

The Guards Museum
Wellington Barrock, Birdcage Walk, Westminster SW1E 6HQ. Tel 0171 414 3271/3428.
£ A £2. Con & groups of 25+ £1. Fam £4.
O Daily 10.00-16.00. Cl Xmas and all Jan and some ceremonial days.
P Meters in Buckingham Gate.
D Lift to enable disabled persons to get down to museum, all one one level. Toilet available for disabled.
• The Guards museum illustrates the story of Her Majesty's Foot Guards. The collection of uniforms, weapons and memorabilia spans 300 years. Large toy soldier centre is especially interesting.

The Michael Faraday Museum and Laboratory
21 Albemarle Street, Westminster W1X 4BS. Tel 0171 4092992
£ A £1. Con 50p.
O Mon-Fri 10.00-16.00. Conducted tours available for pre-booked parties.
• The Michael Faraday Museum houses his apparatus, manuscripts, pictures, personal memorabilia. His magnetic laboratory has been restored on it's original site.

The Museums of the Royal College of Surgeons (Hunterian and Odontological)
35-43 Lincoln's Inn Fields WC2A 3PN Tel 0171 973 2190
£ Free, donations welcomed
O Mon-Fri 10.00-17.00 Cl weekends, BHs and other days when College is closed
P Meters in Lincoln's Inn Fields. Underground Holborn and Temple. Numerous buses
D Access can be arranged by telephoning before visit
• The Hunterian Museum contains about 3,500 anatomical and pathological preparations both human and animal from the collection of John Hunter F.R.S. (1728-1793)
• The Odontological Museum is about teeth with displays on dental anatomy and pathology both human and animal., dental instruments and dentures. There are about 70 video tapes available for viewing in the museum.

GREATER LONDON

Alexander Fleming Laboratory Museum
St Mary's Hospital, Paddington., W2 1NY Tel 0171 725 6528
£ A £2 C/OAP/Students and Con £1
O Mon-Thur 10.00-13.00 Cl BHs
P Public car park or take tube to Paddington, Buses-7,15,27,36
• See the small laboratory where Fleming discovered penicillin, now restored to its cramped condition of 1928 when a petri dish of bacterias became contaminated with a mysterious mould. Displays and video trace the story of Fleming, the man and scientist.

Allhallows by the Tower, Undercrypt Museum
Byward Street, Whitchapel EC3R 5BU Tel 0171 481 2928
£ A £2.50 C/OAP £1
O Mon-Sat 11.00-16.30 Sun 12.00-16.30
P Public car park at Tower Palace
C Children's Guide and study room available
T Yes
D Wheelchair access and toilets
• School parties dealing with Roman and Saxon London and Medieval cities especially welcome. Related material to National Curriculum.

Arsenal Football Club

Arsenal Stadium, Highbury N5 1B4 Tel 0171 704 4000
£   A £2 C under 16 and OAP £1
O   Fri 09.30-16.00 Matchdays for approx two hours before game (North Bank ticket holders only)
P   Local street parking except on matchdays
C   A number of 'hands on' exhibits including a London Bus, interactivities
R   None on site except matchdays when refreshment bars are open.
T   Yes
D   Lift access and toilet facilities, museum is on one level
•   Tells the story of Arsenal F.C. in conventional and some rather unconventional ways.

The Baden Powell Story

Baden Powell House, Queen's Gate, Kensington SW7 5JS Tel 0171 584 7030
£   Free
O   24 hours a day, 7 days a week!
P   Meter and public car parks nearby, but better to get tube to Gloucester Road
R   Yes
T   Yes
D   Yes
•   Tells life story of Baden-Powell the founder of Scouting and Guiding.

Bank of England Museum

Threadneedle Street, City EC2 R8AH
£   Free
O   Mon-Fri 10.00-17.00 Cl weekends & BHs
P   Very limited and expensive parking in the City, best take the tube to Bank
C   Activity sheets, interactive videos, foreign exchange and dealing simulation
T   Yes
D   Access not easy, but ramp available, toilet facilities, please give prior notice of visit
•   Story of Bank of England from its foundation in 1694 to its role today as the central bank of the U.K. Exhibits include gold bars, coins, bank notes, pictures, prints, drawings and cartoons.

Bethnal Green Museum of Childhood

Cambridge Heath Road, Whitechapel EC2 9PA Tel 0181 980 2415 (recorded info)
£   Free
O   Mon, Thur and Sat 10.00-17.50 Sun 14.30-17.50
P   12 free parking spaces at museum
C   Activities in holidays and art workshops most Saturdays
R   Licensed Cafe
T   Yes
D   Please telephone prior to visit, portable ramps for entrance, goods lift to upper floor, adapted toilet.
•   One of the world's largest toy and nursery collections including enchanting displays of dolls, doll's houses, teddies, toy soldiers, games, trains, puppets, children's costume and nursery antiques.

Bruce Castle Museum

Lordship Lane, Haringay N17 8NU Tel 0181 8088772

£   Free

O   Wed-Sun 13.00-17.00

P   Free parking

C   Special activities for children on summer Sunday afternoons. half term, Easter and Summer weekdays.

T   Yes

D   Wheelchair access to ground floor only, no lift, disabled toilets on ground floor

•   Bruce Castle is a Grade 1 listed building built in 1514. The main museum has exhibitions and collections. on local history (ranging from the Highgate Roman Kiln to Victorian costume) and includes a major collection of postal history.

The Chartered Insurance Institute

20 Aldermanbury, London City EC2V 7HY. Tel 0181 9898464/0171 4174425.

£   Free

O   Mon-Thur 10.00-17.00. Fri 10.00-16.00. Cl BHs & Xmas period.

P   NEC & meters. Nearest tube Moorgate.

T   Yes

•   Early firefighting equipment incl hand-drawn fire-engines, helmets, leather buckets, etc. Large collection of memorabilia incl fire-marks, a reminder that early fire-brigades were operated by the insurance companies.

Church Farmhouse Museum

Greyhound Hill, Hendon NW4 4JR. Tel 0181 2030130.

£   Free

O   Mon-Thur 10.00-12.30, 13.30-17.00. Sat 10.00-13.00, 14.00-17.30. Sun 14.00-17.30. Cl Xmas, Boxing & N.Y days & Gd Fri.

P   Yes, free

C   Activity sheets produced for certain exhibitions

R   Pub next door admits children and serves food all day

T   Yes

D   Access difficult. No adapted toilet.

•   17th century farmhouse with Victorian period farmhouse kitchen, laundry and dining room. Local history gallery. Small public garden. Continuous programme of temporary exhibitions, incl Christmas exhibitions for children, often with events.

Crystal Palace Museum

Anerley Hill. Crystal Palace SE19 2BA. Tel 0181 6760200.

£   Free

O   Every Sun & BH.Mons

P   Yes, free

T   Yes

•   The museum tells the story of the Crystal Palace from 1851-1936 in audio/visual displays. Well stocked shop.

Croydon Clock Tower

Katharine Street, Croydon CR9 1ET. Tel 0181 2531030.

£   A £2. Con £1. Prices vary for special exhibitions.

O   Mon-Sat 11.-17.00. Suns & BHs 12.00-17.00.

P   Nearby in town centre car parks, Surrey Street or Fairfield.

C   Hands-on activities, Saturday creche, special exhibitions, quiz sheets.
R   Cafe
T   Yes
D   Full wheelchair access. Large print brochure. Toilets.
•   Lifetimes is a unique museum about Croydon people, having won several national awards. Touchscreen computers and lots of fun, hands-on activities. Special temporary exhibitions each year for all ages, please ring for details.

The Cuming Museum
155-157 Walworth Road, Walworth SE17 1RS. Tel 0171 7011342.
£   Free
O   Tue-Sat 10.00-17.00. Cl public hols.
P   Stead Street car park
C   A range of treasure hunts for children to fill in which take them around the various displays. Various events during school holidays
D   Museum on 1st floor, no special access.
•   History of the Cuming family and their world-wide collections. Collection of local objects illustrates Southwark's growth and development throughout the area's history.

Erith Museum
Erith Library, Walnut Tree Road, Erith DA8 1RS. Tel 01322 526574
£   Free
O   Mon,Wed 14.15-17.15. Sat 14.15-17.00. Cl BHs.
P   Limited free street parking nearby
R   Cafes nearby in town centre
D   Museum is on 1st floor, no wheelchair access.
•   Geology, archaeology and history of the Erith area, featuring the River Thames, local industries, civilian life in WW.II and model of a 1894 flying machine.

The Fan Museum
12 Crooms Hill, Greenwich SE10 8ER. Tel 0181 3051441.
£   A £3. Con £2. Fam £8.50
O   Every day except Mons & Xmas & Boxing days.
P   Nearby
C   Handling boxes and activity sheets
R   Only for groups
T   Yes
D   Wheelchair access, lift, toilets
•   The award winning museum is the first and only one in the world devoted to all aspects of the fan

Forty Hall Museum
Forty Hill, Enfield EN2 9HA. Tel 0181 3638196.
£   Free
P   Free parking in grounds
C   With specific temporary exhibitions
R   Cafe
T   In grounds next to museum
D   Wheelchair access to ground floor museum. Paved pathways around museum. Toilets in grounds.
•   Set in fine parkland with lakes and woods, the museum exhibits social history of the

area. Forty Hall is close to the M25 and A10.

effrye Museum

ingsland Road, Hackney E2 8EA. Tel 0171 7399893
  Free
  Tue-Sat 10.00-17.00. Suns & BAH. Mon 14.00-17.00
  Limited parking in nearby streets
  Quiz sheets, school sessions, holiday activities
  Coffee bar
  Yes
  95% wheelchair accessible. Toilets.
  Fine collection of English furniture and decorative arts arranged in a chronological series of period rooms from 1600-1950. Set in elegant Georgian almshouses surrounded by mature gardens. Tranquil walled herb garden, open Apl-Oct.

range Museum

easden Lane, Brent NW10 1QB. Tel 0181 4528311
  Free
  June-Aug Tue-Fri 11.00-17.00. Sat 10.00-176.00. Sun 14.00-17.00. Sept-May Mon-Fri 11.00-17.00. Sat 10.00-17.00
  Yes
  Ball pool
  Cold drinks machine
  Yes
  Access to ground floor only
  Local history of Brent viewed through the eyes of it's people

Greenwich Borough Museum

232 Plumstead High Street, Greenwich SE18 1JT. Tel 0181 8553240
  Free
  Mon 14.00-19.00. Tue. Thur. Fri. Sat 10.00-13.00. 14.00-17.00
  Local street parking
  Saturday club 10.30-12.15, term time. Holiday activities
  1st floor location but no special wheelchair access
  Local and natural history, temporary exhibition galleries, children's Saturday club, adult lecture/workshop programme. Sales point.

Gunnersbury Park Museum

Gunnersbury Park, Popes Lane, Ealing W3 8LQ. Tel 0181 9921612
  Free
  Mar-Oct, Mon-Fri 13.00-17.00. weekends & BHs 13.00-18.00. Nov-Feb, Mon-Fri 13.00-16.00. weekends & BHs 13.00-16.00. Cl 24-26 Dec.
  Yes
  Depends on exhibition showing
  Cafe in park
  In park
  Wheelchair ramps, seats in the galleries, some large print texts to exhibits. Toilets in park.
  The home of the Rothschild family in the 19th century, the house contains fine interiors and Victorian kitchens, general social history collection, carriages and costume collections, archaeology, childhood memorabilia, local industries.

Hampstead Museum

Burgh House, New End Square, Hampstead NW3 1LT. Tel 0171 4310144

£   Free to museum but donations appreciated and needed!! Various entry fees for lectures, concerts etc.
O   Wed-Sun 12.00-17.00. BHs14.00-17.00. Cl 2 weeks over Xmas.
P   No on-site parking
C   Only by advance arrangement, small groups due to small space (museum is run by volunteers), regret no clipboards etc.
R   Licensed buttery in basement, light meals, teas, cakes, etc.
T   Yes
D   Wheelchairs by arrangement, ground floor only. Toilet
•   Local history of Hampstead old village, environs, heath, famous inhabitants etc. Useful study resource (key stage 2). Temporary exhibitions.

Harrow Museum and Heritage Centre

Headstone Manor, Pinner View, Harrow HA2 6PX. Tel 0181 8612626

£   Free
O   Sat, Sun & BHs 10.30-17.00. Wed-Fri 12.30-17.00. Open Tue for talks only. Closes at dusk in winter.
P   Free car park near entrance
C   Dependant on current exhibition
R   Hot and cold drinks and confectionery. Wine and beer bar for Sunday concerts and special events
T   Yes
D   Wheelchair access to most areas. Hearing loop in tithe barn. Toilets.
•   Moated manor house, barns and granary. Local collections and visiting exhibitions, themed rooms. Popular Sunday lunchtime jazz bands. Tue afternoon talks, special events, group and school visits by arrangement.

Inns of Court & City Yeomanry Museum

10 Stone Buildings, Lincoln Inn, London City WC2A 3TG. Tel 0171 4058112

£   Free
O   Only by prior appointment. Museum is contained within a T.A. drill hall.
P   Lincoln Inn fields
T   Yes
•   Museum of the Inns of Court and City Yeomanry and T.A. unit with close links back to 1584. The unit has close association with the legal profession.

Livesay Museum

682 Old Kent Road, Southwark SE15 1JF. Tel 0171 6395604

£   Free
O   Tue-Sat 10.00-17.00
P   Street parking on Peckham Park Road and Commercial Way
C   Interactive temporary exhibitions, hands-on exhibits, worksheets, colouring sheets
R   Picnic area in courtyard only
T   Yes
D   Access to lower gallery only. Toilets.
•   'Going Underground' a highly imaginative hands-on experience about all that lives, uses, and is, beneath our feet, from large scale anterys, wormerys, to exploring tunnels and caves.

MCC Museum

Lord's Cricket Ground, St Johns Wood Road, St John's Wood NW8 8QN Tel 0171 289 1611

£   Match Days - ticket holders A£2 Con 50p
    Non Match Days - via tour of Lords (0171 432 1033) A £5.50 Con £4 Fam £17.00
O   Match days 10.00-17.00, other times via tour
P   Street parking (Meters)
R   Lord's Tavern adjacent to ground
T   Yes
D   Limited for wheelchairs, will provide help with lifting if notice given
•   The history of cricket from 1550 to present day. Major exhibits-The Ashes, Widen Trophy, Prudential Cup. Cricketing art and memorabilia.

Museum of Artillery

The Rotunda, Repository Road, Woolwich SE18 4BQ Tel 0181 316 5402

£   Free
O   Mon-Fri 13.00-16.00 Cl Weekends & BHs
P   Museum car park
T   Yes
D   Yes
•   The building is a Georgian masterpiece built by John Nash, the collection holds artillery from 14th Century to present day plus many rare models.

Museum of Fulham Palace

Bishops Avenue, Fulham SW6 6EA Tel 0171 736 3233

£   A 50p Accompanied children free Con 25p
O   March-Oct Wed-Sun & BH.Mons 14.00-17.00 Nov-Feb Thur-Sun 13.00-16.00
P   Parking by meter in Bishops Avenue a few minutes walk
C   Quizzes, word searches for several age groups, architectural game. Children's activities during half term and school holidays.
R   Cafe in park nearby
T   Public toilets in park nearby
D   Wheelchair access, sound guide for visually impaired and those with learning difficulties.
•   The museum in the former home of the Bishops of London tells the story of this ancient site, displays include archaeology, paintings, stained glass and a mummified rat. Herb garden and large grounds.

Museum of Garden History

5 Lambeth Palace Road, Westminster SE1 7LB 0171 261 1891

£   Free but donations welcome
O   March-Dec Mon-Fri 10.30-16.00 Sun 10.30-17.00
P   Meters in Lambeth Road and High Street
R   Yes, groups please notify in advance
T   Yes
D   Wheelchair access and ramps, no adapted toilet
•   Large collection of historic tools, pictorial panels of plant-hunters, artefacts, exhibitions of paintings, replica 17th Century garden.

Museum of Richmond

Old Town Hall. Whittaker Avenue, Richmond TW9 17P Tel 0181 332 1141

£   A £1 C/OAP/ Student/Con 50p
O   Tue-Sat 11.00-17.00 All year May-Oct Sun 13.00-16.00

P   Parking available around Richmond Green and Paradise Road
C   Regular children's activities
T   Public toilets in basement
D   Wheelchair access and toilet facilities
•   The local history museum for Richmond and Kew. Features permanent exhibits and a changing programme of temporary displays.

National Postal Museum

King Edward Building, King Edward Street, City, EC1 1LP
£   Free
O   Mon-Fri 09.30-16.30 Cl Weekends & BHs
P   N.C.P. Car park nearby, no parking outside the building
C   'Stamp as you go' souvenir card -an activity for all ages. Hand outs available for most exhibits.
T   Yes
D   Yes
•   Museum holds the Post Office collection of stamps of the world, British 20th Century stamps and archival philatelic material exhibitions and displays of postal related items-posting boxes, vehicles, writing equipment and ephemera etc.

The Old Operating Theatre and Herb Garret

9a St Thomas's Street, Southwark SE1 9RY Tel 0171 955 4791
£   A £2.50 Con £2
O   Mon-Sun 10.00-16.00 All year except Xmas Day
P   Parking on Weston Street under London Bridge, nearest tube-London Bridge
C   'Hands -on' facilities
T   Yes
•   The only operating theatre in this country that was in use before anaesthetics and antiseptics which reveals the horror of medicine in those days. Display of medical instruments.

Petre Museum of Egyptian Archaeology

University College, Gower Street, Euston WC1E 6BT. Tel 0171 3877050 Ext 2884.
£   Free, donation appreciated
O   Mon-Fri 10.00-12.00. 13.15-17.00. Open some Sat mornings. Cl Xmas week, Easter and 4 weeks during summer.
P   Meter parking nearby
C   To purchase - childrens trail and teachers' pack
R   In college refectories
T   Yes
D   Wheelchair access. Toilets
•   A wealth of archaeological material illustrating ancient Egyptian culture, technology and daily life. Museum houses world's largest dresses and monumental lions. Forty of the Famum portraits, all excavated by Flinders Petrie.

Pitshanger Manor & Gallery

Mattock Lane, Ealing W5 5EQ. Tel 0181 56721227
£   Free
O   Tue-Sat 10.00-17.00. Cl Xmas,N.Y & Easter
P   On-street parking, also at shopping centre multi-storey car park.
R   Hot and cold drinks machine

T   Yes
D   On-site parking. Ramp into museum and gallery. Lift for small wheelchairs to all floors. No wheelchair
•   1768 Grade I listed house mostly rebuilt by architect Sir John Soane for his country villa. Houses large collection of Martinware pottery. Art gallery has changing programme of contemporary exhibitions.

Queen Elizabeth's Hunting Lodge

Rangers Road. Chingford E4 7QH. Tel 0181 5296681
£   A 50p. Accompanied children free
O   Wed-Sun 14.00-17.00(dusk in winter)
P   Nearby
C   Quiz. Various handling objects on show
R   Cafe and kiosk nearby
T   Yes
D   Wheelchair lift for stairs. Toilet
•   The only remaining royal hunting grandstand in the world, built for Henry VIII to view the game, and is the only survivor of all his royal timber-framed buildings.

Ragged School Museum

46-50 Copperfield Road, Tower Hamlets E3 4RR. Tel 0181 9806405
£   Free
O   Wed. Thur 10.00-17.00. Also 1st Sun in month 14.00-17.00.
P   Street parking
C   On the Sun openings and during school holidays there is a varied programme of events for children, adults and families, i.e. treasure hunts, art workshops, story-telling and re-enacted Victorian lessons.
R   Cafe
T   Yes
•   Victorian canal-side warehouses converted for use as a Ragged School by Dr Barnardo. Experience how Victorian children were taught. Displays of local history, industry and East End life.

The Royal London Hospital Archives and Museum

The Royal London Hospital Whitechapel E1 1BB Tel 0171 377 7608
£   Free
O   Mon-Fri 10.00-14.30 Cl Public Hols
P   Meter parking (Parking is difficult)
R   In Out-Patients Dept near to Archives
T   In Out-Patients
D   Wheelchair access to Archives
•   The story of the London Hospital founded in 1740 is told in the Crypt of the former hospital Church and includes its contribution to the health and welfare of millions of Londoners and the work of pioneers like James Parkinson, Frederick Treves and Edith Cavell. Many interesting exhibits and videos on hospital history and modern developments such as London's Helicopter emergency medical service.

Sir John Soane's Museum

13 Lincoln's Inn Fields, Holborn WC2A 3BP. Tel 0171 4300175
£   Free admission to museum. Guided tours Sat afternoons(tickets sold at 14.00 for 14.30) £3. Students, under 18s & UB40's free. Groups by arrangement.

O   Tue-Sat 10.00-17.00. Cl Xmas & BHs
P   NCP Drury Lane, meters Mon-Sat in Lincoln Inn Fields(expensive). Close to Holborn underground and various bus routes
C   Children welcome under supervision in view of the nature and vulnerability of displays. Regret no buggies or carry-packs
R   Cafes and sandwich bars nearby. Picnics possible in central garden in square of Lincoln Inn Fields.
T   Yes
D   Very limited access (please phone for details). No wheelchair access or adapted toilet.
•   The house and museum of Sir John Soane, one of England's greatest architects. Rooms appear almost exactly as they did on the day of his death in 1837.

Spelthorne Museum
Old Fire Station, Market Square, Staines TW18 4RH. Tel 01784 461804.
£   Free
O   Wed & Fri 14.00-16.00 Sat 13.30-16.30
P   Public car parks in town centre (5 mins walk)
R   In town
T   None in museum, nearest Old Town Hall Arts Centre, next door
D   Access to ground floor
•   Constantly chaning programme of exhibitions relating to archaeology, social history and local industries. Extensive collection of items from Roman town of Staines. 1738 fire engine.

Vestry House Museum
Vestry Road, Walthamstow E17 9NH. Tel 01815091917.
£   Free
O   Mon-Fri 10.00-13.00. 14.00-17.30. Sat 10.00-13.00. 14.00-15.00. Cl BHs
P   Street parking opposite
C   Facilities only for special events and exhibitions
T   Yes
D   Ramp access to ground floor only
•   Based in 18th century workhouse in Walthamstow village conservation area, the museum covers many aspects of life in Waltham Forest. Displays include Victorian police cell and 1894 Brener car.

Wandsworth Museum
The Courthouse, 11 Garratt Lane, Wandsworth SW18 4AQ. Tel 0181 871 7074/7075
£   Free
O   Tue-Sat 10.00-17.00. Sun 14.00-17.00
P   Shoppers car parks nearby
C   Hands-on facilities, questionnaires, fun/activity sheets
T   Yes
D   Wheelchair access throughout. Lift. Tactile plans of building. Toilet.
•   Exhibitions tell the story of Wandsworth's growth from country village to London's biggest borough. Try on a Roman helmet, become a Celtic chieftain, peer into a yuppie house.

Westminster Dragoons Museum
Cavalry House, Duke of York's Headquarters, Kings Road, Chelsea SW3 4SC. Tel 0181 8567995(curator)
£   Free
O   By arrangement
P   By arrangement
T   Yes
D   Access. No adapted toilet
•   Regimental museum housed within a barracks. Display shows the regiments predecessors and it's history from an Imperial Yeomanry Regiment to it's present roll in the Territorial Army.

Wimbledon Lawn Tennis Museum
Church Road, Wimbledon SW19 5AE. Tel 0181 9466131.
£   A £2.50. Con £1.50. Discount for pre-booked groups.
O   Tue-Sat 10.30-17.00. Sun 14.00-17.00. Also open BH.Mons Easter-late summer. Cl Fri, Sat. Sun prior to Championships, also middle Sun. Phone for Xmas & N.Y openings.
P   Ample free parking Aug-May, drive in the museum gates.
C   Quizzes and databanks.
R   Yes, open half an hour before museum
T   Yes
D   Full facilities
•   Videos show the great players in action and highlights of last year's championship. Collection of paintings, jewellery and costume. Historic collection of rackets, balls and paraphernalia of the modern game. View of centre court.

Wimbledon Society Museum of Local History
22 Ridgway, Wimbledon SW19 4QN. Tel 0181 2969914.
£   Free
O   Sat only, 14.30-17.00
•   A unique museum of local history of the parish and electoral district of Wimbledon.

MERSEYSIDE

BIRKENHEAD

'The Birkenhead Packet'

Williamson Art Gallery & Museum - Wirral Museum - Birkenhead Priory - St May's Tower
Birkenhead Tramways - Pacific Road Transport Museum - Egerton Bridge - Shore Road
Pumping Station all c/o Wirral Museum, Birkenhead Town Hall, Hamilton Street, Birkenhead
LA1 5BR. Tel 0151 65664010

£   A £2.50. C £1.25. Fam £6.50. (all admittances + tram rides)
O   Sat & Sun 13.00-17.00. School hol Tue & Sun 13.00-17.00. Groups at all times by
    arrangement
P   No charge, available at all venues except Wirral Museum
C   For school visits only
T   Yes
D   Facilities at Priory-Williamson-Wirral Museum only
•   The Birkenhead Packet features a number of related venues which offer a variety of
    family experiences. Ride on trams, climb St Mary's Tower. The museums trace the
    growth, history and development of Wirral-Birkenhead.

LIVERPOOL

Museum of Archaeology

University of Liverpool, 14 Abercromby Square L69 3BX Tel 0151 794 2467

£   Free
O   Wed during term time 13.30-16.00. Contact Sec re other times
P   Yes but permit required. Contact Sec
R   Refreshment area in Guild of Undergraduates
T   Yes
•   The collections consist of about 40,000 objects mainly from excavations of Professor J
    Garstang in Egypt and the Near East. Also collections of classical Aegean and prehistoric
    antiquities and coins from the Barnard and Chevasse collections

Merseyside Maritime Museum

Albert Dock, Liverpool L3 4AQ. Tel 0151 4784499

£   A £3. Con £1.50 (for unlimited 12 months entrance to all 8 museums and galleries

O   Daily 10.00-17.00

P   Kings Dock, 2 mins walk

C   Yes

R   Yes

T   Yes

D   Yes

•   Museum has galleries on the Battle of the Atlantic, transatlantic slavery and the Titanic amongst others and contain H M Customs and Excise national museum and museum of Liverpool life.

ST HELENS

Pilkington Glass Museum

Prescot Road, St Helens, Merseyside WA10 3TT. Tel 01744 692499/692014

£   Free

O   Mon-Fri 10.00—17.00. Sat Sun BH 14.00-16.30. Closed Xmas-N.Y

P   Yes

C   Some hands-on, workshops and quiz available

R   Vending machines

T   Yes

D   Toilet and stair lift but the lift does not accommodate a wheelchair

•   A colourful experience for all the family, working periscope, lighthouse optic, interactive display, 4000 years of glass making. See your body shape in the distortion mirror. Collection of rare and exotic glass exhibits from around the world.

SOUTHPORT

British Lawnmower Museum

106-114 Shakespeare Street, Southport PR8 5AE. Tel 01704 501336.

£   A £1 C 50p

O   All year exc Suns & BHs, 09.00-17.30. Tours for parties/schools by appointment.

P   Yes, 50 metres away

•   Over 150 restored rare and vintage lawnmowers dating from 1850's - a tribute to the garden machine industry over the last 150 years. Also large collection of vintage toy lawnmowers and games.

NORFOLK

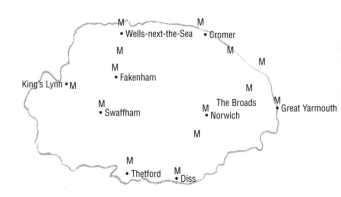

M

• Wells-next-the-Sea   M • Cromer

M   M

M   M

King's Lynn • M   • Fakenham

M   The Broads   M
M   • Swaffham   M • Norwich   • Great Yarmouth

M

M

• Thetford   M • Diss

CROMER

Cromer Museum
East Cottages, Comer NR27 9NJ Tel 01263 511722
£ A-£1.10p, C-50p, Con- 60p Group rates available
O Mon-Sat 10.00-17.00 (Cl Mon 13.00-14.00) Sun 14.00-17.00
P Nearby in town
C Activity sheets. Beachcombers shed available for schools, allowing hands on activity
T Yes
D Disabled access poor due to architectural design
• Atmospheric museum housed in row of tiny fishermens cottages beside Church. It tells the story of a Norfolk seaside resort and the landscape around it.

R.N.L.I. Lifeboat Museum
The Gangway, Cromer, NR27 0HY Tel 01263 511294
£ Free
O Easter-Oct 10.00-16.00
P In town
C Tasks can be arranged
R next door
T nearby
D Wheelchair access all round
• Building houses the lifeboat H.F. Bailey which served from 1935-1945 and saved 812 lives. Lifeboat history from 1804. Films showing current lifeboat.

Elizabeth House Museum
4 South Quay, Great Yarmouth NR30 2QH Tel 01493 855746
£ A.70p C.30p Con.40p. Joint tickets available if also visiting Maritime and Tolhouse Museums.
O 2 weeks over Easter then 25 May-26 Sept. 10.00-17.00. Cl Sat

Free on Quay or pay & display in King Street car park.
Yes
Limited
Victorian kitchen and toy room

Maritime Museum
25 Marine Parade, Great Yarmouth, Norfolk Tel 01493 842267
A.70p C 30p Con 40p. Joint tickets available if also visiting Elizabethan House &
Tolhouse Museums
2 weeks over Easter then 25 May-26 Sept. 10.00-17.00. Cl Sat.
Public car parks & parking in side streets
Yes

Tolhouse & Brass Rubbing Centre
Tolhouse Street, Great Yarmouth NR30 2SK Tel 01493 858900
A 70p C30p Con 40p. Joint tickets available if also visiting Elizabethan House & Maritime
Museums
2 weeks over Easter than 25 May-26 Sept 10.00-17.00 Cl Sat
Nearby public car parks
Quiz sheets. Brass rubbings from £1.
Victorian prison cells - brass rubbings

DISS

Diss Museum
The Market Place, Diss IP22 3AB Tel 01379 650618
Free
All year Wed, Thur 14.00-16.00 Fri, Sat 10.30-16.30 Cl BHs, Gd Fri & Xmas-NY
Car park in town
Wheelchair access
Housed in the historic shambles building, award winning Diss Museum provides visitors
with a variety of changing displays on local history and prehistory.

FAKENHAM

Fakenham Museum of Gas and Local History
Hempton Road, Fakenham Tel 01328 863150
A £1.50 C 25p OAP £1
8th-11th Apl,6th-9th May, 27th May-19th Sept Tue, Thur and BHs
Public car park in Bridge Street
Yes
Limited
The only remaining (non working) gas works in England and Wales, housed in a
scheduled ancient monument. The works give insight into the making of gas and the
working conditions of the men who made it.

GREAT YARMOUTH

Elizabethan House Museum
4 South Quay, Great Yarmouth Tel 01493 855746
A £1.90 C 90p Cons £1.40 Fam £4.70

O   Easter for two weeks Cl Gd Fri and Sat May-Sept Mon-Fri & Sun Cl Sat
P   On Quayside
T   Yes
D   Very limited
•   Complete re display for 1998. house through Tudor, Stuart and Victorian times. Family friendly upstairs and downstairs.

KINGS LYNN

The Old Goal House
Saturday Market Place, Kings Lynn PE30 5DQ Tel 01553 763044
£   A £3 C under 14 and OAP £2
O   Daily 10.00-16.15 Cl Xmas & NY
P   Town centre pay and display car park
C   Yes
T   Yes
D   Most of exhibition accessible to wheel chair. Toilet facilities
•   Records crime and punishment in King's Lynn over 300 years. In the Regalia room there is the famous King John's Cup and Sword and four town maces plus charters and artefacts of civic interest.

The North End Trust
Trues Yard, North Street, Kings Lynn, PE30 1QW Tel 01553 770479
£   A £1.90 C £1.50 Con £1. Parties £1 per head.
O   Every day, except Xmas
P   Coach & carparks 100 metres
C   Full hands on science activities
T   Yes
D   Toilets and lift to upper floors
•   King's Lynn's last remaining fishermen's yard housed in two restored fishermen's cottages telling the story of how life was lived from the mid 19th Century to early 20th Century. New extension opened May 97 including two new galleries.

LITTLE WALSINGHAM

The Shirehall Museum
Common Place, Little Walsingham, NR22 6BP Tel01328 820510
£   Museum only A 60p C/OAP 40p. Abbey grounds & museum A £2 C/OAP £1.
O   Easter-Oct every day except Suns. 10.30-16.30. Abbey grounds 10.30-16.30 Sun 14.00-17.00
P   within easy reach
R   within easy reach
D   Wheelchair access suitable to grounds
•   Early 19th Century courtroom with original fittings. Exhibits depicting the history of Walsingham.

MUNDESLEY

Mundesley Maritime Museum
Beach Road, Mundesely, NR118BG Tel 01263 720879
£   50p children free if accompanied by adult

O Easter weekend then daily from 1st May-30 Sep 11.00-13.00 & 14.00-16.00
P across the road
T across the road
D Ground floor only therefore no charge for disabled. Toilet across the road
• Photos illustrating maritime history, trade, ship wrecks, lifeboat activity. Exhibits of breeches buoy, foghorn, etc. 1st floor reinstated as Coastguard lookout (binoculars available) coastwatch lookouts in attendance.

NORWICH

Bridewell Museum
Bridewell Alley NR2 1AQ Tel 01603 667228
£ A £1.20 C 50p Con 80p
O Apl-Sept, Tue-Sat 10.00-17.00
P St Andrews car park, 5 mins walk
C Quiz, colouring sheets and hands-on activities
T Yes
• Working life of Norwich over last two hundred years. Reconstructed chemist, pawnbrokers and smithy.

Sainsbury Centre For Visual Arts
University of East Anglia, Norwich NR4 7T5 01603 593199/456060
£ A £2 C under 5 free Con £1
O Tue-Sun 11.00-17.00
P U.E.A. West and Central car parks ask at Porter's Lodge
C Activity sheets and questionnaires. Special children's activities first Sunday of month
R Cafe, also Buffet and Restaurant open Mon-Fri lunchtime only
T Yes
D Wheelchair access and disabled toilets

St Peter Hungate Church Museum & Brass Rubbing Centre
Princes Street Norwich NR3 1AE Tel 01603 667231
£ Free
O Apl-Sept, Mon-Sat 10.00-17.00
P Limited on-street but public parking at Monastery car park (Elm Hill) and St Andrews car park
C Activity sheets, handling material, brass rubbing
D Wheelchair ramps
• Fine 14th century Church with displays illustrating local history

POTTER HEIGHAM

Museum of the Broads
The Broads Haven, Bridge Road, Potter Heigham NR29 5JD Tel 01692 581900
£ Free- Donations requested
O Easter-Oct Wed-Sun 12.00-16.00
P Yes free
C Yes
T Yes
D Yes
• Museum in development stage. Exhibition showing items from collection plus displays

and demonstrations, videos etc.

SWAFFHAM

Swaffham Museum
Town Hall, 4 London Street, Swaffham PE37 7DQ Tel 01760 721230
£   A 50p C Free
O   Easter-Oct Tue-Sat 11.00-16.00
P   In Market Place
C   Yes
T   Yes
•   Small friendly social history museum, exhibitions changed annually, houses Symonds collection of 68 figures from Dickens, Shakespeare, Tolkien Commedia and De'Larte. Guided tours of town available.

THETFORD

Ancient House Museum
21 White Hart Street, Thetford, IP24 1AA Tel 01842 752599
£   Free except Jul & Aug A 70p C 30p Con 40p
O   Mon-Sat all year 10.00-17.00 plus Suns in Jun Jul & Aug 14.00-17.00
P   Yes
C   Activity sheets, hands on display of local countryside
R   town centre
T   town centre
•   Grade 1 list Merchants house showing Thetford & Breckland life, flints, timbers, mammoth teeth, herbs.

WALSINGHAM

Walsingham Shirehall, Common Place
Walsingham, NR22 6BP Tel 01328 820510
£   A 60p museum A£2 grounds & museum Con museum 40p grounds & museum £1
O   May-Oct Mon-Sat
P   Outside museum 50p per hour. Public car park 300 metres
R   Available in village
T   In Abbey grounds and High Street
D   Wheel chair entrance via High Street. Toilet facilities in Abbey grounds
•   Georgian Court Room in original state. Museum of local history including ruins of Augustinian Priory. Bridewell prison 1/4 mile walk -free.

WELLS NEXT THE SEA

Wells Maritime Museum
The Old Lifeboat House, West Quay, Wells next the Sea NR23 1AT Tel 01328 711646
£   A 75p C 25p under 6years free
O   Easter, July-Oct Tue Fri 14.00-17.00 Weekends 10.00-13.00 14.00-17.00 during schools hols during Aug open daily morning, afternoon and evening
P   Wells Harbour Quay car park £1.50 per day
C   School pack
T   Public toilets 50 metres

Housed in the old Lifeboat House the museum provides a history of Wells.

WYMONDHAM

The Wymondham Heritage Museum
Norwich Road, Wymondham, NR18 0NS Tel 01953 600205
A £1 C 50p cons 75p (prices to be revised in 1998
March-Nov Mon-Sat 10.00-16.00 Sun 14.00-16.00
Free car park
Yes please telephone for details
Tea Room
Yes
Yes
The museum tells the story of the building from its foundation in Elizabethan times to its reformed prison in 1785. Also relates the growth of Wymondham from the foundation of the Abbey in 1107 through to the present day.

NORTHAMPTONSHIRE

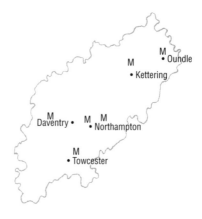

M
• Oundle

M
• Kettering

M
Daventry • M M
• Northampton

M
• Towcester

ASHTON

The National Dragonfly Museum at Ashton Mill
Ashton Wold, Ashton, Nr Oundle PE8 5LZ Tel 01832 272427
£ A £2.50 C 75p Fam ticket £5 2 A season £10 Fam Season £12
O 14th June-29th Sept 10.30-17.00 Weekends and BHs Open Thur & Fri by appointment-groups
P Yes
C Questionnaires
R Tea rooms
T Yes
D Yes access to all areas except tea rooms which has two steps but help available. Toilet facilities.
• Europe's first dragonfly museum. Inside are exhibitions, information, videos and live larvae. Outside there is a dragonfly trail. Also at the mill is a Victorian Engine Hall, vintage farm machinery and 'Room of the Five Craftsmen'.

DAVENTRY

Daventry Museum
Moot Hall, Market Square, Daventry NN11 5AF Tel 01327 302463
£ Free
O Apl-Sept 10.00-17.00 Mon-Sat Oct-March 10.00-15.30
P Public car park directly outside
C Sometimes available. special activities arranged in some school hols telephone first
• A local history museum including nearby Iron Age Hill Fort and the former BBC transmitter station at Daventry. Also regular arts and crafts temporary exhibitions.

EARLS BARTON

Earls Barton Museum of Local Life

Barkers Factory Complex, Station Road, Earls Barton NN6 OHD Tel 01604 811735

Free

Feb-Nov Sats 10.00-16.00 Cl Xmas & NY

Yes

Children very welcome, school parties etc. Talks and guided walks to suit age and ability

Local coffee shop

Yes

Wheel chair access to ground floor, prior notice preferred

A major part of the display depicts the interior of a shoe-workers cottage at the turn of the century. There is also a corner shop, a display of lace and a temporary exhibition area.

KETTERING

Manor House Museum

Sheep Street, Kettering Tel 01536 534381/534219

Free

Mon-Sat 09.30-17.00 Cl BHs

Car park next door or town centre parking

Yes please phone for details

Confectionery shop only

Yes

Wheel chair access Toilet facilities next door on Market Place

Explore Kettering's history at the museum, collection includes archaeology, social and industrial history. Temporary exhibition area.

NORTHAMPTON

Abington Museum

Abington Park, Park Avenue South, Northampton NN1 4LW Tel 01604 31454

Free

Thur 13.00-17.00 Sun 13.00-17.00 BH Mon

Parking available on street

Cafe in park

Yes

Wheel chair access to ground floor, toilet facilities, parking, wheel chair available

The museum is housed in a 15th century manor house. displays include the social history of the house along with a Victorian cabinet of curiosities, Northamptonshire's military history, a 19th Century fashion gallery and Northampton life from cradle to grave.

Central Museum and Art Gallery

Guildhall Road, Northampton NN1 1DP Tel 01604 39415

Free

Mon-Sat 10.00-17.00 Sun 14.00-17.00 All year

Public car park 400 metres

Yes available from the shop

Tea Room adjacent

T   Yes
D   Wheel chair access, lifts and toilet facilities
•   Displays feature - Northampton's history, audio and visual, decorative arts, the larges collection of boots and shoes in the world. Leathercraft gallery. Art gallery feature Italian and British art.

OUNDLE

Oundle Museum
The Drill Hall, Benefield Road, Oundle PE8
£   Free. Donations welcome
O   March-Nov Weekends 14.00-17.00 Other times by prior arrangement
P   Yes
C   Questionnaires
T   Yes
•   The main display is changed annually- 1997 was 'the Pubs and Breweries of Oundle'

TOWCESTER

The Canal Museum
Stoke Bruerne. Towcester NN12 7SE Tel 01604 862229
£   A £2.70 C and OAP £1.80 Fam £6.30
O   Easter-Oct All week 10.00-18.00 Oct-Easter Tue-Sun 10.00-16.00 Last admission 3 mins before closing
P   Adjacent parking, charge £1.20 (£1 refundable against admission fee)
C   Activity book, worksheet
R   Yes
T   Yes
D   Limited access to museum but good surface for canalside walks. toilet facilities
•   Comprehensive collection of inland waterways related artefacts housed in restored grai mill next to the Grand Union canal. Boat trips available.

WEST HUNSBURY

Northamptonshire Ironstone Railway Trust
Hunsbury Hill Country Park, West Hunsbury Tel 01604 890229 Or 403526
£   Admission is free. Train rides from Easter-Sept A £3 C £1.50 Fam £7
O   Easter-Sept Weekends 10.00-16.00
P   Public car park free next to museum
C   Access to engine cab and static engine
R   On Sundays Sweets and cans of drink etc
T   In car park
D   Limited
•   Features Nothamptonshire's ironstone industry and working industrial type railwa engines, static units and models of the railway industry and artefacts of the ironston industry.

WOLLASTON

The Wollaston Museum
102 High Street, Wollatston
£   Free
O   Easter Sun-last Sun in Sept 14.30-16.30
P   Free
•   This is a small village museum containing archaeological finds, own maps, prints and photographs, Victorian toys and treasures, handmade lace, bobbins, tools used in making footwear by hand. Paintings by local artists. Industrial and agricultural equipment and aspects of life in the village.

NORTHUMBERLAND

ASHINGTON

Woodhorn Colliery Museum & Narrow Guage Railway
QE II Country Park, Ashington NE63 9YF. Tel 01670 856968

£   Free to museum. Railway A 70p. Con 40p

O   May-Aug, Wed-Sun & BH Mons 10.00-17.00. Sept-Apl, Wed-Sun & BH Mons 10.00-16.00

P   Yes

C   Activity sheets. Play area. Narrow gauge railway

R   Yes

T   Yes

D   Limited access for wheelchair users. Toilet

•   The only coal mining museum in Northumberland, set in a country park. Railway and play area particularly attractive to children. Very near to the beautiful Northumberland coast.

BAMBURGH

Grace Darling (RNLI) Museum
Radcliffe Road, Bamburgh NE69 7AE. Tel 01668 214465

£   Free, donations to RNLI appreciated

O   Easter-end Oct daily 10.00-17.00

P   Nearby in village

T   In village

D   Wheelchair access

•   A living memorial to the bravery of Grace Darling who risked her life to rescue others from certain death in a terrible storm. An impressive collection of original relics of the Darlings.

ERWICK-UPON-TWEED

Berwick Borough Museum & Art Gallery
The Barracks, The Parade, Berwick-upon-Tweed TD15 2TQ. Tel 01289 330933
- A £2.30. Con £1.10. incl admission to 2 other museums
- End Mar/Easter-end Oct, daily 10.00-18.00. End Oct-end Mar, Wed-Sun 10.00-16.00
- Yes
- 'Window on Berwick' is exploratory
- Yes
- Limited

Local history & arts (from Burrell Collection) presented with sound/music & figures, 54 ft dragon, summer exhibitions. Family orientated with many interactives.

Regimental Museum of The King's Own Scottish Borderers
The Barracks, Berwick-upon-Tweed TD15 1DG. Tel 01289 307426
- A £2.30. C £1.20. Con £1.70. incl admission to 2 other museums
- Mon-Sat 09.30-16.00. Cl Easter & Xmas
- Public car park 50 metres
- Yes

The museum tells the story of the Borderer from 1689 to the present day through the use of audio-visual displays, diorama and tableaux.

Lindisfarne Ltd
Palace Green, Berwick-upon-Tweed
- Free
- Open all year but variable depending on tide times
- Yes, drop-off only for buses

The museum houses artefacts from the wine and spirit industry, see potters working, visit the pot shop and perfumery, and an original chemist's shop. Adults may sample Lindisfarne mead.

CORBRIDGE

Corbridge Roman Site
Corbridge NE45 5NT Tel 01434 632349
- A £2.50 C £1.30 Con £1.90
- Apl-Sept 10.00-18.00 Oct-March 10.00-16.00 Cl Mon-Tue Nov-March
- Yes
- Yes Hadrian's Wall activity pack £1.99
- Yes
- Limited please telephone for details

The museum houses a large and varied collection of Roman sculpture, glass and pottery, all found at Corbridge.

HEXHAM

Border History Museum
Old Gaol, Hexham NE46 3NH. Tel 01434 652349
- A £1.60. Con 80p. Fam £4.
- Easter-end Sept. daily 10.00-16.30. Oct. Nov. Feb-Easter, Sat-Tue 10.00-16.30
- Wentworth car park

C   Worksheets
R   Nearby
T   Nearby
D   No wheelchair access. Induction loops, large print & Braille guides
•   Come and meet the Border Reivers, families who fought, feuded, stole, raided and blackmailed across the border between England and Scotland in Tudor and Stuart times

Housesteads Roman Fort and Museum
Haydon Bridge, Hexham NE47 6NN Tel 01434 344363
£   A £2.70 C under 16 £1.40 Cons £2
O   Apl-Oct 10.00-18.00 (dusk in Oct) Nov-March 10.00-16.00
P   Half mile from site. Pay and Display £1 (run by Northumberland Nat Park)Housestead's
C   Activity book on Hadrians Wall available price £1.99, based on Housesteads, Chester and Corbridge sites
R   Kiosk at car (Summer only) Cold drinks, biscuits, icecream available from Museum all year
T   In car park
D   Car park on site. Toilet in car park. Steep steps up to museum., strong pushers for wheelchairs needed around site.
•   Substantially excavated fort on dramatic site, contains the only visible example of a Roman Hospital in Britain. Well preserved Roman Military latrine and granaries plus superb views along Hadrians Wall.

WOOLER

Earle Hill Household & Farming Museum
Earle Hill Head Farm, Wooler NE716H. Tel 01668 281243
£   A £1.50. C 50p
O   Jun-Sept, Fri pm & BHs.
P   Yes
T   Yes
•   Rare collection of household and farm antiquities incl kitchen range, quilts, china, jewellery & toys. Farming tools, implements, records and photos

WYLAM

Wylam Railway Museum
Falcon Centre, Falcon Terrace, Wylam NE41 8EE Tel 01661 852174 Or 01661 853520
£   Free but donation requested
O   Tue-Thur 14.00-17.00 17.30-19.30 Sat 09.00-12.00 All year Cl Easter, Xmas and NY days
P   Nearby
T- Public toilets including disabled within 100 metres
D   Level access from 'The Dene'
•   This attractive small museum illustrates Wylam's unique place in railway history. Famous 'Father of Railways' George Stephenson was born in Wylam. The world's oldest locomotive 'Puffing Billy' was built in Wylam.

NOTTINGHAMSHIRE

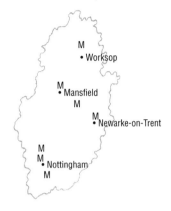

M
• Worksop

M
• Mansfield
M

M
• Newarke-on-Trent

M
M
• Nottingham
M

EASTWOOD

D H Lawrence Birthplace Museum
8a Victoria Street, Eastwood, NG16 3AW. Tel 01773 763312
£   A £1.75. Con £1.
O   Daily Apl-Oct 10.00-17.00. Nov-Mar 10.00-16.00. Cl 24 Dec-1 Jan incl.
P   Yes
C   Questionnaires available
T   Yes
D   Wheelchair access to ground floor only
•   Carefully restored and refurbished Victorian home reflecting working class lifestyle.
    Various exhibition rooms depicting D H Lawrence's 'Country of My Heart'

MANSFIELD

Mansfield Museum & Art Gallery
Leeming Street, Mansfield,. NG18 1NG. Tel 01623 663088
£   Free
O   Mon-Sat 10.00-17.00. Cl Suns & BHs
P   Public parking within 5 mins walk
C   Activity corner with puzzles, activity sheets and object handling
R   Cafe next door
T   Yes
D   Fully accessible to wheelchairs.
•   Museum shows local history and fine & decorative arts. Temporary exhibitions.

NEWARK

Millgate Museum

48 Millgate, Newark. NG24 4TS. Tel 01636 79403

£ Free

O Mon-Fri 10.00-17.00 (last admission 16.30). Sat-Sun 13.00-17.00. Please phone re BHs.

P Nearby

C Activity booklet on request

R Yes

T Yes

D Wheelchair access to ground floor only but photo album of other floors available. Toilet

• Visit Newark Castle, Gilstrap Centre and Newark Museum to discover the history of Newark and it's castle. The Mezzanine Gallery shows work of local artists, designers and photographers.

Upton Hall Clock & Watch Museum

Upton Hall, Upton, Newark. NG23 5TE. Tel 01636 813795.

£ A £2.50. C over 11 yrs £1.00. Con £2.00.

O Easter Sun-Aug BH. Sun-Fri 13.30-17.00

P Yes

R Yes

T Yes

D Ground floor access only

• Upton Hall houses the British Horological Institute's intriguing clock and watch collection. See the first successful electric clock, the actual watch worn by Capt Scott, the first self-winding wrist watch and many, many more items of fame and interest.

Vina Cooke Museum of Dolls & Bygone Childhood

The Old Rectory, Cromwell, Newark NG23 6JE. Tel 01636 821364.

£ A £2.50. C £1. Con £2.

O Sat-Thur 10.30-12.00. 14.00-17.00. Other times by appointment

P Yes

C Aspects of display are explained verbally where appropriate

R By prior arrangement and for booked parties

T Yes

D Facilities very limited

• Large display of dolls, toys, costumes, prams, etc. in historic setting. Garden and gift shop.

NOTTINGHAM

The Canal Museum

Canal Street, Nottingham NG1 7ET. Tel 0115 9156870.

£ Free

O 10.00-17.00 Wed-Sun & BHs. Cl Xmas & Boxing days.

P City centre parking nearby

C Self-operated audio/visual show of trip along river Trent. Various activity sheets

T Yes

D Wheelchair access (one helper per wheelchair for access to first floor). No access to wharf

Situated on two floors of a former canal warehouse, displays relate to river Trent and local canals. Two former working narrowboats.

The Caves of Nottingham

Drury Walk, Broadmarsh Centre, Nottingham NG1 7LS. Tel 0115 9241424

£ A £2.95. Con £1.95. Fam £8.50
O Mon-Sat 10.00-16.15. Sun 11.00-16.00
P Broadmarsh shopping centre car park
C Audio tour plus pub games etc
T In shopping centre
D Due to nature of attraction we are unable to admit wheelchairs. Induction loop available
• 35 min audio tape tour of 700 year old caves beneath modern shopping centre. Air raid shelter, medieval tannery, cesspit and remains of Drury Hill. Choose a hard hat and descend into the caves.

The Lace Hall

High Pavement, Nottingham NG1 1HN. Tel 0115 9484221

£ A £2.85. Con £1.85. Group rate available.
O Every day exc Xmas day, 10.00-17.00(last admission 16.00)
P Limited forecourt parking. Coach & disabled parking by arrangement
C Educational visits welcome. Hands-on and activity sheets provided. Role play, dressing up.
R Yes
T Yes
D Wheelchair access throughout. Toilets
• Learn how lace developed from cottage craft to become the toast of the industrial revolution. See lace being made on 100 year old working machines in 'The Story of Lace' exhibition

Brewhouse Yard - The Museum of Nottingham Life

Castle Boulevard, Nottingham NG7 1FB. Tel 0115 9153600

£ Weekdays free. Weekends and BHs A £1.50. Con 80p. Passport to leisure holders A £1. Con 50p (prices will differ for special events)
O Daily 10.00-17.00. Cl Xmas & Boxing days and Fri mornings 1 Nov-28 Feb.
P Within walking distance
C Hands-on in some areas. Questionnaires available
T Yes
D Access to ground floor on
• Discover many fascinating locally made or used objects shown in a mixture of period rooms, recreated shops and 'between the wars' shopping street

Museum of Costume & Textiles

Castle Gate, Nottingham NG1 6AF

£ Free
O Daily 10.00-17.00. Cl Xmas & Boxing days and Fri mornings 1 Nov-28 Feb.
P Nearby
D Access to ground floor only
• A series of atmospheric period rooms displaying costume from 1790 to mid-20th century.

Castle Museum & Art Gallery
Nottingham NG1 6EL. Tel 0115 9153700
£   Mon-Fri free. Weekends & BHs, A £1.50. Con 80p. Passport to leisure holders A £1. Con
    50p Fam £3.80. (charges will differ for special events)
O   Daily 10.00-17.00. Cl Xmas& Boxing days and Fri mornings 1 Nov-28 Feb.
P   Within walking distance
C   Range of exhibits. Activities and facilities designed for younger visitors
R   Yes
T   Yes
D   Lift provides access to all floors. Parking for wheelchair users. Access guides available
    by tel 0115 9153684. Toilet
•   Nottingham Castle has a reputation for its friendly, warm atmosphere, lively exhibitions
    innovative displays. Fun activities and events for all. Also enjoy the beautiful gardens and
    craft shop.

Sherwood Foresters Regiment Museum
Nottingham Castle
£   Free
O   Mon-Sun 10.00-16.30
P   Public car park on Friar Lane by castle gates
C   Yes
R   Yes
T   yes
D   Yes
•   The museum tells the history of the Regiment from 1741 to 1970.

RAVENSHEAD

Longdale Craft Centre Museum
Longdale Lane, Ravenshead, NG15 9AH. Tel 01623 794858.
£   A £1.95. C £1.75
O   Daily 09.00-18.00. Cl Xmas & Boxing days
P   Yes
C   Yes
R   Yes
T   Yes
D   Wheelchair access
•   See craftspeople working on a range of crafts incl pottery, jewellery and printmaking in
    authentic period workshops housed in recreated Victorian streets. Also the Gordon
    Brown sculpture collection.

RUDDINGTON

Nottingham Heritage Centre
Mere Way, Ruddington. NG11 6NX. Tel 0115 9405705.
£   A £2.50. C £1.50. Con £2. Fam £7.
O   Mar-mid Oct Sun & B.H.
P   Yes
R   Yes
T   Yes
D   Wheelchair access.

The centre is managed and run completely by volunteers and is an ever expanding facility.

Ruddington Framework Knitters Museum

Chapel Street, Ruddingto. NG11 6HE. Tel 0115 9846914

A £2. Con £1.25. Fam £5.25

Easter-mid Dec, Wed-Sat 11.00-16.30. Sun Easter-end Sept 13.30-16.30

Nearby

Knitting on Griswold circular machines also sitting at historic frames

By prior arrangement for booked parties

Yes

Due to historic nature of site wheelchair access to ground floor only

Working museum - all machines demonstrated to visitors. Unique purpose-built knitters yard, cottages, workshops around courtyard with communal facilities. Contemporary Primitive Methodist Chapel adjacent.

Ruddington Village Museum

St Peter's Rooms, Church Street, Ruddington NG11 6HA

A £1 C under 5 free Con 50p

Apl-Sept Wed-Thur 14.00-16.30 Sat 14.30-16.30 & BHs

Car park opposite (100 metres)

Yes

Yes

Yes and toilet facilities

The museum depicts the community life of Ruddington and includes several reconstructed shops - Edwardian fish and chip shop, pharmacy, cobbler, ironmonger and toy shop.

SNEINTON

Green's Mill & Science Centre

Windmill Lane, Sneinton. NG2 4QB. Tel 0115 9156878.

£ Free

Wed-Sun 10.00-17.00 Cl Xmas & Boxing days.

P Yes

C Majority of exhibits are hands-on

T Yes

D Wheelchair users can gain access to all exhibits. Sloping cobbled courtyard may cause difficulties for some unaccompanied visitors but museum staff are on hand to help.

• Explores windmills, milling and achievements of George Green, through interactive hands-on exhibits, models, audio visual. Visitors may also see the restored windmill at work.

The William Booth Birthplace Museum

The Salvation Army William Booth Memorial Complex, 14 Notintone Place, Sneinto. NG2 4QZ. Tel 0115 9503927

£ Free
O By appointment
P Rear of complex or windmill car park
R Booked in advance
T Yes
D No access for wheelchairs
• Museum showing the life of William Booth.

WOLLATON PARK

Industrial Museum (incl Stable Block Gallery)

Courtyard Buildings, Wollaton Park. NG8 2AE. Tel 0115 9153910.

£ Weekdays free. Weekends & BHs, A £1.50. Con 80p. Fam £3.80
O Apl-Sept, Mon-Sat 10.00-16.30. Sun 13.00-16.30. Oct-Mar, Thur-Sat 10.00-16.30. Fri & Sun 13.00-16.30
P Yes
R Cafe in grounds
T In grounds
D Access available to ground floor level. Toilet in grounds
• Museum offers insight into Nottingham's rich industrial heritage. Beam engines to bicycles and the best collection of lace machines in the country.

Wollaton Hall Natural History Museum

Wollaton Park. NG8 2AE. Tel 0115 9153900.

£ Weekdays free. Weekends & BHs, A £1.50. Con 80p. Fam £3.20.
O Mon-Sat 10.00-16.30. Sun 13.00-16.30 Cl Xmas & Boxing days & Fri mornings 1 Nov-28 Feb
P Yes
C Hands-on within nature quest room
R Cafe in grounds
T In grounds
D Wheelchair access to ground floor. Toilet .
• Striking example of renaissance domestic architecture, once home of Sir Francis Willoughby. Now houses city's natural history collection. Set in more than 500 acres of parkland. Beautiful gardens rich in wildlife.

WORKSOP

Museum of Telecommunications

Qeeen Street, Worksop. Correspondence to Tim Toulson, 30 Old Park Avenue, Greenhill, Sheffield SB 7DR Tel 01909 483680

£ Free
O By appointment only
P Public car park 500 metres
C Guided tours, hands on and working models
R Drinks biscuits normally available, Buffets by arrangement
T Yes
D Access to all areas but no toilet facilities

- Shows all aspects of telecommunications from origins to modern day. A very friendly and comfortable environment to explore a complex subject. Suitable for 6 to 60 year olds.

Worksop Museum

Public Library, Memorial Avenue, Worksop S80 2BP Tel 01909 472408/501148
£ Free
O Mon,Tue, Wed & Fri 09.30-18.00 Thur, Sat 09.30-13.00 All year
P Parking in Memorial Avenue
T Continental style in Memorial Avenue!
D Yes
- The main exhibit is a display on the Pilgrim Fathers whose roots lay in North Nottinghamshire, this exhibit is presided over by life-size model of William Brewster one of the leaders of the movement.

OXFORDSHIRE

ABINGDON

Abingdon Museum
The County Hall, Market Place, Abingdon OX14 3HG Tel 01235 523703
£   Museum Free roof visits A £1 C 50p
O   Apl-Oct Tue-Sun 11.00-17.00 Nov-March Tue-Sun 11.00 16.00. Roof open last Sun June-Aug
P   Public car park within 5 minutes walk
C   Some specials for the summer holidays contact museum for details
R   Drinks, crisps and biscuits available in gallery. Cafes etc in town centre
T   By request only, key at desk. Public toilets in town
•   A lively and friendly museum in a spectacular building

Pendon Museum of Miniature Landscape & Transport
Pendon Museum Trust Ltd, Long Wittenham, Abingdon OX14 4QD Tel 01865 407365
£   A £3 C £2 (over 6 years) OAP £2.50
O   All year Weekends 14.00-17.00 Cl Dec June-Aug Wed 14.00-17.00 BHs 11.00-17.00 Cl Xmas and N.Y
P   Small car park on site, free to visitors
R   Drinks, biscuits and sweets
T   Yes
D   Limited, please telephone in advance
•   Fine quality models, depicting Vale of White Horse in 20's and 30's. Dartmoor scene with working railway and pioneering 'Madder Valley' railway (static) and railway relics.

BANBURY

Banbury Museum
8 Horsefair Banbury OX16 0AM Tel 01295 259855
£   Free

O Apl-Sept Mon-Sat 10.00-17.00 Oct-March Tue-Sat 10.00-16.30
P Pay and display car park behind museum
C Yes, quiz and questionnaire
R Coffee bar
T Yes
D Yes
• Housed in the former boardroom of the Poor Law Guardians the museum tells the story of 'Banburyshire'. There is a large collection of photographs and glass plate negatives of the region. Also has programme of temporary exhibitions.

BURFORD

Tolsey Museum

126 High Street, Burford OX18 4QU
£ A 50p C 10p Cons 20p
O May-Sept Sat, Sun, Fri and BHs 11.00-17.00 March-Nov Weekdays 14.00-17.00
P Public car park 50 metres
C Yes
• Wide ranging collection illustrating Burford's social and industrial past, including town maces, seals and charters from 1350, exhibits from a variety of trades and an unusual doll's house.

HENLEY ON THAMES

River and Rowing Museum

Mill Meadows, Henley on Thames RG9 1BF Tel 01491 415600
£ Unknown at time of printing. Please telephone museum
O Museum opens June 1998
P Yes on site
C Yes Lots
R Yes
T Yes
D Yes
• Celebrates the fascinating stories of the River Thames, the international sport of rowing and the historic riverside community of Henley on Thames.

OXFORD

Ashmolean Museum of Art and Archaeology

Beaumont Street, OX1 2PH Tel 01865 278000
£ Free. Donations appreciated
O Tue-Sat 10.00-16.00 Sun 14.00-17.00 & BHs Cl Xmas, NY & St Giles Fair in Sept
P Public car parks nearby
C Holiday activities Please telephone for details
R Yes
T Yes
D Wheelchair ramp into museum. Lift to all floors (Four steps down to antiquities galleries on first floor)
• Fascinating and rich array of art and archaeology including Egypt, Greece, Asia and Europe. Paintings, ceramics, coins, furniture, sculpture, glass, silver, tapestries, musical instruments and casts of classical sculpture.

Museum of Oxford
St Aldates, Oxford OX1 1DZ Tel 01865 815559
£ A £1.50 C under 8 years 50p Con £1 Fam £3.50
O Tue-Fri 10.00-16.00 Sat 10.00-17.00 All year
P Parking at Westgate Shopping Centre or Park and Ride
C Yes
T In adjacent building
• This town centre museum houses the town's first charter of 1192, models of the Saxon walled town and the Norman castle. Treasures from local archaeological excavations. Tools and products of the crafts people who supplied the University. Atmospheric room settings - an inn parlour, a students lodging and many more.

Museum of the History of Science
Broad Street, Oxford OX1 3AZ Tel 01865 277280
£ Free
O Tue-Sat 12.00-16.00
P Parking in Broad Street, Multi-storey car park, or Park and Ride
• Collection of antique scientific instruments, especially strong in early material i.e. medieval - 19th Century.

Oxford University Museum of Natural History
Parks Road, Oxford OX1 3PW Tel 01865 272950
£ Free
O Mon-Sat 12.00-17.00
P Town parking or Park and Ride
C At half term
T Yes
D Access to court area only using lift
• Magnificent Victorian Gothic style building housing the natural history collections of the University - Zoology, Entomology, Geology and Mineralogy.

Pitt Rivers Museum
South Parks Road, Oxford OX1 3PP Tel 01865 270927
£ Free
O Mon-Sat 13.00-16.30 Cl Xmas & Easter Please telephone for details
P Town parking or Park and Ride
T In the Natural History Museum
D Wheel chair access, no toilet facilities, please telephone in advance of visit
• World famous collection in a unique Victorian setting, includes jewellery, weaponry, textiles, toys, head-hunting trophies, masks and musical instruments. Audiguide by Sir David Attenborough. Programme of special exhibitions.

UFFINGTON

Tom Brown's School Museum
Broad Street, Uffington SN7 7RA Tel 01367 820259
£ Adults 60p Con 30p
O Easter-Oct Weekends & BH Mon except August 14.00-17.00
P By the Church
C Victorian slates to use
D Access to ground floor only

- Local exhibits housed in 1617 schoolroom. Nearest museum to the White Horse at Uffington.

WALLINGFORD

Wallingford Museum
Flint House, High Street, Wallingford OX10 0DB

£   A £1.75 C Free
O   March-Nov Tue-Fri 14.00-17.00 Sat 10.30-17.00 Suns-(June-Aug) BHs 14.00-17.00
P   Public car park off High Street or on street parking opposite museum
C   Yes
T   Nearest in St Aldates public car park
- A colourful and delightfully intimate local history museum, exciting sight and sound experience, Victorian street scene, feature on prehistory, River Thames, Wallingford Station. Special exhibitions. Small shop.

WITNEY

Witney and District Museum
Gloucester Court Mews, High Street, Witney OX8 6LX Tel 01993 775915

£   A 50p C Free
O   Apl-Sept Wed-Sun 10.00-16.00 Mon & Tue by appointment for groups
P   Public car parks nearby
C   Yes
R   Drinks only
T   Yes
D   Access to ground floor for wheel chairs, no lift to first floor, hand rails. Toilet facilities
- The museum is an amenity for the local area, highlighting the social, educational, historical and industrial heritage of Witney and district. Tours can be arranged and specific topics catered for.

WOODSTOCK

Oxfordshire County Museum
Fletchers House, Park Street, Woodstock OX20 1SN Tel 01993 811456

£   A £1.50 C 50p Con £1 Fam and Annual tickets available
O   May-Sept Tue-Sat 10.00-16.00 Sun 14.00-17.00 Oct-Apl Tue-Fri 10.00-16.00 Sat 10.00-17.00 Sun 14.00-17.00
P   On street or public car park in town
C   Planned for new galleries, please telephone for details
R   Light
T   Yes
- Museum tells the story of Oxfordshire from earliest times to present day. Varied programme of temporary exhibitions. Skeletons in museum which particularly appeal to children.

RUTLAND

COTTESMORE

Rutland Railway Museum

Cottesmore Iron Ore Mines Sidings, Ashwell Road, Cottesmore, Rutland LE15 7BX. Tel 01572 770935

£   Weekends for casual viewing, donations requested. Steam Days - A £2.50. C 5-16 £1.50 Con £1 Fam £6.50
O   Weekends for casual viewing. Please phone for special steam days.
P   Free
C   Only on special children's events
R   Steam days only and some mid summer weekends
T   Yes
D   Site mostly flat but steep slope to toilets
•   Open air industrial railway museum with lineside walkway and various picnic areas. Large collection of locos and wagons. Unlimited train rides on steam days. Close to Rutland Water and Oakham.

OAKHAM

Rutland County Museum

Catmos Street, Oakham LE15 6HW Tel 01572 723654

£   Free
O   All year Mon-Sat 10.00-17.00 Sun (Summer) 14.00-17.00 Sun (Winter) 14.00-16.00
P   Free public car park adjacent
R   Cafe (subject to confirmation)
T   Yes
D   Wheelchair access and toilets
•   Museum of Rutland Life, with farm equipment, vehicles, rural tradesmen's tools, domestic collections, local archaeology. Late 18th Century riding school. Volunteer Soldier gallery. Education service.

SHROPSHIRE

ACTON SCOTT

Acton Scott Historic Working Farm
Wenlock Lodge, Acton Scott SY6 6QN Tel 01694 781306/7
£   A £3 C (5-16) £1.50 OAP £2.50 Fam £9.50 Season tickets and group rates available
O   Apl-Oct Tue-Sun & BHs 10.00-17.00
P   Free on site
C   Build a wheel, build a drill, build a cruck, quizzes, painting comps
R   Cafe
T   Yes
D   Yes Wheelchairs available, ramps, toilet facilities and parking
•   Farming at turn of century (1860-1920) All work by horse or hand. Norfolk four course crop rotation, rare breeds of animals. Crafts - blacksmith, woodland, farrier, wheelwright. Craft shop.

BISHOP'S CASTLE

The House on Crutches
4 Tan House, Church Street, Bishop's Castle SY9 5AA Tel 01588 630 007
£   A 50p
O   Easter-Sept Weekends & BHs 12.00-16.00
P   Public car parks in town
C   Children's guide and Museum/House trail
T   Public toilets opposite museum
•   The House on Crutches is a 'town' museum housed in one of Bishop Castle's oldest buildings. It is a private museum with no pretensions and plenty to interest both the dedicated and the browser.

BRIDGNORTH

Northgate Museum

The Burgess Hall, Northgate, High Street, Bridgnorth WV16 4ER Tel 01746 761859
£   Free
O   Easter-Sept Weekends & BHs plus Mon-Wed during school hols 14.00-16.00
P   Public car park in Innage Lane
T   Public toilets in car park Innage Lane
•   Museum houses collection of coins, tokens, cameras and firemarks. Local history
    depicted by, photographs and postcards. Domestic and agricultural memorabilia.

LUDLOW

Ludlow Museum

Castle Street, Ludlow SY8 1AS Tel 01584 875384
£   A £1 C 50p
O   Apl-Oct Mon-Sat 10.30-13.00 14.00-17.00 Weekend & BHs June-August
P   On street parking or public car park off Castle Square
C   Yes
R   Cafe upstairs in Assembly Rooms complex
T   Public toilet in car park off Castle Square
D   Yes access and toilet facilities
•   Ludlow museum tells the story of Ludlow from 450 million years ago to present day-
    starting in the geology gallery 'Reading the Rocks' moving through archaeology in to
    'Ludlow' the planned town. Changing displays in final gallery.

MUCH WENLOCK

Much Wenlock Museum

The Square, High Street, Much Wenlock TF13 6HR Tel 01952 727773
£   A 50p C, OAP and Con free as are Museum Association members
O   Apl-Sept Mon-Sat 10.30-13.00 14.00-17.00 June-August Sun 10.30-13.00 14.00-17.00
P   Public pay and display in St Mary's Road nearby
C   Yes
R   None on site but plenty nearby
T   Public toilet in St Mary's Road car park
D   Access but no toilet facilities
•   Working display showing how Wenlock Edge formed. Display on William Penny
    Brookes-Modern day Olympics.

SHREWSBURY

Clive House Museum

College Hill, Shrewsbury SY1 1LT Tel 01743 354811
£   A £2 C 50p OAP and Students £1
O   Mid May-Sept Tue-Sat & BHs 10.00-16.00 Cl 21st Dec-5th Jan
P   Public car park town centre 5 mins walk
C   Children's room with hands on toys, aquarium and natural history table
R   None on site but walled garden for picnics
D   Limited wheelchair access via cobbled lane to ground floor and garden
•   Typical Shrewsbury town house with a long history displaying aspects of Victorian

domestic life and natural history, Temporary exhibitions with a natural history 'theme'.

oleham Pumping Station
ongdon, Coleham, Shrewsbury Tel 01743 362947

A £1 Con 50p

Apl-Sept 4th Sunday each month 10.00-16.00

Public car park nearby off English Bridge

Yes

Wheelchair access

Two steam driven beam engines by Renshaws of Stoke installed in 1984 to solve Shrewsbury's sewerage problem

owley's House Museum
arker Street, Shrewsbury SY1 1QH Tel 01743 361196

A £2 C 50p OAP and Students £1

Mid May-Sept Tue-Sat 10.00-17.00 Sun & BH. Mon 10.00-16.00 Cl 21st Dec-5th Jan

Short stay public car park adjacent, long stay public car park few minutes walk

Yes at holiday periods

Limited ramped access only to ground floor, reception and shop

A major regional museum with varied collections, including important material from Roman Wroxeter, costume, log boats, mediaeval Shrewsbury. Changing programme of temporary exhibitions of general interest .

hropshire Regimental Museum
he Castle, Castle Street, Shrewsbury SY1 2AT Tel 01743 262292/358516

A £2 C 50p OAP and Student £1

Easter-Sept Tue-Sun 10.00-16.00 Oct-Easter Tue-Sat 10.00-16.00

Public car park in town centre less than 3 minutes walk

Yes

Yes

Wheelchair access to 95% of museum. Toilet and parking facilities

The museum has recently been re structured in an easy to understand display in date order from 1090 to the present day, including displays on the Castle, the Shropshire Regiments including the Shropshire Volunteers and Militia.

ELFORD

ronbridge Open Air Museum of Steel Structure
herry Tree Hill, Coalbrookdale, Telford TF8 7EF Tel 01952 433152

A £2 C and OAP £1.50 Fam £6 Reduced rates for groups of 10 or more

Tue-Sun & BHs 10.00-17.00

On site free car park and free coach parking if booked in advance

None but picnic site in grounds

Facilities on request

Much of the site is accessible by electrically powered outdoor wheelchairs, some areas are difficult for manually operated wheelchairs. Visually impaired visitors may touch the sculptures.

A unique collection of 60 sculptures, by several leading artists, sited throughout 10 acres of exceptionally beautiful landscape. Featuring a substantial number of works by Museum Founder-Roy Kitchin.

Staffordshire

Stoke-on-Trent • M

M
• Stafford

• Burton-on-Trent

M
• Lichfield

LICHFIELD

Lichfield Heritage Exhibition and Treasury
Market Square, Lichfield WS15 6LG Tel 01543 256611
£   A £1.30 Con 80p Spire £1 Con 80p
O   Mon-Sat 10.00-16.00 Sun 10.30-16.00 Cl Xmas, Boxing & NY Days
P   Public pay and display car park 50 metres
R   Coffee Shop
T   Yes
D   Yes
•   Lichfield and the Civil War exhibition. Two audio visual presentations. Wonderful display of silver in the Treasury. Document display in Monument room. Guided tour of spire and ringing room.

STAFFORD

Ancient High House, Greengate Street, St16 2HS Tel 01785 240204
£   A £1.60 Con £1 Fam £4
O   All year Mon-Fri 09.00-17.00 Apl-Oct Sat 10.00-16.00 Nov-March Sat 10.00-15.00
P   Public car parks near by
C   Children's guide 80p
R   McDonalds next door or tea rooms etc in town
T   Yes
•   The largest timber framed town house in England. Permanent collection displayed in period room settings which relate to the house's history. Staffordshire Yeomanary Museum on top floor. Gift Shop and video room. Temporary exhibition programme

Izaak Walton's Cottage

Worston Lane, Nr Stone, Stafford ST15 OPA Tel 01785 760278 (April-March) 01785 240204 (Nov-March)

£   A £1.60 Con £1 Fam £4
O   Apl-Oct Tue-Sun 11.00-16.30 Cl Mon except BHs
P   Free on site
C   Children's guide 80p
R   Light refreshments
T   Yes
D   Access to cottage difficult, museum guides will help as mush as possible Toilet facilities
•   Timber framed cottage in the heart of mid Staffordshire countryside. Bequeathed by Izaak Walton it has displays on the history of angling. Ground floor rooms set in 17th Century style. Events programme during the summer. Souvenir shop.

Stafford Castle and Visitor Centre

off Newport Road, Stafford ST16 1DJ Tel 01785 257698

£   A £1.60 Con £1 Fam £4
O   Castle grounds all year admission free
O   Visitor centre Apl-Oct Tue-Sun & BH. Mon 10.00-17.00 Nov-March 10.00-16.00
P   Free on site
C   Yes
T   Yes
D   Wheel chair access and toilet facilities
•   The site of a Norman Motte and Bailey castle. The visitor centre is set out as a Norman guard room. an imaginative audio-visual presentation describes the castle's mixed fortunes. Gift shop.

STOKE ON TRENT

City Museum and Art Gallery

Bethseda Street, Hanley, Stoke on Trent ST1 3DW Tel 01782 232323

£   Free
O   Mon-Sat 10.00-17.00 Sun 14.00-17.00 Cl 25th Dec-1st Jan
P   Public car parks within 5 minutes walk
C   Yes
R   Tearoom
T   Yes
D   Wheelchairs available, toilet facilities, minicom service induction loop in lecture theatre
•   Sound-alive tape guide to our ceramic galleries. Dazzling display of over 5,000 pieces of English pottery. A MK16 Spitfire. Meet 'Ossie' the famous owl jug. A programme of events and exhibitions throughout the year.

Spode Museum

Spode Works Church Street, Stoke on Trent St4 1BX Tel 01782 744011

£   £ A2 C under 5 Free C under 12 and Con £1
O   Mon-Sat 09.00-17.00 Sun 10.00-16.00
P   Some free on site parking
C   In the craft centre - paint or lithograph your own saucer dish
R   Blue Italian Restaurant
T   Yes
D   Wheel chair access to museum

- Collection relates all aspects of the manufacture of Spode and Copeland wares. Factory and Connoisseur Tours by appointment, please telephone for details.

The Royal Doulton Visitor Centre
Royal Doulton, Nile Street, Burslem, Stoke on Trent ST6 2AJ Tel 01782 292434/292292
£   A £2.50 C under 5 Free C 5-9 £1 C 10-16 OAP and Con £2 Fam £7
O   Mon-Sat 09.30-17.00 Sun 10.00-16.00
P   Please telephone for details
C   Please telephone for details
R   Yes
T   Yes
D   Yes at Visitor Centre Parking available
- The museum traces the history of Royal Doulton right through from 1815 with a wide variety of exhibits and rare pieces. Factory tours available please telephone for details.

Etruria Industrial Museum
Lower Bedford Street, Etruria, Stoke on Trent St4 7AF Tel 01782 287557
£   Free
O   Wed-Sun 10.00-16.00
P   Small car park 100 metres from site- free
C   Yes
R   Yes
T   Yes
D   Limited Toilet facilities available in 1998
- Collection includes a steam powered bone and flint mill with 1820's beam engine, also a blacksmith's forge. New visitor centre completed end 1997 with tea room, shop, reception and toilets. New car park and foot paths planned for 1998.

SUFFOLK

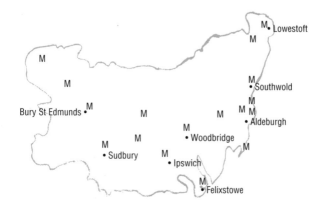

ALDEBURGH

Moot Hall Museum

Aldeburgh, IP15 5DS. Tel 01928 453295

£   A 50p C free if accompanied by adult

O   Apl, May, early Sept, Oct weekends only 14.30-17.00. June & early Sept daily 14.30-17.00. Jul & Aug daily 10.30-12.30 & 14.30-17.00

P   Free car park nearby

C   Activity sheet. Teaching box.

T   Nearby

D   Unsuitable, narrow doorways and steep stairs. R.N.I.B. labelling.

•   Anglo Saxon urns and other finds, early maps, fishing exhibitions & local history.

BECCLES

William Clowes Printing Museum

Beccles NR34 9QE, Tel 01502 712884

£   Free

O   1st week in June till last week in Aug, Mon-Fri 14.00-16.30

P   400 metres

T   Factory toilet available

•   Museum covers all areas of printing. Range of iron presses dating from 1834 and other machinery. Fine collection of old books and memorabilia. Collection of wood and metal engravings.

BRANDON

Brandon Heritage Centre

George Street, Brandon, IP27 0BX. Tel 01842 813707

£   A 50p C, students and Con 40p. Wheelchair users & children under 11 free.

O   Apl-Oct, Sat 10.30-17.00. Sun 14.00-17.00 - June, Jul & Aug - also open Thur 10.30 17.00
P   Free on opposite side of road
C   Questionnaire available. Some items can be touched.
T   Staff toilet available if necessary
D   Wheelchair access. Toilet approx 250 metres
•   Old industries of the area - flint mining and knapping, warrening, fur skin factories forestry. Collection of pre 1950 items. Exhibition of specific topic each year.

BURY ST EDMUNDS

Manor House Museum

Honey Hill, Bury St Edmunds, IP33 1HF Tel 01284 757076
£   A £2.50 C & Con £1.50
O   All year Tue-Sun 10.00-17.00 Cl Xmas, Boxing &Gd Fri Open BH Mons
P   weekend parking
C   Activity sheets, hands-on facilities & workshops
R   Licensed cafe
T   Yes and disabled
D   Access and lifts
•   Beautiful restored Georgian house with collections of longcase clocks, watches costumes, paintings,etc.

Moyses Hall Museum

Cornhill, Bury St Edmunds, IP33 1DX Tel 01284 757488
£ A £1.25. C & Con 75p. Fam ticket £4.00
O   Mon-Sat 10.00-17.00. Sun 14.00-17.00. Cl Xmas, Boxing & Gd Fri
P   Ram Meadow and Parkway car parks
C   Quizzes, weekends & holiday periods. Museum trail. Hands-on facilities. Regular activity sessions.
D   Limited to ground floor only
•   "Murder in the Red Barn" relics, gibbet cage, barrel organ, nationally important archaeological collection incl artefacts found at West Stow and mediaeval relics connected with Abbey.

DUNWICH

Dunwich Museum

St James Street, Dunwich, IP17 3ED Tel 01728 648796
£   Donations welcomed
O   Mar Sat-Sun 14.00-16.30, 1st Apl-30 Sept daily 11.30-16.30, Oct daily 12.00-16.00.
P   Beach car park 100 metres, free but any donations to Church.
T   Yes incl disabled
D   Yes
•   History and model of Dunwich before it was eroded away by the sea.

FELIXSTOWE

Felixstowe Museum

Landguard, Felixstowe - c/o Mr C Brown, Secretary, 44 Wentworth Dr, Felixstowe, IP11 9LB
Tel 01394 277985

£   A £1.00 C 50p
O   BH Suns & Mons, every Sun in Apl, Wed & Sun May-Sept 14.00-17.00
P   Harbour View & Landguard Fort car parks - both free
C   Questionnaires and activity sheets
R   Tea, coffee & biscuits served outside, weather permitting
D   Wheelchair access
•   9 rooms incl areas on Roman Britain, local history, naval room, Wiseman room (RAF),
    paddle steamer room, Darrel room (11th-18th cent), Landguard room (history of
    Landguard Fort.)

FRAMLINGHAM

The Lanman Museum

The Castle, Framlingham, Woodbridge, Suffolk. Tel 01728 723214

£   A 40p C & Con 20p. Fam ticket £1.00
O   Easter to 30 Sept. Daily except Sun & Mon 10.30-13.00 & 14.00-16.30
P   Castle car park, 300 metres
C   Hands-on facilities
R   In town
T   In castle
D   Museum situated in Poor House of Castle and therefore not accessible
•   Collection of items relating to Framlingham & surrounding villages. Farming tools and
    pictures.

IPSWICH

390th Bomb Group Memorial Air Museum

101 Avondale Road, Ipswich IP3 9LA. Tel 01473 711275

£   Free
O   1st Sun in Mar-last Sun in Oct & BH Mons 11.00-18.00. Also Weds in Jun, Jul & Aug
    11.00-16.00
P   Yes
C   on-going
R   Light refreshments
T   Yes
D   Limited access for wheelchairs but always welcome
•   Bomb group memorabilia. RAF involvement in East Anglia and good collection of
    engines and other artefacts.

Wattisham Airfield Historical Collection

Wattisham Airfield, Bldg 144, Ipswich IP7 7RA. Tel 01449 728307, 728399 or 678189

£   Free
O   Apl-Oct every Sun afternoon or by appointment
P   Yes
T   Yes
D   Access only

Ipswich Museum

Ipswich Borough Council Museums & Galleries
High Street, Ipswich,, IP1 3QH. Tel 01379 213761

£   Free
O   Tue-Sat 10.00-17.00. Cl Gd Fri, 24 & 25 Dec & 1 Jan.
P   Charles Street car park 3 mins. Disabled parking in High Street, phone for details.
C   Work sheets, holiday activities programme, inter-active computer in Anglo-Saxon gallery.
T   Yes
D   Step-crawler access to first floor, hand operated by attendant staff. Disabled access via side door. No toilet for disabled users.
•   Town museum featuring "People of the World" gallery, Roman Suffolk, The Anglo-Saxons in Ipswich, Gallery of British birds and Victorian natural history gallery. Suffolk wildlife gallery features life-size reconstruction of woolly mammoth.

Christchurch Mansion

Ipswich Borough Council Museums & Galleries
50 Anne Street, Ipswich IP4 2BE. Tel 01473 253246

£   Free
O   Throughout year Tue-Sat 10.00-17.00(16.00 winter). Sun 14.30-16.30(16.00 winter) BH Mon 10.00-17.00. Cl Gd Fri, 24 & 25 Dec & 1 Jan.
P   Charles Street car park-5 mins walk. Parking for disabled, please phone for details.
C   Work sheets, holiday activities
T   Yes
D   Access to ground floor only. No toilet facilities for disabled users.
•   1548 Tudor mansion in Christchurch Park. Period room settings, good collection of fine art, furniture & ceramics, Suffolk artists gallery, Wolsey Art gallery, exhibition programmes.

LEISTON

The Long Shop Museum

Main Street, Leiston, IP16 4ES. Tel 01728 832189

£   A £2. Con £1.50. C 75p(under 5 free)
O   Apl-end Oct, 10.00-17.00
P   Free parking on site
C   Yes
R   Can be ordered and delivered to our picnic garden
T   Yes incl wheelchair access
D   Ramps to most of the museum
•   Discover the magic of steam through a visit to the world famous traction engine manufacturer of Richard Garrett. Soak up the atmosphere of the Long Shop built in 1852 as one of the first production line engineering halls in the world. An award winning museum with three exhibition halls full of items from our glorious age of steam.

LOWESTOFT

East Anglia Transport Museum

Chapel Road, Carlton Colville, Lowestoft NR33 8BL. Tel 01502 518459

£   A £3. C (5-15) & Con £2. Price includes rides on trams, trolleybuses & railway.
O   Easter weekend then Sun & BH Mon May-Sept 11.00-18.00. Wed from Jun-Sept & every

day last 2 weeks Jul-1st week Sept 14.00-17.00. (last admission 1 hr before closing)
Free parking
Rides on vehicles
Light refreshments and picnic area
Yes
Limited wheelchair access
Working trams and trolleybuses in a reconstructed street scene, also narrow gauge railway, battery powered vehicles, commercial vehicles, steam rollers, cars, buses, etc. Special events, please phone for details.

westoft Maritime Museum

napload Road, Lowestoft NR32 1XG. Tel 01502 561963
A 50p. C & Con 25p
Easter then May-Oct daily, 10.00-17.00
Free parking opposite
Hands-on facilities and questionnaires
Cafe in park
In park
Wheelchair access. Toilet in park.
History of Lowestoft fishing fleet from early sail to steam and through to modern diesel. Fine picture gallery and collection of shipwrights & coopers tools. Exhibition of the evolution of lifeboats. Museum attendants are always available to answer questions about the museum and its exhibits.

westoft Museum

oad House, Nicholas Everitt Park, Oulton Road,Lowestoft NR33 9JR Tel 01502 511467
Free, donations appreciated
Easter- 2 weeks Mon-Fri 10.00-17.00 Weekends 14.00-17.00 Easter-Sp BH. Weekends 14.00-17.00 Sp BH-Sept Mon-Sat 10.00-17.00 Sun 14.00-17.00 Oct-Weekends 14.00-16.00 Open Oct half term
Pay and display 200 metres
Yes
Park Cafe
Public toilet in park
Wheel chair access to ground floor only, Braille descriptions on display cases
Archaeology, domestic history and trades area. The third largest collection of Lowestoft porcelain in the world. Groups including schools (up to 50) welcome by appointment.

yal Naval Patrol Service Assn, Naval Museum,

arrows Nest, Lowestoft,. Tel 01502 536250
Free but donations welcomed
Mon-Fri 10.00-12.00 & 14.00-16.30. Sat & Sun 14.00-16.30 Cl 2nd week in May & Oct.
Free parking 2 mins walk away
Must be accompanied by adults. Colouring posters available.
Restaurant adjacent
Adjacent
Model ships, naval uniforms, photos, documents, medals etc.

MILDENHALL

Mildenhall & District Museum
6 King Street, Mildenhall, IP28 7QP. Tel 01638 716970 (during opening hours only)
£   Free
O   1st Mar-25 Dec. Wed, Thur. Sat. Sun 14.30-16.30. Fri 11.00-16.30.
P   Free parking 100 metres
C   Activity sheet/quiz
D   Wheelchair access to ground floor only.
•   Displays of natural history of Fenland & Breckland. Aviation incl. RAF Mildenha‹ Occasional special exhibitions. Roman silver tableware, penny farthing, Victorian kitche‹ range, etc. Please note that as a voluntary museum the telephone is only manned durir‹ opening hours.

ORFORD

Suffolk Underwater Studies
c/o S Bacon, Front Street, Orford, IP12 2LN. Tel 01394 450678
£   50p
O   Daily 11.00-17.00
P   Free
R   Yes
T   Yes
•   Exhibition on underwater exploration off the Suffolk coast incl the reclaimed town ‹ Dunwhich, now under the sea.

SOUTHWOLD

Southwold Museum
9-11 Victoria Street, Southwold, IP18 6HZ. Tel 01502 722437.
£   Free
O   Easter - 30 Sept daily 14.30-16.30 also 11.00-12.30 Aug.
P   Few spaces opposite with 2 hr limit. Free unlimited parking on nearby common.
C   Hands-on and questionnaires
T   200 metres
D   Wheelchair access. Toilet 200 metres
•   Natural and local history. Battle of Sole Bay 1672. Flints, fossils, pottery. Southwo‹ railway 1879-1929. Victorian dolls house. Ships figureheads. Pictures, photos etc.

STOWMARKET

Mechanical Music Museum & Bygones
Blacksmith Road, Cotton, Nr Stowmarket, IP14 4QN. Tel 01449 613876. (ar‹ correspondence to Mrs P Keeble, 27 St Peters Close, Stowmarket, Suffolk IP14 1LF)
£   A £3. C £1
O   Suns only from May BH.to end of Sept. 14.30-17.30. Private parties during the week ‹ arrangement. Fair organ enthusiasts day-please phone for details.
P   Yes
C   Welcome
R   Yes
T   Yes

Wheelchair access but no toilet
Unique collection of music boxes, polyphons, street pianos, barrel organs, fair organs, gigantic cafe/dance band organ, wurlitzer theatre pipe organ plus many unusual items, all played.

useum of East Anglian Life
owmarket, IP14 1DL
phone for details
phone for details
Yes
Bread & butter trail. Animals, Hands-on exhibits. Adventure playground being planned.
Yes
Yes incl for disabled
not all exhibits are accessible
70 acres of exhibits and farmland. Displays of rural, industrial and social history of East Anglia incl several historic buildings, watermill, windpump, smithy, farmhouse. Riverside walk

lid Suffolk Light Railway Museum,
ockford Station, Wetheringset, Stowmarket, IP14 5PW. Tel 01499 766899
A £1. C 50p
Easter Sun-End Sept. Sun & BHs & Wed in main school holidays
Yes
Yes
Yes
Yes
Yes

UDBURY

ue Ryder Foundation Museum
avendish, Sudbury CO10 8Ay. Tel 01787 280252
A 80p. C (12 & under) & Con 40p
Daily 10.00-17.30
Yes
Yes
Yes
Yes
Small museum set in beautiful surroundings depicts the remarkable story of how the foundation was established, its work today and its hopes for the future.

VOODBRIDGE

Suffolk Horse Museum
he Market Hill, Woodbridge, IP12 4LV Tel 01394 380643
A £1.50. C & Con £1.
Easter Mon end Sept 14.00-17.00
nearby
nearby
nearby
Access difficult due to exterior stone staircase.

- The story of the Suffolk Punch heavy working horse. Models, paintings and photograph showing all aspects of rearing and training.

WOOLPIT

Woolpit & District Museum

The Institute, The Street, Woolpit.(Any correspondence to Woolpit Museum, c/o Walnut Tre Cottage, Green Road, Woolpit, Suffolk IP30 9RF)

£ Free
O Sat, Sun & BHs 14.30-17.00
P Yes
R Shop opposite
T Yes
D Chair lift
- Small museum with a personal touch. Displays change annually.

URREY

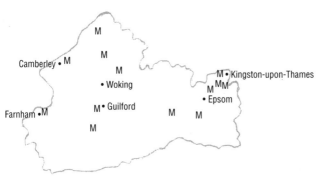

Camberley • M
M
M
M
• Woking
M • Kingston-upon-Thames
M M M
M
• Epsom
Farnham •M
M • Guilford
M
M
M

AMBERLEY

Royal Logistic Corps Museum
Deepcut, Camberley GU16 6RW Tel 01252 340871/984
Free
Mon-Fri 10.00-16.00 Sat 10.00-15.00 Cl Sat & BHs
Yes free adjacent to museum
Questionnaires on request
Yes
Yes, access, parking and toilet facilities
The story of support to the Army- transport, ordinance, pioneers, catering and postal over 500 years of history-explained in words, pictures and artefacts.

ARSHALTON

Honeywood, The Hertitage Centre
Honeywood Walk, Carshalton SM5 3NX Tel 0181 773 4555
A £1 C 50p
Wed-Fri 10.00-17.00 Weekends & BH. Mons 10.00-17.30
On street parking in Honeywood Walk, public car park 500 metres in High Street
Special events and holiday activities including workshops, quizzes and trials
Tea Room Tue-Sun 10.00-17.00
Yes
Wheelchair access to ground floor only, toilet facilities
A local history museum next to the picturesque Carshalton Ponds, in a 17th Century listed building. Permanent displays on aspects of local history plus a changing programme of exhibitions and events on a wide range of subjects.

Little Holland House

40 Beeches Avenue, Carshalton SM5 3LW Tel 0181 770 4781
£ Free
O First Sun of month plus BH Weekends 13.30-17.30
P Parking in side streets such as Barrrow Hedges Way
T Yes
D Access to ground floor and garden only
• Built in 1902 the Arts and Crafts style by artist, designer and craftsman Frank Dickinson who designed and built and furnished the house himself. Grade 11 listed interior features - handmade furniture and fittings, carvings, metalwork and paintings by Dickinson.

CHEAM

White Hall

1 Malden Road, Cheam SM3 8QD. Tel 0181 643 1236.
£ A £1. C 50p.
O Apl-Sept, Tue-Fri & Sun 14.00-17.30. Sat. 10.00-17.30. Oct-Mar, Wed, Thur, Sun 14.00- 17.30. Sat 10.00-17.30.
P Pay and display opposite
C Fun/activity sheets and trails plus special one-day themed events
R Light refreshments incl home-made cakes available in the beamed tea room
T Yes
D Wheelchair access to part of ground floor plus garden. No adapted toilet
• 16th century timber-framed house. Twelve rooms open to view include displays of Henry VIII's Nonsuch Palace, Cheam pottery and William Gilpin. Changing programme of exhibitions and special events.

CHERTSEY

Chertsey Museum

The Cedars, 33 Windsor Street, Chertsey KT16 8AT Tel 01932 565764
£ Free
O Tue-Fri 12.30-16.30 Sat 11.00-16.00
P Street parking or Sainsbury's car park within 5 minutes walk
C Yes, activity sheets, monthly club and holiday activity days
R None on site but picnic tables in museum grounds, cafes etc. nearby
T Yes
D Ground floor access only, parking space on site, no disabled toilet facilities
• Regency House with museum of local history and archaeology. Olive Matthew collection of historic costume, clocks, Messier porcelain and glass. Lively exhibition and events programme complements the permanent display.

EGHAM

Egham Museum

Literary Institute, High Street, Egham TW20 9EW Tel 01344 843047
£ Free
O Tue, Thur and Sat 10.00-12.30 14.00-16.30
P Public car park nearby
T Yes
• Permanent displays include 'Magna Carta', Thomas Holloway (Royal Holloway College

and Holloway Sanitorium). Other displays include the Thames and other local topics.

EWELL

Bourne Hall Museum
Spring Street, Ewell KT17 1UF Tel 0181 394 1734
£   Free
O   Mon-Sat 09.00-17.00 Cl Xmas and BHs
P   Car park adjoining (200 spaces)
C   Activites and questionnaires for special exhibitions only at present
R   Cafe next door
T   Yes and baby changing facilities
D   Yes access to all parts
•   The museum houses memories of Epsom and Ewell from Sone Age to Edwardian times, plus a general collection of early kitchenware, radios and photography.

FARNHAM

Museum of Farnham
38 West Street, Farnham GU9 7DX Tel 01252 715094
£   Free
O   Tue-Sat 10.00-17.00
P   Public car park at The Hart off West Street
C   Children's guide 50p
R   No but plenty in town
T   Yes
D   Access to ground floor only, toilet facilities
•   Tells the story of Farnham and its people, housed in a Grade I listed Georgian townhouse with fine walled garden. See Charles I's embroidered night-cap and a Georgian dolls house.

Rural Life Centre
Old Kiln Museum Trust
Reeds Road, Tilford, Farnham GU10 2DL tel 01252 795571/792300
£   £ A£3 C £1.50 OAP £2.50
O   Apl-Sept Wed-Sun & BHs 11.00-18.00
P   Yes on site free
C   Yes 1960's playground, activity sheets, I-Spy sheets and animals on certain days
R   Yes
T   Yes
D   Yes
•   Pleasantly distributed over ten acres of fields, woodland and barns this museum comprises all aspects of village life and rural activities-trades, crafts, and domestic.

GODALMING

Godalming Museum
109a High Street, Godalming GU7 1AQ Tel 01483 426510 Fax 01483 869495
£   Free
O   All year 11.00-18.00 Cl Xmas
P   Public car park in South Street

C   Yes
R   Coffee and tea
T   Yes
D   Access to ground floor only.
•   Godalming museum is housed in a medieval house with Victorian additions. Local personalities including Gertrude Jekyll and Edwin Lutyens are featured and there is a Jekyll style garden. Redevelopment planned for Sept-Jan 1997/98.

GUILDFORD

British Red Cross Museum
Barnett Hill, Wonersh, Guildford GU5 0RF Tel 01483 898595
£   Free
O   Mon-Fri 10.00-16.30 Cl BH. Admission by appointment only
P   On site free
C   Talks and guided tours available on request
T   Yes
•   The museum depicts the humanitarian work of the Red Cross from 1863 to its vital continuation today. Exhibits include the 2nd World War Changi Quilt.

Guildford Discovery Science Centre
The Old Chapel, Ward Street, Guildford GU1 4LH Tel 01483 537080
£   A £2.50 C £2 OAP £2 Student £2
O   All year Sat 10.00-17.00 Sun 14.00-17.00 Tue-Sat School Hol & Half Term 10.00-17.00
P   Town centre car park or Park and Ride at the Spectrum which has a drop off very close to museum
C   Yes lots of hands on and interactive science exhibits aimed at 5 to 12 year olds
T   Yes but only one
D   Yes help available to get wheelchairs up the steps.
•   We are a small friendly hands on science centre, the emphasis is on fun, experimenting, exploration and discovery.

Guildford Museum
Castle Arch, Guildford GU1 3SX Tel 01483 444750
£   Free
O   Mon-Sat 11.00-17.00 Open most BHs Cl Xmas
P   Public car parks near by
C   Activity sheets and seasonal quizzes
T   Yes
•   Museum houses a collection of local history from Surrey, also a collection of needlework from all over the country.

The Queen's Royal Surrey Regiment Museum
Clandon Park, Guildford GU4 7RQ Tel 01483 223419
£   Free
O   Apl-Oct Tue-Thur, Sun & BHs 12.00-17.00
P   Yes
C   School visits in process of being planned
R   Licensed restaurant
T   Yes
D   Yes easy access and toilet facilities

• The museum relates the long and distinguished service of the two Infantry Regiments of Surrey in a comprehensive display of Colours, uniforms, medals, pictures and other artefacts.

KINGSTON UPON THAMES

Kingston Museum
Wheatfield Way, Kingston upon Thames Kt1 2PS Tel 0181 546 5386
£   Free
O   Mon, Tue, Thur, Fri, Sat 10.00-17.00
P   Public car park at Cattle Market
C   Saturday, half term and holiday activities (a small charge is made for materials volunteer assistance)
T   Disabled facilities only
D   Lift to first floor. Toilet
•   The museum housed in Grade II listed building tells the story of Kingston from its ancient origins to the present by means of permanent and changing displays, lots of special events and exhibitions. Museum gift shop.

LEATHERHEAD

Leatherhead Museum
Hampton cottage, 64 Church Street, Leatherhead KT22 8DP Tel 01372 386348
£   Free
O   Apl-Dec Thur 13.00-16.00 Fri 10.00-13.00 Sat 10.00-16.00
P   Public car parks in town
C   Quiz sheet available from late 1997
•   Main theme is local history of Leatherhead, Ashtead, Fetcham, Bookham and surrounding area. Small souvenir shop, selling local history publications, postcards etc.

REIGATE

Reigate Priory Museum
Bell Street, Reigate RH2 7RL Tel 01737 245065
£   Free for individuals, School parties £15 per class of 30, Adult groups - donation according to programme requested.
O   Wed & Sat during term time only 14.00-16.30
P   Public car park adjacent
C   Arranged for visiting school parties on request
T   Yes
D   Yes
•   The museum presents changing exhibitions on a wide range of subjects- For example 'Happy and Glorious' which opened in April 1997 describes Queen Victoria's Diamond Jubilee and holiday times in 1897

WEYBRIDGE

Elmbridge Museum
Church Street, Weybridge K113 BDE Tel 01932 843573
£   Free
O   Mon, Wed, Thur 11.00-17.00 Sat 10.00-13.00 14.00-17.00

Surrey

P   Parking available in Churchfield Road at rear of museum
C   Children's corner with feely box, dressing up box and a craft area
T   Yes
D   Limited
•   The museum was refurbished in 1996, the new look museum has a permanent gallery on the history of the Elmbridge area from prehistoric to present day. Programme of temporary exhibitions, local history room and museum shop.

SUSSEX

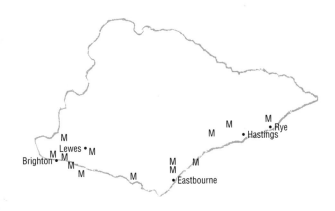

Brighton

Lewes

Eastbourne

Hastings

Rye

EAST SUSSEX

BATTLE

Battle Museum of Local History
Memorial Hall, High Street, Battle TN33 0TA Tel 01424 775955
£   A 80p. Accompanied child free.
O   Easter-Sept. Mon-Sat 10.30-16.30. Sun 14.00-17.00
P   Yes
•   Museum telling history of Battle of Hastings with diorama of reproduction of Bayeux tapestry. Remains from local sites, iron and other industries.

BEXHILL ON SEA

Bexhill Museum
Egerton Road, Bexhill on Sea TN39 3HL Tel 01424 787 950
£   A £1 Under 12s free. Con 50p
O   Tue-Fri 10.00-17.00 Sat-Sun 14.00-17.00
P   Parking in Egerton Road
C   Pre-booked school parties and educational groups welcome. Work sheets and talk by Curator available. Small class room.
T   Public toilets in Egerton Park
D   Yes
•   Local history, dinosaurs, archaeology and natural history are just some of the themes covered. Displays are complemented by a temporary exhibition programme that explores various local topics.

Bexhill Museum of Costume and Social History
Manor Gardens, Upper Sea Road, Bexhill-on-Sea TN40 1RL Tel 01424 210045
£   A £1.50 C/Student 50p

O   Apl.May.Oct.,daily 10.30-17.00. June.July.Aug.Sept. - Weds only.
P   Public car park
D   Yes
•   Costume from mid 18th Centrury, plus dolls and toys, lace, embroidery etc. Victorian kitchen and schoolroom.

BRIGHTON

Barlow Gallery of Chinese Art
The Library, University of Sussex, Falmer BN1 9QL Tel 01273 606755 ext 3506 or 2038
£   Free
O   Tue.Thur,11.30-14.30 Cl Easter.Aug.Xmas & University closure days.
P   Yes on campus
C   No special programme, but we are always happy to tell them about the collection and show them around.
R   Available on campus
T   Yes
D   Wheel chair access and toilet facilities
•   Over 400 Chinese works of art covering every period from 12th Century BC,-incl. archaic ritual bronzes, ceramic tomb figures, burial vessels, fine porcelains, Jades and small number of Korean celadon ware.

Booth Museum of Natural History
194 Dyke Road, Brighton Bn1 5AA tel 01273 292777
£   Free
O   Mon.Tue.Wed.Fri.Sat.10.00-17.00. Sun.14.00-17.00
P   Roadside
C   Some available
T   Yes
D   Rear access. No adapted toilet.
•   A natural history museum originally built in 1874 to house Mr Booth's colection of stuffed birds. Now we have skeletons, insects, fossils, minerals. A museum shop and many temporary exhibitions.

Brighton Museum and Art Gallery
Church Street, Brighton BN1 1VE Tel 01273 290900
£   Free
O   Mon.Tue.Thur.Fri.Sat 10.00-17.00. Sun.14.00-17.00 Cl Gd Fri, Xmas and N.Y.
P   Public car park in Church Street
C   For school groups during term-time.
R   Yes
T   Yes
D   Access to ground floor only
•   Rich collections of both national and local importance. Art Nouveau and Art Deco. Non Western arts and culture from textiles to masks. Archaeology, a fashion gallery, toy cabinet. Exhibitions and events.

Preston Manor
Preston Drive, Brighton Tel 01273 292770
£   A £2.95 C £1.80 Con £2.45 Fam £7.70
O   Mon 13.00-17.00. Tue-Sat 10.00-17.00. Sun 14.00-17.00 BH Mons 10.00-17.00. Cl Gd

Fri.Xmas & N.Y. days.
P   Parking vouchers, tickets from newsagent
C   Role playing and guided tours available
T   Yes
•   Manor house which evokes the life of an Edwardian home, both 'upstairs' and 'downstairs'. Explore restored servants quarters, kitchen, butlers pantry and boothall. Collections of furniture, portraits, silver and family memorabilia.

Sussex Toy and Model Museum

52-55 Trafalger Street Brighton BN1 4EB Tel 01273 749494
£   A £3 C under 16 Student and OAP £1.50 Fam ticket £6
O   Mon-Fri 10.00-17.00. Sat 11.00-13.00 14.00-17.00. Cl Xmas & Boxing days
P   Multi Storey car park near museum, special arrangements for disabled if telephone in advance
C   Available for school parties
T   Yes
D   Wheel chair access and disabled toilets
•   Exhibits include a priceless toy and model train collection, planes, boats, Mecanno, dolls and specimens of Evans & Cartwright dolls house furniture. We also have a working 1930s Model Railway.

DITCHLING

Ditchling Museum

Church Lane, Ditchling BN6 8TB Tel 01273 844744
£   £ A 2 C 50p OAP £1.50. Discount for 10+
O   Nov-Mar. Sat 10.30-16.30. Sun 14.00-16.30. Apl-Oct. Mon-Sat 10.30-17.00. Sun 14.00-17.00.
P   Car park in village. Disabled parking on site
C   Workshops, holiday activities. Young friends group 'The Wyveins'
R   Tea, coffee and cakes
T   Yes
D   Yes
•   Housed in Victorian village school. Farm tools, costumes, period room settings, local history. Gallery of work by 20th century workmen. Special exhibitions.

EASTBOURNE

'How We Lived Then' Museum of Shops

20 Cornfield Terrace, Eastbourne BN21 4Ns Tel 01323 737143
£   A £2.50 C up to 15 £1.50. Cons £2
O   Feb-Dec. daily 10.00-17.30. Cl Xmas & Boxing days.
P   On street limited to 2 hours, public car parks nearby
C   Worksheets availble on request
R   Many nearby
T   Yes
D   Ground floor access only for which there is no charge
•   Displays of authentic Victorian-style shops and room settings shown on three floors., over 75,000 exhibits collected during the past 35 years.

Lifeboat Musem

King Edward Parade, Eastbourne BN21 4BY Tel 01323 730717
£   Free
O   Easter-end Apl. 10.00-16.00. May-Sept 10.00-17.00. Oct-Dec 10.00-16.00.
P   Public car park nearby (charge) Free parking on sea front, spaces sometimes available
R   Near by kiosk for light refreshments and restuarant 2 mins walk
T   Public toilets within I min walk
•   Memorabilia and photos of old lifeboats and crews, descriptions of notable rescues over the years. Selection of lifeboat models. Well stocked shop.

The Sussex Combined Services Museum

The Redout Fortress, Royal Parade, Eastbourne Bn22 7AQ Tel)1323 410300 Fax 01323 732240
£   A £1.85. Con £1.05 Fam £5
O   Easter-Nov. daily 09.30-17.30.
P   Off street parking
C   Yes, activity sheets
R   Yes
T   Yes
•   South East England's most comprehensive military museum.

Towner Art Gallery and Museum

High Street, Old Town, Eastbourne BN20 8BB Tel 01323 417961
£   Free, although charge for some exhibitions. Parties of over 15 please book in advance.
O   Tue-Sat 12.00-17.00. Sun & BH Mons14.00-17.00. (Nov-Mar close 16.00). Cl over Xmas, N.Y day, Gd Fri.
P   Street parking
C   Occasionally, please telephone for details
T   Yes
D   Access to ground floor galleries, toilet facilities. Staff willing to be of assistance.
•   Museum depicts the history and development of Eastbourne from prehistory. Programme of temporary art exhibitions.

HASTINGS

Hastings Fishermen's Museum

Rock-A-Nore, Hastings TN34 3DW Tel 01424 461446
£   Free but donations welcome
O   Daily 11.00-17.00 except Xmas day.
P   Public car park adjacent
C   Museum crossword for children
R   Several cafes in Rock A Nore Road
T   Public toilets nearby
D   Wheel chair access to main museum
•   Housed in former fishermen's Church, with the centrepiece 'Enterprise', last of the Hastings sailing luggers. Many photographs, paintings, model boats, old fishing gear and the history of Hasting's fishing industry.

Hastings Old Town Hall Museum of Local History

High Street, Hastings. Tel 01424 781166
£   Free

O   Mar - daily exc Wed. 14.00-16.00. Apl-Sept. Tue-Sun 10.00-13.00. 14.00-17.00.
P   On street
R   Cafes nearby
•   History of Hastings from Palaeolithic to 20th cenrtury incl Cinque Ports, smugglers, wrecks, famous people. Please check opening times as museum is likely to be closed during 1998 for alterations.

Hastings Museum and Art Gallery
Johns Place, Cambridge Road, Hastings TN34 1ET. Tel 01424 781155.
£   Free
O   Mon-Fri 10.00-17.00. Sat 10.00-13.00. 14.00-17.00. Sun 15.00-17.00. Cl Xmas & Boxing days & Gd Fri.
P   Yes
C   Activity sheets available on request
T   Yes
D   Ramp access to part of ground floor. Toilets not accessible to wheelchairs.
•   Local dinosaurs, natural history, American Indians & Grey Owl, ceramics, paintings, Indian Durbar Hall and temporary exhibition programme.

HOVE

Hove Museum and Art Gallery
19 New Church Road, Hove. BN3 4AB. Tel 01273 290200.
£   Free
O   Tue-Fri 10.00-17.00. Sat 10.00-16.30. Sun 14.00-17.00.
O   On street
C   Quiz sheets/worksheets available at front desk. Handling kit for teaching sessions.
R   Tea room open Wed. Thu. Sat. Sun.
T   Yes
D   Wheelchair access. Toilets.

LEWES

Anne of Cleves House
52 Southover High Street, Lewes. BN7 1JA. Tel 01273 474610.
£   A £2. C £1. Fam £5.
O   Mar-Dec. Mon-Sat 10.00-17.00. Sun 12.00-17.00. Jan-Feb Tue.Thu.Sat. 10.00-17.00.
P   400 metres at train station
C   Education department.
R   Yes
T   Yes
D   Very limited.
•   Displays take the story of Lewes from 16th century to present day and the kitchen and bedroom re-create their original setting. Gallery of Wealden Ironwork.

POLEGATE

Filching Manor & Motor Museum
Filching Manor, Filching, Polegate BN26 5QA. Tel 01323 487838.
£   A £3. C over 5 £2.50.Fam £9.
O   Easter-end Apl. Thu-Sun. May-Sep, every day. Oct Thu-Sun.

P   Yes
C   School visits with guided tour
R   Tea, coffee & biscuits. Fast food at track. Other facilities nearby.
T   Yes
D   Wheelchair access. Toilet.
- Museum exhibits range from 1893 to 1995 Grand Prix car, K3 Bluebird and Campbell artefacts. Oldest part of Wealden Hall Manor House. 500 mtr outdoor karting track.

PORTSLADE

Foredown Tower
Foredown Road, Portslade BN41 2EW. Tel 01273 292092.
£   A £2. Con £1.50. C £1. Fam £5.
O   Apl-Sep. daily 10.00-17.30. Oct-Mar. Thu-Sun 10.00-dusk. Cl 24 Dec-1 Jan
P   Yes
C   CD-ROM, interactive computers
R   Yes
T   Yes
D   Wheelchair access to ground floor only.
- Camera obscura, exhibitions on weather etc. School visits by appt. Talks on Astronomy, countryside walks, local history.

ROTTINGDEAN

The Grange
The Green, Rottingdean BN2 7HA. Tel 01273 301004.
£   Free
O   Mon-Sat 10.00-16.00. Sun 14.00-16.00
P   Nearby
R   During summer months
T   During summer months
D   Wheelchair access to ground floor onlyt.
- Art gallery shows exhibitions covering a wide range of subject and artists. Reconstruction of Rudyard Kipling's study and shows aspects of his life and work. Local history.

RYE

Rye Castle Museum
Ypres Tower, Gungarden, Rye. TN31 7HH. Tel 01797 225728.
£   A £1.50. Con £1. U/16s 50p. U/7s free. Fam & party rates by arrangement.
O   Apl-Oct, daily, 10.30-17.30. Nov-Mar, Sat & Sun 10.30-17.30.
P   Nearby car parks.
C   Education programme with activity sheets etc.
T   50 metres away.
D   Ancient monument with circular stone staircase, therefore unsuitable to most disabled persons.
- If lottery bid is successful exhibition site will be doubled and will also have full facilities for disabled

SEAFORD

Seaford Museum of Local History
Martello Tower, Esplanade, Seaford. Tel 01323 898222. Correspondence to 58 High Street, Seaford BN25 1PP. Tel 01323 898853.

£ A £1. Con 50p.

O Sun & BHs 11.00-13.00. 14.20-16.30. also in high season from Easter, Wed & Sat 14.30-16.30.

P On adjacent seafront

C Special times for school parties (please phone to arrange). Educational packs available prior to visits.

T On seafront, 50 metres

D Regretfully the nature of the building (coastal defence) has too many steps, stairs, etc.

• 6000 sq ft of display area incl walled-in dry moat area. Exhibitions include Rueben the Shepherd, life in 1950's. Victorian kitchen with bath by the fire. Souveniers on sale.

SUSSEX

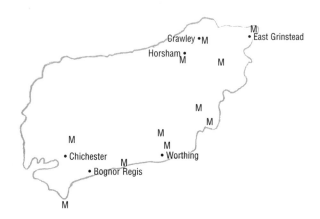

WEST SUSSEX

CHICHESTER

Chichester District Museum

29 Little London, Chichester PO19 1PB

£   Free but charge for special workshops and events

O   Tue-Sat. 10.00-17.30. Cl Xmas,Boxing & N.Y days & Gd.Fri.

P   Public car parks nearby

C   Yes

R   Tea shops nearby

D   Access to ground floor only

•   Chichester museum tells the story of local people and places through geology, archaeology and local history. Annual programme of temporary exhibitions, children and adult events and special openings.

Royal Military Police Museum

Roussillon Barracks, Chichester PO1 94BN Tel 01243 534225 Fax 01243 534288

£   Free

O   Apl-Sep. Tue-Fri 10.30-12.30. 13.30-16.30. Sat.Sun 14.00-18.00. Oct-Mar. Tue-Fri 10.30-12.30. 13.30-16.30. Cl Jan.

P   On street parking

C   Yes

D   Wheel chair access but no toilet facilities

•   Modern display techniques provide an intriguing journey based on the world wide activities of Military Police from Tudor times to present day.

Mechanical Music and Doll Collection

Church Road, Portfield, Chichester PO19 4HN Tel 01243 372646

£   A £2. C 75p

O   Easter-Sept. Sun-Fri 13.00-17.00. Oct-Easter, Sun 13.00-17.00.
P   Yes
D   Yes but no toilet facilities
•   See and hear mechanical instruments playing just as they did 100 years ago. Musical boxes, organettes, street pianos, fair organs etc.Also 100 beautiful Victorian dolls.

CRAWLEY

Crawley Museum Centre
Goffs Park House, Old Horsham Road, Southgate, Crawley RH11 8PE Tel 01293 539088
£   Free
O   Sun & Wed 14.00-16.00
P   Yes
T   Yes
D   Parking bay outside museum. Wheel chair access
•   Small purpose built museum attached to a Victorian house in a park setting. Programme of exhibtions illustrating the history of Crawley and surrounding countryside.

Ifield Watermill
Hyde Drive, Ifiled, Crawley RH11 OPL Tel 01293 539088
£   Free
O   May-Sept. last Sun in month & national mill days, 14.30-17.00.
P   Free public car park at end of lane
C   Yes
D   Limited access, stairlift to first floor. Please telephone for details
•   Partly restored waterrmill in an attractive setting. Walks around hammer pond, working water wheel. Displays of milling machinery and local history.

CUCKFIELD

Cuckfield Museum
Queens Hall, High Street, Cuckfield RH17 5EL Hon Curator 01444 483107
£   Free
O   Jun-Sept. Wed&Sat 10.00-12.30. 14.00-16.30. End Mar-Jan.Tue.Wed.Sat 10.00-12.30
P   Yes
T   Yes
•   Concerned primarily with village of Cuckfield and Mid-Sussex. Temporary exhibitions.

EAST GRINSTEAD

East Grinstead Town Museum
East Court Mansion, College Lane, East Grinstead RH19 3LT Tel 01342 712087
£   Free
O   All year Wed-Sat 14.00-16.00
P   Free on site
C   Work sheets available
T   Yes
•   Small museum relating to the history of the town. Large collection of photographs and of local pottery. Moving to new premises in 1998, therefore please telephone before visit.

HENFIELD

Henfield Museum

Village Hall. High street, Henfield BN5 9DB Tel 01273 492546

£   Free
O   Mon.Tue.Thur.Sat. 10.00-12.00. Wed.Sat 14.30-16.30. Cl BHs.
P   On-street parking
T   Yes
D   Yes
•   Small village museum illustrating life in a typical Sussex village, showing domestic objects, costume, farm implements, local paintings and photographs.

HORSHAM

Horsham Museum

9 The Causeway, Horsham RH12 1HE. Tel 01403 254959.

£   Free
O   Mon-Sat, 10.00-17.00. Cl BHs.
P   Nearby
R   Cafes nearby
T   Yes
D   Ramps to ground floor. Toilets
•   Set in a timber-framed medieval house with two gardens. Displays include unique dinosaur bones, local crafts, bicycles, farming, shoping, domestic life and geology exotica.

LITTLEHAMPTON

Littlehampton Museum

Manor House, Church Street, Littlehampton BN17 5EP. Tel 01903 715149.

£   Free
O   Tue-Sat.& BH Mons 10.30-16.30. Cl Xmas, Boxing & NY days & Gd Fri.
P
C   Each temporary exhibition usually has a children's quiz. Some hands-on facilities.
T   In adjacent car park.
D   Wheelchair access - all displays are on ground floor.
•   Small museum close to High Street. Displays of social history and archaeology, and perhaps some surprises. Children and families very welcome.

SELSEY

Selsey Lifeboat Station & Museum

Kingsway, Selsey. Tel -1243 602833/605601.

£   Free
O   Boathouse open 365 days. Museum, Easter-Oct. 10.00-13.00. 14.00-15.00.
P   On-street parking
R   Local Lifeboat Inn
T   Yes
D   Access to museum and inshore boathouse only.
•   Video room showing rescue videos and workings of the RNLI. Annual 'Launch Day'

when sea safety demonstrations are given and all day activities for all the family. Please phone for date.

SHOREHAM-BY-SEA

Marlipins Museum
High Street, Shoreham BN43 5DA. Tel 01273 462994.
£   A £1. Child over 5 50p. Con 75p.
O   May-Sept. Tue-Sat 10.00-13.00. 14.00-16.30. Sun 14.00-16.30.
P   On and off street nearby.
T   Public toilets within 1 min walk.
D   Wheelchair access to one gallery only.
•   Marlipins is Norman in origin with an impressive 14th century chequerwork facade. It contains geological, archaeological, local and maritime history collections, the latter including some fine ship portraits and models.

STEYNING

Steyning Museum
Church Street, Steyning BN44 3YB. Tel 01903 813333.
£   Free
O   Apl-Sept Tue.Wed.Fri.Sat. 10.30-12.30. 14.00-16.30. Sun 14.00-16.30. Oct-Mar Tue, Wed.Fri.Sat. 10.30-12.30. 14.30-16.00. Sun 14.30-16.00.
P   Public car park nearby free
D   Yes
•   The museum depicts Steyning's history, the crafts and industries of Steyning which traditionally have been linked to the agricultural wealth of the Downs and the Adur valley.

WORTHING

Worthing Museum and Art Gallery
Chapel Road, Worthing BN11 1HP Tel 01903 239999 ext 2528 or 01903 204229 (Sat)
£   Free
O   Apl-Sept Mon-Sat 10.00-18.00 Oct-March Mon-Sat 10.00-17.00
P   Public car parks nearby. On site parking for disabled
C   Special events throughout the year
T   Yes. (Museum loo of the year award 1996)
D   Wheel chair access to all displays. Wheel chair available. Toilet facilities.
•   Friendly museum with displays including geology, archaeology, local history and art. Our costume and doll collections are outstanding. Programme of temporary exhibitons and special events.

TYNE AND WEAR

GATESHEAD

Bowes Railway Centre
Springwell Village, Gateshead, NE9 7QJ Tel 0191 416 1847
£   A £2.75 C£1.75 OAP £2.25 Special prices for Santa Specials Non train days-free
O   May-Aug BH 1st & 3rd Sun in month (all Suns in Aug)12.00-17.00
    All year Mon-Sat (non operating days) 11.00-16.00
P   Free on site car park
C   Questionnaires and activity sheets subject to availability
R   Yes
T   Yes
D   Limited, toilet facilities
•   Historic workshop with permanent exhibition, engineering shops only surviving example in North East of typical courtyard layout. The railway is the only preserved standard gauge rope haulage railway in the world. Steam locomotives take visitors to the winding house that operates rope haulage.

JARROW

Bede's World
Church Bank, Jarrow NE32 3DY Tel 0191 489 2106
£   A £3 Con £1.50 Fam £7.20
O   Apl-Oct Tue-Sat 10.00-17.30 Sun 14.30-17.30 May-Sept Sun & BH Mons 12.00-17.30 Nov-March Tue-Sat 10.00-16.30 Sun 14.30-17.30.
P   Yes on site free
C   Small handling collection
R   Yes
T   Yes
D   Wheelchair access except to upper floor of Jarrow Hall
•   Remains of Anglo-Saxon monastery site-home of the venerable Bede. Exhibitions

relating to excavations and the golden age of Northumbria, recreated Anglo-Saxon farm with timber buildings, crops and rare breeds of animals.

NEWCASTLE UPON TYNE

Discovery Museum
Blandford Square, Newcastle NE1 4JA Tel 0191 232 6789
£   Free
O   Mon-Sat 10.00-17.00 Sun 14.00-17.00 Open BH Mons
P   Charge for parking
C   Yes
R   Yes
D   Yes wheel chair access, toilet facilities and lift to all floors
•   A fun day out for all! Displays include fashion works, science factory, time tunnel and 'Turbine' once the fastest ship in the world now housed in her own hands-on gallery.

Military Vehicle Museum
Exhibition Park Pavilion, Newcastle upon Tyne NE2 4PZ 0191 2817222
£   A £2 C & OAP & Con £1 under 5s free
O   Summer 10.00-16.00 Winter 10.00-15.30 Cl Xmas, Boxing & NY Days
P   Car park outside Exhibition Park
C   Questionnaires and guided tours for school parties by arrangement
R   Cafe in park, drinks machine on site
T   Yes
D   Yes
•   The museum houses up to 50 vehicles including field guns. Also 65 cabinets displaying artefacts and mannequins depicting the military from W.W.1 to present day.

Shefton Museum of Greek Art And Archaeology
University of Newcastle, Classics Dept, (Armstrong Building) Newcastle upon Tyne NE1 7RU Tel 0191 2227966
£   Free
O   All year Mon-Fri 09.30-13.00 14.00-16.00 Cl Xmas, Easter and other BHs If travelling from far away please check opening times first
P   Parking difficult as in town centre, advise take public transport -metro to Haymarket
T   Yes
D   Wheelchair access and toilet facilities
•   We have a small but choice collection of Greek and Roman antiquities, including Greek painted vases. architectural terracotta's and arms and armour; also a giant porphyrx foot (Roman)

Museum of Antiquities
University of Newcastle upon Tyne, NE1 7RU Tel 0191 2227849
£   Free
O   Mon-Sat 10.00-17.00 Cl Xmas, NY Days & Gd Fri
P   Public car park in Percy Street or Claremont Road
C   Quiz sheets available for Key Stage 2 and Keystage 3
R   None on site, plenty in town
T   Available in adjacent building
D   Wheelchair access, no disabled toilet facilities, open access to Roman sculpture for visually handicapped and large print guides available.

- The ideal place to start a tour of Hadrian's wall. Famous reconstruction of Temple to Mithras, models of Hadrian's Wall, its forts, turrets and milecastles. world famous prehistoric Roman, Anglo-Saxon and medieval collections. Well stocked bookshop.

SOUTH SHIELDS

Arbeia Roman Fort
Baring Street, South Shields NE33 2BB Tel 0191 454 4093
£   Site free Quest Gallery A £1 others 50p
O   Apl-Sept Mon-Sat 10.00-17.30 Sun 13.00-17.00 Oct-March Mon-Sat 10.00-16.00
P   On street parking outside museum no charge
C   Time quest interactive display, activity sheets and special event days
R   Drinks machine, picnic area and small shop
T   Yes
D   Ramp access to Time Quest, some parts of site have difficult access. Disabled toilets
- Re-enactment group Quinta appear on special days. Archaeological digs to view summer weekdays and guided tours (fee payable) by prior arrangement.

South Shields Museum and Art Gallery
Ocean Road, South Shields NE33 2JA Tel 0191 456 8740
£   Free
O   Easter-Sept Mon-Sat 10.00-17.30 Oct-Easter Mon-Sat 10.00-17.00 Cl Gd Fri
P   Free multi storey car park in Ocean Road and another in Mile End Road
C   Yes telephone for details
R   Drinks machine
T   Yes
D   Yes wheelchair ramp and lifts, toilet facilities, audio guides in exhibitions
- Two permanent galleries both focusing on the historical and social development of South Shields using interpretative techniques including film, simulation, traditional displays and hands on features. A programme of temporary exhibitions. Catherine Cookson gallery.

William Wouldhave Lifeboat
Ocean Road, Southshields
- Exhibition often changing and lifeboat on permanent display throughout the year.

SUNDERLAND

Monkwearmouth Station Museum
North Bridge Street, Sunderland SR5 1AP Tel 0191 567 7075
£   Free
O   Fri 10.00-17.00 Sat 10.00-16.30 Sun 14.00-17.00
P   Free car park outside museum
C   Activity sheets, exhibitions aimed at family audience, play area for under 5's
R   Soft drinks machine and sweets
T   Yes
D   Access and disabled toilet facilities
- Restored Victorian station Of 1848.

North East Aircraft Museum
Old Washington road, Sunderland SR5 3HZ Tel 0191 519 0662
£   A £2 C& Con £1
O   Daily 10.00-17.00 Cl Xmas & NY
P   Car park on site
T   Yes
•   Over 35 exhibits including the Vulcan bomber, Lightning fighter and record breaking Swift. Nearly all exhibits are housed in our three hangers.

Ryhope Engines Museum
Ryhope Pumping Station, Ryhope, Sunderland SR2 0ND Tel 0191 521 0235
£   A £1.20 C/OAP 60p maximum of two children in any one party charged for
O   Easter-Dec Sun 11.00-16.30 In steam most BH Weekends
P   Free on site parking
C   Some hands on activity sheets
R   Only on steam days
T   Yes
D   Limited, no toilet facilities

Sunderland Museum and Art Gallery
Borough Road, Sunderland SR1 1PP Tel 0191 565 0723
£   Free
O   Mon-Fri 10.00-17.00 Sat 10.00-16.30 Sun 14.00-17.00
P   Free parking on site for disabled, public car park close by
C   Yes
R   Tea room
T   Public toilets outside museum
D   Ramped access, lift to all floors, toilet and parking facilities
•   Museum and Art Gallery celebrates the people, industries and skills that have made Sunderland famous world wide. As well as looking at the natural environment, displays include coalmining, glass, pottery, shipbuilding, geology and local wildlife.

WARWICKSHIRE

BAGINTON

Midland Air Museum

Coventry airport, Baginton CV8 3AZ Tel 01203 301033

£   A £3 C £2 (5-16 years) OAP/Student £2.75 Fam £8
O   Apl-Oct Mon-Sat 10.30-17.00 Sun & BHs 10.30-18.00
P   On site parking
C   Yes
R   Yes and picnic area
D   Wheelchair access and toilet facilities
•   The museum houses a unique collection of aircraft, engines and related exhibits illustrating the story of the jet age. Local aviation history is relayed in the 'Wings over Coventry' gallery.

Lunt Roman Fort

Coventry Road, Baginton Tel 01203 832381

£   A £2.60. C £1.30 incl tape tour guide. Admission only, A £1.80. C 80p. Group rates for pre-booked parties
O   Easter-Oct Weekends & BHs 10.00-17.00 Open daily late July and all Aug
P   On site free
R   Picnic area on site
T   Yes
D   Yes wheelchair access and toilet facilities
•   Unique 1st Century turf and timber Roman Fort. Regular programme of visits by X1111 Geminae Legion.

COVENTRY

Coventry Toy Museum

Whitefriars Gate, Much Park Street, Coventry CV1 2LT Tel 01203 227560
£ A 1.50 C £1 OAP £1
O Daily 12.00-18.00
P Street parking opposite restricted to 30 mins also Pay & Display
• Toys of every description. Housed in a 14th Century Monastery Gatehouse.

Herbert Art Gallery and Museum

Jordan Well, Coventry CV1 5QP Tel 01203 832381
£ Free
O Mon-Sat 10.00-17.30 Sun 14.00-17.00
P Public car parks in Gosford Street and Whitefriars Street
C Many interactives free. Some free or paid for activity sheets
R Tea Room open 10.00-16.00 Mon-Sat 14.00-16.30 Sunday
T Yes
D Access via automatic entrance door, lift to first floor, toilet facilities
• 'Godiva City' exhibition is an ward winning display with many interactive features. All temporary exhibitions include workshops, demonstrations or talks.

LEAMINGTON SPA

Leamington Spa Art Gallery & Museum

Avenue Road, Leamington Spa CV31 3PP Tel 01926 426559
£ Free
O Mon, Tue,Thur,Fri & Sat 10.00-13.00 14.00-17.00
P Parking outside museum limited to 2 hours, disabled parking 10 metres
C Activity sheets, holiday activities, discovery chest, education resource packs for art & local history
T Disabled toilet only
D Yes
• Discover the rich history of Leamington and its people. Explore the world of art through themed displays and interactive games. Paintings by major British artists and old masters.

NUNEATON

Nuneaton Museum & Art Gallery

Coton Road, Nuneaton Cv11 5TU Tel 01203 350720
£ Free
O All year Tue-Sat 10.30-16.30 Sun 14.00-16.30 Also open BH Mons (Please ring for Xmas opening times)
P 100 metres away. Parking adjacent for badge holders
C Yes. Please ring for details of special events
R Tea-room open Mon-Sat 10.30-16.30 Sun 14.00-16.30
T Yes including disabled and baby changing
D Yes, lift to upper galleries
• A friendly and accessible museum and art gallery set in award winning Riversley Park. Regularly changing art exhibitions. George Eliot display, local history. Please ring for details of current exhibitions.

RUGBY

HM Prison Service Museum
Newbold Revel, Rugby CV23 OTH Tel 01788 834168
£   Free
O   Mon-Fri 10.00-16.00 by appointment only
P   Free on site
C   Education packs, book related to National Curriculum for sale
T   Yes
D   Toilet facilities, please telephone for wheelchair access details
•   Housed in a converted stable block containing reconstruction's of Victorian prison architecture, the museum holds the prison service's national historical collection, exhibits illustrate the history of imprisonment from medieval time to present day.

Rugby School Museum
10 Little Church Street, Rugby CV21 3AW Tel 01788 574117
£   Museum £1.50 Tours £2 Combined £3 Con £1 Tours £1.50 Combined £2 Fam £5 and £7.50
O   Tue-Sat 13.30-16.30 Cl Xmas & N.Y
P   Car park 100 metres
R   By prior arrangement only, local cafes near to school
T   Yes
D   Assistance provided
•   History of one of the most famous schools in Britain, where the game of Rugby began and which numbers many famous names as pupils, from Lewis Carroll to Rupert Brooke and Chamberlain.

STRATFORD UPON AVON

RSC Collection
Royal Shakespeare Theatre, Stratford CV37 6BB Tel 01789 296655
£   £1.50 Con £1
O   Mon-Sat 09.30-20.00 Sun in Summer 12.00-16.30 Winter 11.00-15.30
P   Bridgefoot car park
C   Theatre exhibitions, paintings, sculpture
T   Yes
D   Access to ground floor of Gallery, toilet facilities
•   Temporary theatre exhibitions including costumes, props, paintings, sculpture from the Royal Shakespeare Theatre collection archives. Dressing-up skip for visitors to try on props- no charge. Backstage tours-please telephone for details.

WARWICK

The Warwick Doll Museum
Castle Street, Warwick CV34 4BP Tel 01926 49556 or 412500 in winter
£   A £1 C and OAP 70p
O   Easter-Sept Mon—Sat 10.00-17.00 Sun 13.00-17.00 Oct-Easter Sat 10.00-dusk
P   Street parking 20 metres
C   Yes
T   Public toilets 30 metres
•   Picturesque 14th Century house with hundreds of dolls, teddies and toys. Video showing

mechanical toys and how they work. Well stocked shop with something for everyone.

St John's House Museum

St John's, Warwick CV34 4NF Tel 01926 412021/412132

£   Free
O   May-Sept Tue, Sat and BHs 10.00-12.30 13.30-17.30 Sun 14.30-17.00
P   On site and nearby at St Nicholas Park
C   Holiday activities please telephone for details. None but picnic area in garden
T   Yes
D   Access to most of ground floor and gardens, toilet facilities
•   Housed in a 17th Century house with gardens. Displays include a Victorian classroom, parlour and kitchen; also a gallery of period costume that is changed annually.

Warwickshire Museum

Market Place, Warwick CV34 4SA Tel 01926 412500

£   Free
O   All year Mon-Sat 10.00-17.30 May-Sept Sun 14.00.17.00
P   Parking limited to 1 hour in Market Place, Westgate multi-storey 200 metres
C   Holiday activities please telephone
T   Public toilets 70 metres
D   Wheelchair access to ground floor. Public toilet for disabled 70 metres
•   Displays of Warwickshire's geology, biology and history include giant fossils, live bees and the famous Sheldon Tapestry Map. Temporary exhibition changes every 4-6 weeks. Well stocked shop.

WEST MIDLANDS

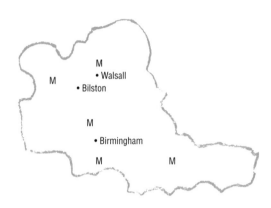

BILSTON

Bilston Art Gallery & Museum

Mount Pleasant, Bilston WV14 7LU. Tel 01902 409143

£ Free
O Mon-Thur 11.00-17.00. Sat 11.00-16.00. Fri, pre-booked groups only. Cl. BHs
P Free public parking nearby.
C Dragon sculpture garden. Education pack. Activities vary with temporary exhibitions.
R No refreshments but you may picnic in sculpture garden
T Yes
D Wheelchair accessible. Dedicated on-site parking.
• Many temporary exhibitions are themed on popular culture and crafts and supported with education programme with activities for children during school holidays. Permanent local history exhibition.

EDGBASTON

Lapworth Museum of Geology

School of Earth Sciences, University of Birmingham, Edgbaston, Birmingham B15 2TT. Tel 0121 4144173

£ Free
O Mon-Fri 09.00-17.00. Cl BHs
P Yes
C Hands on facilities
R Facilities adjacent
T Yes
• Rocks, minerals and fossils from around the world, incl fossil fish, dinosaur remains and footprints.

HOCKLEY

Jewellery Quarter Discovery Centre
75-79 Vyse Street, Hockley, Birmingham. Tel 0121 5543598
£   A £2. Con £1.50. Fam £5. Special rate for pre-booked groups of 10+
O   Mon-Fri 10.00-16.00. Sat 11.00-17.00.
P   Pay and display on street parking
C   Activity sheets, puzzles, holiday workshops and activities
R   Yes
T   Yes
D   Fully accessible
•   Award winning working museum, built around a preserved jewellery factory. Visitors can enjoy a guided tour of the Smith and Pepper factory and see a real jeweller at work.

SMETHWICK

Avery Historical Museum
Avery Berketl, Foundry Lane, Smethwick B66 2LP. Tel 0121 5581112 Ext 1951.
£   Free
O   Mon-Tue 09.00-16.30 with prior appointment only
P   Yes
C   Unsuitable for small children
R   Yes
T   Yes
•   History of weighing over 6000 years. Based on the historical factory site of Matthew Boulton & James Watt.

WALSALL

Birchills Canal Museum
Old Birchall, Walsall WS3 8QD. Tel 01922 6445778/653116.
£   Free
O   All year, Tue 09.30-12.30. Wed-Sun 13.00-16.00. Cl. BHs
C   Facilities available
R   Pub approx. 50 metres
T   Yes
D   Ramp entrance, stairs to first floor
•   Small museum about life on the canals, housed in a former boatman's rest at the top of the 8 Walsall   locks on the Walsall canal.

Walsall Leather Museum
Littleton Street West, Walsall WS2 8EQ. Tel 01922 721153.
£   Free
O   All year Tue-Sat 10.00-17.00 Sun 12.00-17.00 (16.00 Nov-March)
P   Public car park in Day Street
C   Programme of events and activities throughout the year. Children are encouraged to 'have a go'
R   Cafe serves excellent range of home cooked meals
T   Yes
D   Fully accessible to disabled persons. Lift to first floor. Toilet.
•   A 'living and working' museum with regular demonstrations of Walsall's traditional

leather crafts. Regular events/activities plus changing exhibitions. 1990 Best Industrial Museum Award. Shop.

Walsall Museum & Art Gallery

Lichfield Street, Walsall WS1 1TR. Tel 01922 653116.

£   Free
O   Tue-Sat 10.0-17.00. Sun 14.00-17.00
P   Car parks within walking distance
C   Jigsaws, games and dressing up facilities. Interactive computer programmes about the art collection.
T   Yes
D   Wheelchair access via lift, although the building is not an easy one in which to move around. Toilet.
•   Lively, friendly museum, always plenty for families to see and do. New lottery funded Art Gallery due to open 1999 which will give more space and excellent visitor facilities.

WEDNESBURY

Wednesbury Art Gallery, Museum & Adult Education Centre

Holyhead Road, Wednesbury WS10 7DF. Tel 0121 5560683.

£   Free
O   Mon. Tue. Wed Fri 10.00-17.00. Thur, Sat 10.00-13.00.
P   Free car park adjacent
C   Activity sheets available
T   Yes
D   Wheelchair access to ground floor only.
•   Edwin Richard collection of oil and water-colour paintings. Ruskin pottery, highly prized art pottery manufactured at West Smethwick. Timestones Gallery (geology) and travels of Lady Helen Caddick.

WILLENHALL

The Lock Museum

54 New Road, Willenhall WV13 2DA. Tel 01902 634542.

£   A £2. Con £1.
O   All year except Xmas period, Tue, Wed, Thu & Sat. 11.00-17.00.
P   Yes
C   Activity days for schools with hands-on experience of lock making and Victorian life.
R   Tea/coffee/biscuits
T   Yes
D   Wheelchair access to ground floor only. Toilet.
•   Museum based on Victorian home and workshop of Hodson family, locksmiths in Willenhall from 1790, with gas lighting and kitchen range where school parties can experience life in a Victorian kitchen.

Willenhall Museum
Willenhall Library, Walsall Street, Willenhall WV13 2EX. Tel 01902 366513.
Free
Mon 10.00-19.00. Tue 09.30-17.15. Thu 9.30-19.00. Fri 9.30-17.15. Sat 9.30-13.30. 14.30-17.00.
Ample free parking
The museum tells about the people of Willenhall and their town, capital of the British lock industry.

WILTSHIRE

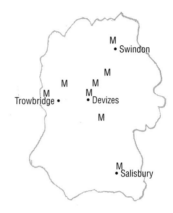

M
• Swindon

M

M   M
M   M
Trowbridge •   • Devizes

M

M
• Salisbury

AVEBURY

The Great Barn Museum
Avebury, Wiltshire SN8 1RF Tel 01672 539555
£   A 95p C, Student and OAP 50p Nat Trust Member 50p Fam £2.30
O   March-Nov daily 10.00-18.00 Dec-Feb weekends only 11.00-16.30
P   Parking nearby
C   Hands on exhibits and special events
R   Yes
T   Yes
D   Wheelchair acces to all museum, toilet facilities
•   The museum of Wiltshire rural life reflecting crafts, trades and domestic life of the county housed in 17th Century thatched threshing barn.

BRADFORD ON AVON

Bradford on Avon Museum
Bridge Street, Bradford on Avon BA15 1BY Tel 01225 863280
£   Free
O   Easter-Oct Wed-Sat 10.30-12.30 14.00-16.00 Sun & BHs 14.00-16.00
    Nov-Easter Wed, Thurs, Fri & Sun 14.00-16.00 Sat 10.30-12.30 14.00-16.00
P   Parking outside museum 20p per hour or other parking nearby
T   Public toilet nearby
D   Access and toilet facilities
•   This is a small volunteer run museum displaying local history of an old picturesque stone town, featuring a complete rebuilt chemist shop.

NE

ell and Wilson Motor Museum

vnside, Stockley Lane, Calne SN11 0NF Tel 01249 813119

A £2 C 75p OAP £1.50

Mon-Thurs & Sun Summer 11.00-17.00 Winter 11.00-16.00 Open Gd Fri

Please telephone for details

Children's play equipment, crayoning sheet and questionnaire by arrangement

Yes

Yes

An ideal venue for car club visits. Over 70 exhibits, plus automobilia.

VIZES

tshire Fire Defence Museum

.H.Q. Manor House, Potterne, Devizes SN10 5PP Tel 01380 731108

Free

Please telephone for details

On site free

'Hands on' facilities

Yes

A collection of 18th -20th Century fire-fighting equipment.

tshire Archaeological & Natural History Museum

Long Street, Devizes SN10 1NS Tel 01380 727369

A £1.75 C 40p OAP/Student £1.25 Mon Free Admission

Mon-Sat 10.00-17.00

Parking on street and in Market Square

Education officer available for school parties

Yes

Independent museum with galleries tracing Wiltshire history from pre-historic to present. Internationally important Bronze Age collection. Art gallery, library, natural history gallery, rolling programme of special exhibtions.

COCK

ckham Country Atrractions

.ckham College, Lacock SN15 2NY Tel 01249 443111

A £3 C £1 Con £2 Fam £7

Easter-Oct daily

On site

Rare breeds and poultry, adventure playground

Tea rooms and restaurant

Yes

Wheelchair access to site, many paths are shingle so difficult for person without aid. Museum of agricultural history with machinery and tools, rural crafts and milking equipment in reconstructed graneries and a barn.

MARKET LAVINGTON

Market Lavington Village Museum
Church Street, Market Lavington Tel 01380 818736
£   Free
O   May-Oct Wed, Weekends & BHs 14.30-16.30
P   Public car park nearby
C   Toy box - educational files
R   Available in village
•   Museum concentrates on the life of the village up to the present incl photograp
documents, etc.

SWINDON

Great Western Railway Museum
Faringdon Road, Swindon SN1 5BJ Tel 01793 466555
£   A and OAP £2.30 C £1.10 Children under 5 free
O   Mon-Sat 10.00-17.00 Sun 14.00-17.00 Cl Xmas and Gd Fri
P   Public car park nearby
C   Yes
T   Yes
D   Wheelchair access to ground floor only
•   A museum dedicated to the history of the Great Western Railway, including
locomotives, nameplates, posters and a restored railwayman's cottage.

Purton Museum
Public Library, High Street, Purton SN5 9AA Tel 01793 770567
£   Free
O   Tues 14.00-17.00 18.00-20.00 Weds 10.00-13.00 14.00-17.00 Fri 14.00-17.00 18.0
20.00 All year
P   Free parking next to museum
C   Yes
R   None on site but plenty nearby
T   Yes
•   Collection includes Neolithic and Roman remains, agricultural hand tools and dai
equipment which reflect the village's past reliance on the land.

Railway Village Museum
34 Faringdon Road, Swindon SN1 5BJ Tel 01793 466553
£   A 85p C 45p (Free to visitors from GWR Museum)
O   Mon-Sat 10.00-17.00 Sun 14.00-17.00 Cl Xmas and Gd Fri
P   Public car park in town centre
D   Access to ground floor only
•   A restored Victorian railwayman's cottage with original features, lit by gas.

SALISBURY

The Royal Glos, Berks and Wilts Regiment Museum
The Wardrobe, 58 The Close, Salisbury SP1 2EX Tel 01722 414536
£   A £2 C 50p OAP and Students £1.50
O   Apl-Oct daily 10.00-16.30 Nov-mid Dec and Feb-March weekdays only

P Limited on site and in the Close. Public car park 600 metres in New Street
R Yes
" Yes
) Wheelchair access but no disabled toilet facilities

A combination of a fine military museum, mediaeval house, relaxing riverside garden and good food await the visitor to the Old Bishop's Wardrobe in Salisbury's renowned Cathedral Close.

Salisbury and South Wiltshire Museum

The King's House,65 The Close, Salisbury SP1 2EN Tel 01722 332151

£ A £3 C 75p under 5 Free OAP, Student and Con £2 Groups £2
Tickets give unlimited free visits throughout the calendar year.
) All year Mon-Sat 10.00-17.00 Sun in July and Aug 14.00-17.00
P Parking in Cathedral Close
; Quiz trails and under 5's trail
R Coffee Shop Mon-Sat
T Yes
) Wheelchair access to ground floor. shops and special exhibitions, toilet facilities, parking by prior booking
• Home of the Stonehenge Gallery-winner of 6 awards. Great archaeology and local history. Pitt Rivers collection, ceramics, Wedgwood, Turner watercolours, costume, lace, embroidery. Salisbury Giant and Hob Nob Exhibitions.

WORCESTERSHIRE

BEWDLEY

Bewdley Museum
Load Street, Bewdley DY12 2AE Tel 01299 403573
£   A £2 C accompanied free unaccompanied £1 OAP £1
O   Apl-Oct daily 11.00-17.00 incl BHs
P   Public car park nearby
C   Yes
R   None on site but tea shops etc in town, picnic area on site
D   Most parts of museum accessible
•   The museum is set in the 18th Century Butchers Shambles making an interesting setting for the craft workshops and sawyard. Picnic area and daily demonstrations including clay pipe making.

BROMSGROVE

Bromsgrove Museum
26 Birmingham Road, Bromsgrove B61 0DD Tel 01527 577983
£   A £1.20 C and OAP 60p
O   Mon-Sat 09.30-17.00 All year
P   Public car park opposite museum
C   Look and see question sheet for children
T   Yes
•   Displays of local and social history. Shop windows, local industry. Group visits can view some of the reserve collection by prior arrangement.

DROITWICH SPA

Droitwich Spa Heritage Centre
St Richard's House, Victoria Square, Droitwich Spa WR9 8DS

Free

Mon-Sat 10.00-16.00 all year

Pay and display car park at rear of museum

Work sheets available for visiting parties

Yes

Access and toilet facilities

The Droitwich Heritage Centre houses a unique permanent local history exhibition, depicting the town's 'salty' past, having an excellent 'Roman' section. Also a comprehensive T.I.C. and brass rubbing centre.

EVESHAM

The Almoney Heritage Centre
Abbey Gate, Evesham WR11 4BG Tel 01386 446944

A £2 OAP £1 C and Students Free

All year Mon-Sat 10.00-17.00 Sun 14.00-17.00 Cl for 2 weeks Xmas & NY

Pay & Display nearby

Work sheets for First Middle and Senior Schools

14th Century home of the Almoner of the Benedictine Abbey. Houses displays relating to the Abbey, Battle of Evesham (1265). Social and economic history of the Vale of Evesham.

KIDDERMINSTER

Hereford and Worcester County Museum
Hartlebury Castle, Hartlebury, Kidderminster DY11 7XZ Tel 01299 250416

A £1.90 C and OAP 90p Fam £5

March- Nov Mon-Thurs 10.00-17.00 Fri and Sun 14.00-17.00 Cl Sat & Gd Fri

On site

Questionnaires to Galleries

Yes

Yes

Wheelchair access to ground floor and toilet facilities

Mainly 19th Century social history and archaeology set in servants wing of Bishop's Palace. Programme of temporary exhibitions.

REDDITCH

Forge Mill Needle Museum & Bordesley Abbey Visitor Centre
Needle Mill Lane, Riverside, Redditch B97 6RR. Tel 01527 62509.

'A £1.80. OAP £1.30. C 55p. Fam £4.20. Season tickets A £4. Fam £10.

Easter-Sept, Mon-Fri 11.00-16.30. Sat-Sun 14.00-17.00. Oct-Mar & Feb-Easter, Mon-Thur 11.00-16.00. Sun 14.00-17.00.

Free parking and bicycle stands

Activity sheets for both museums

Ice creams and cold drinks, water for dogs

Yes

D   Partial disabled access (not top floors). Toilet. Hard surface in car park for wheelchair users. Adapted picnic table. Painted lines on stairs. Large text museum information sheet.

- Needle Museum - Displays about Redditch needle industry. Working, water-powered machinery, dummies, open displays.
- Visitor Centre - Abbey ruins and finds from 25 years of excavations at the adjacent medieval Cistercian Abbey.

TENBURY

Tenbury Museum

Cross Street, Tenbury.

£   A 25p C 5p
O   May-Sept Tue 10.30-12.30 13.00-17.00 Sat 10.30-14.30 Sun & BHs 14.30-17.00
P   Car park at swimming pool
C   Music box etc which attendant will work for children
D   Yes

- Tenbury Advertisers from 1896. Hop crib, relics of spa and cobblers shop.

WORCESTER

The Elgar Birthplace Museum

Crown East Lane, Lower Broadheatth, Worcester WR2 6RH Tel 01905 333224

£   A £3 C 50p OAP £2 Student £1
O   May-Sept 10.30-18.00 Oct-Jan15th 13.30-16.30 Feb16th-Apl 13.30-16.30 Cl Wed
P   Free on site
C   Yes
T   Yes
D   Wheelchair access to ground floor

- The cottage in which Elgar was born, now housing a wonderful collection of furniture, memorabilia, books, photographs and original manuscripts spanning his whole lifetime.

Museum of Local Life

Friar Sreet, Worcester WR1 2NA Tel 01905 722349

£   A £1.50 Con 75p Fam £3.25
O   Mon, Tue,Wed Fri and Sat 10.30-17.00
P   Public car park
T   Public toilets
D   Limited please telephone prior to visit

- The museum is situated in a medieval timber framed building and our displays show life in the city during the past two centuries. Temporary exhibitions and events are held throughout the year.

The Worcestershire Regiment Museum

Worcester City Museum and Art Gallery
Foregate Street, Worcester WR1 1DT Tel 019005 25371

£   Free
O   Mon,Tue, Wed, Fri 09.30-18.00 Sat 09.30-17.00
P   Public car park in town
R   Cafe
T   Yes

D   Access via lift from street and toilet facilities
*   The museum houses a wide variety of uniforms, weapons, medals, pictures and artifacts which illustrate the Regiment's record of over 300 years of service at home and overseas in peace and war.

Museum of the Worcestershire Yeomanry Cavalry
City Museum and Art Gallery
Foregate Strret, Worcester WR1 1DT Tel 01905 25371
£   Free
O   Mon,Tue, Wed and Fri 09.30-18.00 Sat 09.30-17.00
P   Public car parks at Pitchcroft and St Martin's Gate
R   Yes
T   Yes
D   Wheelchair access via lift, toilet facilities
*   Collection spans the history of the Yeomanary Cavalry from the 18th century to present day.

YORKSHIRE

WEST YORKSHIRE

BATLEY

Bagshaw Museum
Wilton Park, Batley, WF17 0AS. Tel 01924 326155.
£   Free
O   All year, Mon-Fri 11.00-17.00. Sat-Sun 12.00-17.00. Cl Gd Fri. Xmas period & N.Y day.
P   Yes, free
C   Wide range of children's and family activities. Hands-on activities.
R   Yes
T   Yes
D   Wheelchair access. Toilet. Induction loop. Tactile features.
•   Find yourself in another world at the Bagshaw museum. Time and space mean nothing when you can step straight from an Egyptian tomb into the tropical enchantment of the rainforest.

BRADFORD

Bolling Hall Museum
Bowling Hall Road, Bradford BD4 2LP. Tel 01274 723057.
£   Free
O   All year, Wed-Fri 11.00-16.00. Sat-Sun 10.00-17.00 BH Mons 11.00-16.00. Cl Gd Fri & Xmas.
P   Yes
C   Facilities for pre-booked parties only
T   Yes
D   Wheelchair access to ground floor. Some Braille labels. Staff trained in sympathetic hearing. Guidebook available in large print, Braille and audio. Toilet.
•   A lovely house, 16th - 18th centuries, with splendid collection of 17th and 18th century

furniture and a huge window with armorial stained glass.

Bradford Industrial Museum & Horses at Work
Moorside Mills, Moorside Road, Eccleshill, Bradford BD2 3HP. Tel 01274 631756.
£   A £2. Con £1. Fam £4.
O   Tue-Sat 10.00-17.00. Sun & BH Mons 12.00-17.00
P   Yes
C   Holiday activities. Horse tram rides.
R   Yes
T   Yes
D   Ramps. Toilet
•   Original worsted spinning mill complete with mill owner's house, workers cottages, mill stables with heavy horses. Textile, mill machinery and horse demonstrations every day.

The Colour Museum
P O Box 244, Perkin House, Providence Street, Bradford, BD1 2PW. Tel 01274 290955.
£   A £1.50. Con £1. Fam £3.75.
O   Tue-Fri 14.00-17.00. Sat 10.00-16.00.
P   On Westgate and Wigan Street .
C   Interactive exhibits for visitors of all ages.
R   Nearby
T   Yes, incl facilities for parents with small children.
D   Ramp to front door and lift access to all floors. Toilet.
•   This unique museum is packed with visitor operated displays on light, colour, dyeing and textile printing. Special exhibitions cover other uses of colour.

National Museum of Photography, Film & Television
Pictureville, Bradford, BD1 1NQ. Tel 01274 727488.
£   Museum free. Charge for IMAX.
O   Re-development in 1997/8, please phone for opening details.
P   Yes
C   Facilities too numerous to mention
R   Cafe/restaurant and picnic gallery
T   Yes
D   Access to all floors, Limited number to IMAX auditorium.
•   A fascinating audio visual journey, taking you from the very first photograph up to the digital wizardry of the 1990's. MAX is Britain's largest cinema screen - prepare to be overwhelmed as you take an ant's-eye view of the world.

BRIGHOUSE

Smith Art Gallery
Halifax Road, Brighouse, HD6 2QJ Tel 01484 719222
£   Free
O   Mon-Fri (Cl Wed) 10.00-12.30 13.00-18.00. Sat 10.00-12.15 13.00-16.00 BHs 14.00-17.00
P   Free car park in Brighouse- 7 mins walk away
C   According to exhibition
D   Access but no toilet facilities
•   The Gallery displays Victorian paintings from permanent collections and temporary exhibitions, supported by an education programme.

DEWSBURY

Dewsbury Museum

Crow Nest Park, Heckmondwike Road, Dewsbury WF13 2SA Tel 01924 468171

£ Free
O Mon-Fri 11.00-17.00 Weekends 12.00-17.00
P On site free parking
C Stamp card system, dressing up box, reading corner and sound tubes
R Cafe on site
T Yes
D Access to ground floor only and toilet facilities
• The magical theme of childhood. Learn about the lives of Victorian child miners and millworkers. Visit the 1940s school room. 'Growing up in Dewsbury' offers a technicolour journey through childhood experiences..

HALIFAX

Bankfield Museum

Akroyd Park, Boothtown Road, Halifax HX3 6HG Tel 01422 354823/352334

£ Free
O Tue-Sat 10.00-17.00 Sun 14..00-17.00 BH Mon 10.00-17.00
P Free car park at front entrance
T Yes
D Limited access-portable ramp for library entrance, please contact museum for more advice
• Fine Victorian mansion, now home to a wonderful collection of international textiles plus the Duke of Wellington's Regimental programme of temporary exhibition workshops and activities.

Calderdale Industrial Museum

Square Road, Halifax HX1 1RE Tel 01422 358087

£ A 1.60 C 75p Con 80p Fam £4.50
O Mon-Sat 10.00-17.00 Sun 14.00-17.00 Cl Xmas & Mons except BHs
P Public car park adjacent
C Yes
R Drinks available
T Yes
D Wheelchair lift and ramps plus toilet facilities
• A working museum reflecting 150 years of Calderdale's industrial history which tells the people's story alongside working machinery.

Piece Hall Art Gallery

The Piece Hall, Halifax HX1 1RE. Tel 01422 3588087

£ Free
O Tue-Sat 10.00-17.00. Sun 12.00-17.00 BH Mons 10.00-17.00. Cl Xmas, Boxing & N.Y. days.
P Woolshops, Eureka car parks also on street parking
C According to current exhibition
R Yes
T Yes
D Wheelchair access via the Square Road entrance. Lift to all floors. Toilets.

- Exhibitions of original works of contemporary art. Regular workshops and other educational activities take place in the gallery making it a lively, fun place to be.

Shibden Hall
Lister's Road, Halifax HX3 6XG. Tel 01422 352246.
£   A £1.60. OAP 80p. C 75p. Fam £4.50.
O   Mar-Nov, Mon-Sat 10.00-17.00. Sun 12.00-17.00.
P   Yes
C   Occasional activity days. Education pack.
R   Yes
T   Yes
D   Access limited, however, for small pre-booked parties we can provide activities. Audio tour.
- Drift into 600 years of history - a world without electricity - where craftsmen worked in wood and iron - a house where you sense the family has just gone out.

HEPSTONSTALL

Hepstonstall Museum
Church Yard Bottom, Hepstonstall HX7 7LY. Tel 01422 719222.
£   A £1. Con 50p.
O   Easter-Oct, weekends & BHs, 13.00-17.00
P   Public parking 100 metres away
C   Occasional activity days
R   In the village
T . Yes
D   Access is fine, toilet is large space but not adapted.

HUDDERSFIELD

Automobilia Transport Museum
The Heritage Centre, Leeds Road, Huddersfield HD1 6QA Tel 01422 844775
£   Donation box - price guide A £2 C £1
O   All year Mon-Sat 09.00-17.00 Sun 11.00-16.00
P   On site free
C   Museum guide 50p
T   Yes
- A collection of bicycle's, motorcucles, cars and other artefacts from the 1900's, 1920's, 1930's, 1940's, also including Grundy Mack classic car sales. Over 100 cars on view.

Colne Valley Museum
Cliffe Ash, Golcar, Huddersfield HD7 4PY. Tel 01484 659762.
£   A £1. Con 50p.
O   Sat. Sun. BHs, 14.00-17.00. Cl Xmas-N.Y.
P   Free in village
C   Activity sheet. Have-a-go days. Hands-on with textiles.
R   Available on craft/working weekends otherwise drinks only.
T   Yes
D   Wheelchair access difficult but special arrangements can be made if advance notice given.
- Museum is housed in three weavers cottages of 1845. Experience handloom weaving -

the flying shuttle and witch loom. Working spinning jenny. Clog making by gaslight. Special facilities for schools.

Tolson Museum

Ravensknowle Park, Wakefield Road, Huddersifled HD5 8DJ. Tel 01484 223830.
£   Free
O   Mon-Fri 11.00-17.00. Sat-Sun 12.00-17.00. Cl Gd Fri & Xmas.
P   Yes
C   Hands-on, fun sheets etc usually available. Special programme of children's events and activities.
R   Drinks machine
T   Yes
D   Access by step and rail, or ramp at rear. Ground floor accessible, first floor accessible by chair lift. Toilet.
•   A general local 'family' museum telling the story of the natural history, archaeology, local history, transport and industry of the Huddersfield area. Special exhibitions.

ILKLEY

Manor House Museum

Castle Yard, Ilkley LS29 9DT. Tel 01943 600066.
£   Free
O   Wed-Sat 11.00-17.00. Sun 13.00-16.00
P   Pay and display 4 mins away.
T   Yes
D   Limited access to ground floor only
•   Furnished house, archaeology and history. Temporary art exhibitions. Varied workshops, activities and events.

KEIGHLEY

Cliffe Castle Museum

Spring Gardens Lane, Keithley BD20 6LH. Tel 01535 618230.
£   Free
O   Tue-Sat 10.00-17.00. Sun 12.00-17.00. Also open BHs
P   Yes
C   Temporary exhibitions often have activities/hands-on. Holiday activities.
R   Privately run cafe (01535 606593)
T   Yes
D   Wheelchair access to 75% of displays on ground floor. Toilet.
•   Cliffe Castle, a former mill owner's mansion set in a park, now houses the district's collections of minerals and crystals, local natural history, geology and bygones, also original Victorian rooms. Special exhibitions and events.

LEEDS

Armsley Mills

Canal Road, Leeds LS12 2QF Tel 0113 2637861
£   A £2 C if accompanied 50p OAP £1
O   All year Tue-Sat 10.00-17.00 Sun 13.00-17.00 tel first in case of essential building work
P   Free on site

c   At exhibition times
R   Tea/coffee machine and catering on BHs and special events
T   Yes
D   Wheelchair lift to main floors, toilet facilities .Parking spaces by shop entrance
•   Housed in Armsley Mill, once the world's largest textile mill, the museum is a green oasis housing the City's important industrial collections. With exciting working machinery you can relive the past in this spectacular Georgian building.

Horsforth Village Museum
5 The Green, Horsforth, Leeds LS18 5JB. Tel 0113 2589411.
£   Free
O   Easter-Xmas, Sat 10.00-16.00. Sun 14.00-17.00. Also open to schools, etc by appointment.
P   Fink Hill car park
C   Workshops. questionnaires, museum trails
R   Last Sat in the month, 10.00-13.00
T   Yes
D   Wheelchair access to ground floor only.
•   Local social history. Special exhibitions.

Leeds City Museum
Municipal Buildings, The Headrow, Leeds LS1 3AA. Tel 0113 2478275.
£   Free
O   Tue-Sat 10.00-17.00. Cl Tue following BHs
P   Several nearby
C   Facilities available
T   Yes
D   Wheelchair access. No adapted toilet.
•   Founded in 1819, the museum has early and valuable material covering natural sciences, archaeology and ethnography, animals, rocks, Romans, Egyptians, etc.

Thwaite Mills Museum
Thwaite Lane, Stourton, Leeds LS10 1RT. Tel 0113 2496453.
£   A £2. Con £1.
O   Mar-Dec, Mon-Sat 10.00-17.00. Sun 13.00-17.00.
P   Yes
T   Yes
D   Fully accessible
•   Working water powered grinding mill, two waterwheels, extensive island grounds between river and canal, mill manager's house.

OTLEY

Otley Museum
The Mechanics' (Civic Centre), Cross Green, Otley LS21 1AL. Tel 01943 461052
£   Free
O   Mon, Tue, Fri, 10.00-12.30. Cl Easter, Aug, Xmas.
P   Licks car park, North Parade.
C   Many objects which children can handle.
R   Cafes/restaurants in Otley
T   Yes

D   Stairwalking wheelchair available if arranged in advance. Toilet.
•   Wharfedale printing machine, large collection of objects from Mesolithic period to 20th century, collection of archives of printing and other Otley industries which may be researched by prior appointment.

PUDSEY

Moravian Museum
55-57 Fulneck, Pudsey. Tel 0113 2564862(Curator)
£   A 50p. C 25p.
O   Easter Wed-Oct, Wed & Sat. 14.00-16.30. If preferred parties can be accommodated at other times by arrangement.
R   Teas nearby in season. Refreshments to order for pre-booked parties
T   Yes
D   Not accessible to wheelchairs as there are 7 steps up to the museum and more to upper storey. Wheelchair access to Church when open for visitors
•   Unique collection of world-wide Moravian Church, history of local Moravian settlement, superb embroidery and lace, 1822 fire engine, ethnography, costume, loom, kitchen, Victorian parlour, Ladakh items.

WAKEFIELD

Castleford Museum Room
c/o Wakefield Museum, Wood Street, Wakefield WF1 2EW. Tel 01924 305351
£   Free
O   Mon. Tue. Thur 9.30-18.00. Wed. Fri 9.30-17.00. Sat 9.30-13.00.
P   Aire Street and Carlton Street pay and display, 2 mins walk.
C   Interactive hands-on exhibition on Victorian Castleford
R   Cafes nearby
D   Sorry, there are 30 steps up to the museum room.
•   Interactive hands-on exhibition of Victorian Castleford, it's industries, homes and people. It's not large but there's plenty to see and do. To avoid overcrowding groups are advised to book.

Stephen G Beaumont Museum
Stanley Royd Hospital, Aberford Road, Wakefield WF1 4DQ. Tel 01924 201688
£   Free
O   Weds only plus BHs, 10.30-16.30, all year.\plain
P   Yes
T   Yes
D   Wheelchair accessible. No adapted toilet.
•   Devoted solely to illustrating the history and development of an asylum/mental hospital, exhibits include padded cell, restraining appliances, model of original 1818 building and interesting documents and records.

Wakefield Museum
Wood Street, Wakefield WF1 2EW. Tel 01924 305351 (minicom)
£   Free
O   All year, Mon-Sat 10.30-16.30.
P   City centre car parks 5 mins walk and on-street parking
C   Hands-on facilities in temporary exhibitions. Free quiz every school holiday

T   Yes
D   Regret 3 steps to ground floor and many more to first floor (no lift). 'Talking' push button labels.
•   From Romans to rationing, the unique history of Wakefield people, incl Charles Waterton's world-famous collection of 1820's South American rainforest animals. Exciting hands-on exhibitions all year round.

YORKSHIRE

EAST YORKSHIRE

BEVERLEY

Beverley Art Gallery
Champney Road, Beverley HU17 9BQ Tel 01482 883903
£   Free
O   Wed, Thur, Fri 10.00-17.00 Weekends 10.00-12.30 13.30-1700
P   Public car park nearby 20p an hour
R   Drinks
T   Available in Library downstairs
•   Situated above Beverley Library, the Art Gallery is best known for its extensive collection of works by Fred Elwell (1870-1958) a local artist.

BRIDLINGTON

Harbour Museum and Aquarium
Bridlington Pier and Harbour, Gunners Wharf, Bridlington YO15 3AN Tel 01262 670148/9
£   A 40p C 20p
O   Easter-Oct daily 10.00 till dusk Weekends only Oct-Jan
P   Public car parks at Langdale Wharf and Gunners Wharf - 50p
C   Activity sheets
R   Refreshment Kiosks adjacent
T   Yes
D   Wheelchair access and toilet facilities
•   The museum contains a wealth of material relating to the history of the Harbour covering many hundreds of years. It also covers the different methods of sea fishing carried out by vessels from the Harbour.

Sewerby Hall and Gardens

Church Lane, Sewerby YO15 1EA Tel 01262 677874

£   A £ 2.50p C £1 OAP £2

O   Apl-Oct 11.00-18.00   Nov-Dec Sat-Tue 11.00-16.00 March Sat-Tue 11.00.16.00 CL Xmas

P   Free on site

R   Cafe and picnic sites

T   Yes

D   Wheelchair access and lift, parking, toilet facilities

•   Sewerby Hall is also the Museum of East Yorkshire and features an East Yorkshire photographic gallery, display of regional history and the East Yorkshire Showcase Gallery

COTTINGHAM

Skidby Windmill and Rural Life

Skidby, Cottingham HU16 5TF Tel 01482 848405

£   A £1.50 C 50p Con 80p

O   May, June Oct, Nov, Dec Wed & Weekends 10.00-17.00 July-Sept   Wed-Sun 10.00-17.00

P   Mill car park 50 metres from entrance

C   Activity sheets for special events, please telephone for details

R   Cafe

T   Yes

D   Ground floor ramped

•   Only working Tower Windmill East of the Pennines. Displays of rural crafts and working force.

HORNSEA

Hornsea Museum

11 Newbegin, Hornsea HU18 1AB. Tel 01964 533443

£   A £1.50. Con £1. Fam £4.95.

O   Easter-Sept, Mon-Sat 11.00-17.00. Sun 14.00-17.00

P   Public car park nearby

C   Hands-on facilities, questionnaires, activity sheets

R   During summer holidays

T   Yes

D   Wheelchair access to ground floor only. Toilet.

•   Award winning folk museum set in historic farmhouse. Room settings show how the family lived, worked and played 100 years ago. Large gardens and many other attractions.

HULL

Hull City Museums

c/o Ferens Art Gallery, Queen Victoria Square, Hull. HU1 3RA. Tel 01482 613902

Seven museums to visit within a few minutes walking distance of each other.

£   A £1. Under 13's free. Fam £3. This is the entrance fee to each museum

O   Mon-Sat 10.00-17.00. Sun 13.30-16.30.

P   Princess Quay.

C   Facilities at some of the museums
R   At 1 & 2.
T   At all sites except Spurn Lightship
D   Nos 1,2,4,5 & 7 are fully accessible to wheelchairs. No.3 is only wheelchair accessible to ground floor. No. 6 not accessible to wheelchairs.
- 1 - Ferens Art Gallery -This award winning gallery houses an extensive collection ranging from Dutch and European old masters to contemporary art.
- 2 - Streetlife - Hull's noisiest museum transports you back to the days of horse drawn carriages, trams, penny farthings, steam and much more.
- 3 - Wilberforce House - Originally the birthplace of 18th century politician, William Wilberforce, this attractive building houses unique collections relating to his campaign to abolish slavery.
- 4 - Town Docks - Discover the secrets of Hull's maritime heritage spanning over 700 years. Whaling, fishing, shipping and an insight into life at sea.
- 5 - Old Grammar School - Formerly the Old Grammar School built in 1583 it now tells the fascinating story of Hull and it's people though the centuries.
- 6 - Spurn Lightship - Welcome aboard the Spurn Lightship built in 1927 and now moored in Hull's marina. It originally guided sailors navigating the treacherous River Humber.
- 7 -Hull & East Riding - This archaeological treasure house displays some of Britain's finest mosaics; discover life in Celtic times and much more.

Yorkshire Water Museum
Springhead Avenue, Willerby Road, Hull HU5 5HZ. Tel 01482 652283
£   Free
O   Jan-Nov. Fri. Sat. Sun. 13.00-17.00.
P   Yes
C   Self activated working models. Teachers information pack.
T   Yes
D   Limited access for wheelchairs. Toilet.
- Many exciting exhibits tell the story of water distribution from before the city's Royal Charter to Elizabethan times. See the famous beam engine which could raise over 4000 gallons of water every minute.

WITHERNSEA

Withernsea Lighthouse Museum
Hull Road, Withernsea HU19 2DY. Tel 01964 614834.
£   A £1.50. OAP £1. Over 5's 75p. Fam £4.
O   Weekends and BHs Mar-Oct 13.00-17.00. Weekdays mid June-mid Sept 11.00-17.00.
P   Car park 100 metres on street parking nearby
C   Activity sheet for school educational visits.
R   Yes also picnic area in garden.
T   Yes
D   Wheelchair access to ground floor only Toilet.
- Museum towers 40 metres above town centre with spectacular views. Many exhibits, R.N.L.I., H.M.Coastguard, ships bells, models and photos recording history of shipwrecks and Withernsea lifeboats and their crews.

YORKSHIRE

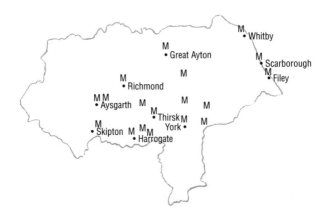

NORTH YORKSHIRE

ALDBOROUGH

Aldborough Roman Town Museum
Aldborough,Broughbridge YO5 9ES Tel 01423 322 768
£   A £1.40 C 70p Cons £1.10
O   Apl-Sept daily 12.00-17.00
P   On street
C   Teachers leaflets and an opportunity to make mosaic pavements
T   Yes
•   A broad range of Roman military and domestic artefacts illustrating the way of life in Isurium Brigantum, capital town of the Brigantes. The grounds contain excavated remains of the town walls and Roman mosaic pavements.

AYSGARTH FALLS

Yorkshire Museum of Horse Drawn Carriages
York Mill, Aysgarth Falls. Correspondence to Mr Keily, Curator, 1 York Cottages, York Mill, Aysgarth Falls, DL8 3SR. Tel 01904 663399
£   A £2. C 75p.
O   All year, 09.30-dusk
P   Pay & display a few minutes walk away
C   Talks given to groups (all ages) by prior arrangement. Fun quiz for younger people.
R   Tea shop adjacent
T   In car park
•   The museum houses a unique collection of horse drawn carts and coaches.

BEDALE

Bedale Museum
Bedale Hall, Bedale, DL8 1AA. Tel 01677 427146
£   Free
O   Easter-Sept, Mon-Sat. Oct-Easter, Tue only, 10.00-16.00. Phone to confirm if travelling any distance
P   Limited parking on site but plenty within 100 metres
C   Limited hands-on. Possibly fun/activity sheets.
R   Cafes within 200 metres
T   In car park, 300 metres
D   Accessible to wheelchairs. Toilet at car park.
•   Bedale 1748 hand drawn line engine. Old documents, photos, clothing, toys, craft tools and household utensils give an absorbing picture of the lives of ordinary people. Smile at the memories evoked.

Museum of Badges and Battledress
The Green, Crakehall, Bedale DL8 1HP. Tel 01677 424444
£   A £1.50. Con £1. C 75p
O   Tue-Fri, 11.00-17.00. Sat-Sun & BH. Mon 13.00-17.00
P   Yes
T   Yes
•   Display of battledress and equipment of the British Forces from 1900. Exhibits to evoke memories of WW11. Parties and guided tours at any time, incl evening, by arrangement.

FILEY

Filey Museum
8-10 Queen Street Filey YO14 9HB Tel 01723 513640
£   A £1 C 50p
O   Late May-Mid Sept Sun-Fri 10.00-12.00 14.00-17.00 Sat 14.00-17.00
P   Adjacent on street parking
D   Limited, please telephone before visit
•   Displays reflect life and times in Filey with particular regard to on-shore fishing and seaside resort.

GREAT AYTON

Captain Cook Schoolroom Museum
101 High Street, Great Ayton TS9 6NB. Tel 01642 722030
£   A £1.50. Con £1. C 75p. Fam £3.50
O   Gd Fri-Oct, daily, 14.00-16.30. Also open in Jul & Aug from 10.30-12.30.
P   Yes in village
C   Activity sheets
R   Cafes & restaurants nearby
T   Opposite museum
•   Started in 1928, the museum occupies two rooms in the old Postage School and houses exhibits related to Cook and the 18th century village where he lived as a boy.

HUTTON LE HOLE

Rizedale Folk Museum

Hutton-le-Hole YO6 6UA tel 01751 417367

£   A £3 C £1.50 under 5 free, OAP and Student £2.50 Fam £7.50
O   March-Oct 10.00-17.30
P   Car park in National Park 100 metres
C   Yes
R   None on site but some in village
T   Yes
D   Yes
•   Yorkshire's finest open air museum 400 years of history-everything from a Manor House to a fire engine.

HARROGATE

Nidderdale Museum

Council Offices, King Street, Pately Bridge, Harrogate HG3 5LE. Tel 01423 711225.

£   A £1. Con 50p.
O   Gd Fri-Oct, daily 14.00-17.00. Aug 11.00-17.00. Nov-Easter, Sat-Sun 14.00-17.00.
P   Yes
C   Quiz sheet. Victorian schoolroom
T   Yes
D   Stairlift (sorry, not suitable for larger wheelchairs). Toilet.
•   Museum of the Year Award 1990. Ten rooms devoted to local life; Victorian sitting room and kitchen, general store, Solicitors office, cobblers shop. New industrial transport displays, workhouse and courthouse scenes.

The Royal Pump Room Museum

Crown Place, Harrogate HG1 2RY. Tel 01423 503340

£   A £1.75. Con £1. Fam £4.50. Group rates for 10+
O   Apl-Oct, Mon-Sat 10.00-17.00. Sun 14.00-17.00. Nov-Mar 10.00-16.00. Sun 14.00-16.00
P   Disc parking nearby
C   Activity days (see details in local press)
R   Cafe nearby
T   Yes
D   Accessible to wheelchairs. Toilet.
•   Housed in Harrogate's premier spa building and site of Europe's strongest sulphur well, the museum tells the story of Harrogate as a spa.

War Room and Motor House Collection

30 Park Parade, Harrogate HG1 5AG. Tel 01423 500704

£   Free but donations welcomed
O   By appointment only
P   On street parking
C   Some hands-on facilities under supervision
T   Yes
D   Access to motor house collection only
•   War room has relics from two world wars. The motor house as some 10,000 die-cast model cars. Both collections are property of founder Brian Jewell or on extended loan.

KNARESBOROUGH

The Old Courthouse Museum

Castle Grounds, Knaresborough HG5 8AS. Tel 01423 503340

£   A £1.75. Con £1. Fam £4.50. Group rates for 10+
O   Easter and May-Sept. Please phone for times
P   Disc parking nearby
C   Activity days during summer (see local press for details)
R   Cafes nearby
T   Nearby
D   Limited access
•   Knaresborough's Royal Castle towers over the river Nidd. Visit the keep and underground sallyport. Discover the legends and characters of this Medieval town.

MALTON

Malton Museum

Old Town Hall, Market Place, Malton YO17 0LT. Tel 01653 695136.

£   A £1. Con 60p. Fam £2.50
O   Easter-Oct, Mon-Sat 10.00-16.00. Sun 14.00-16.00
P   Pay and display adjacent
C   Mosaic making, corn grinding, display quiz
D   Wheelchair access to Roman display on ground floor only
•   Roman collection showing lifestyles of centurions and civilians who lived in Malton's fort, town and nearby villas. Marvel at the evidence and objects gathered from a long history of local excavation.

POCKLINGTON

Stewart's Burnby Hall Gardens and Museum

The Balk, Pocklington YO4 2QF Tel 01759 302068

£   A £2.20 C (5-15) 75p OAP £1.70 Parties 20+ £1.30, Admission price for gardens, museum is free
O   Apl-Sept
P   Free on site
R   Tea room for light refreshments
T   Yes
•   A unique display of sporting trophies, religious and other artefacts gathered by the late Major P M Stewart in the course of his many world wide expeditions.

PICKERING

Beck Isle Museum of Rural Life

Bridge Street, Pickering YO18 8DU. Tel 01751 473653

£   A £2. Con £1.50. C 5-15 £1. Fam £5.
O   Apl-Oct, every day 10.00-17.00. Last entry 16.30.
P   Parking for disabled at museum, free. Council car parks 200 metres & 400 metres.
C   Hands-on. Educational teachers' packs
R   Cafes 100 metres
T   Own toilet being planned. Nearest at present 100 metres
D   Wheelchair access to 60% of museum. Nearest toilet 100 metres at Ropery car park

Experience years gone by - 27 display areas each with a specific theme and filled with items showing changes in social, domestic and working life from the 18th century.

RICHMOND

The Green Howards Regimental Museum

Trinity Church Square, Richmond DL10 4QN. Tel 01748 822133

£   A £2. Under 16's £1.
O   Apl-Oct, Mon-Sat 09.30-16.30. Sun 14.00-16.30. Feb, Mon-Fri 10.00-16.30. Mar & Nov, Mon-Sat 10.00-16.30
P   Free disc parking in Market Place
C   Limited facilities
R   Adjacent
T   Public toilets 100 metres
D   Chairlift to all floors
•   Set in converted 12th century church, the museum tells the story of 300 years of the Green Howards' history with audio guides, interactive videos and modern display techniques.

Richmondshire Museum

Ryders Wynd, Richmond DL10 4JA. Tel 01748 825611

A   A £1. Con 70p. Fam £2.75
O   Apl-Oct, daily 11.00-17.00. Other times by appointment
P   Council car parks nearby
C   School parties catered for
R   Sweets only
T   Yes
D   Wheelchair access throughout. Lift to all floors. Toilet. Low level displays. Gulbenkian award winner for provision for visitors with disabilities
•   Fascinating museum presenting the story of Richmondshire and it's people. Medieval Cruck House, local industry, geology, toy cupboard, domestic bygones, transport in the dales, James Herriot surgery set.

Swaledale Folk Museum

The Green, Reeth, Richmond DL11 6QT. Tel 01748 884373

£   A £1.50. C 50p. Fam £3.50
O   Gd Fri-Oct, daily 10.30-17.00. Other times for parties by appointment
P   On village green
R   On village green
T   On village green
D   Wheelchair access
•   Museum depicts way of life of Swaledale folk, farming implements, lead mining tools, pastimes, stone walls, religion, village life and traditions and much more.

SCARBOROUGH

Rotunda Museum of Archaeology and Local History

Museum Terrace, Vernon Road, Scarborough YO11 2NN. Tel 01723 374839

£   Free
O   Spr BH—mid Oct, Tue-Sun 10.00-17.00. mid Oct-Spr BH., Fri-Sun 11.00-16.00, additional opening for school and BH.

P   Pay & display at South Bay
- Georgian museum with original gallery and moving stage. Displays of finds from Mesolithic lakeside camp at Star Carr and a Bronze Age oak-trunk burial. Temporary exhibitions. Shop.

Wood End Museum of Natural History
The Crescent, Scarborough YO11 2PW. Tel 01723 367326

£   Free
O   Spr BH-mid Oct, Tue-Sun 10.00-17.00. Mid Oct-Spr BH, Fri-Sun 11.00-16.00. Other times for schools and BHs
P   Nearby
C   Questionnaire - Test your Knowledge
- Displays of local wildlife, rocks and fossils. Former home of the literary Sitwell family, featuring the Sitwell library and an unusual two-storied Victorian conservatory. Shop.

SKIPTON

The Craven Museum
Town Hall, High street, Skipton BD23 1AH Tel 01756 794079

£   Free
O   Apl-Sep Mon. Wed, Thur, Fri 10.00-17.00 Oct-March Sat 10.00-12.00 13.00-16.00
P   Pay and display car park 50 metres
C   Yes
T   Downstairs in Town Hall
D   Stairlift as museum is on first floor, wheelchair available, toilet facilities in Town Hall
- This museum is crammed full of exhibits, a treasure house guaranteed to have something of interest for everyone. A good introduction to the history and character of the Craven Dales.

Upper Wharfedale Folk Museum
6 The Square, Grassington Nr Skipton BD23 5AQ

£   A 60p C and OAP 30p Fam £1
O   Easter-Oct 14.00-16.00 daily Winter weekends 14.00-16.00
P   Public car park Hebden Road
- 18th Century dales cottage housing items of local interest - farming, geology, archaeology, lead mining. Attractive kitchen and dairy with displays. Three rooms downstairs and two up.

THIRSK

Thirsk Museum
16 Kirkgate, Thirsk YO7 2LZ Tel 01845 522755

£   A £1 C 50p Fam £2.50
O   Easter-Oct Mon-Sat 10.00-17.00 Sun 14.00-16.00
P   Free car park 100 metres Millgate
C   Many items on display can be handled
T   None on site nearest public toilet Millgate car park and Market Square
D   Wheelchair access to ground floor only, no toilet facilities
- Cricketing memorabilia in birthplace of founder of Lord's Cricket Ground. James Herriot veterinary and farming bygones. Infamous 'Bushy stoop' chair. Victorian rooms, illustrating life and times of Thirsk,

WENSLEYDALE

Dales Countryside Museum

Station Yard, Hawses, Wensleydale DL8 3NT Tel 01969 667450

A £2 C and Con £1 Fam £5

O   Easter-Oct daily 10.00-17.00 Please telephone for winter openings

P   Car park adjacent

C   Objects to handle, low tech interactives being developed

R   Cafe adjacent

T   In car park

D   Wheelchair access, toilet facilities in car park

•   Making the link between the people and landscape of the Yorkshire Dales. Time tunnel takes visitors from prehistoric dales to the 1990s. New exhibits on Dales resources, makers and menders, farming past and present.

WHITBY

The Captain Cook Memorial Museum

Grape Lane, Whitby YO22 4BE Tel 01947 601900

£   A £2.20 C £1.50 OAP £1.70 Fam £6 Prebooked school parties £1.20 per pupil, teacher free

O   Apl-Oct daily 09.45-17.00

P   Pay and display nearby

•   The former house of 18th Century Quaker shipowner John Walker, now a museum to celebrate the life of Captain James Cook who lived here as an apprentice. The museum has displays, artefacts and models of James Cook's Whitby years and subsequent achievements.

Whitby Lifeboat Museum

Pier Road, Whitby, Tel 01947 602001

£   Please check with museum

O   Easter-Oct 10.00-17.00 (subject to weather)

P   Public car park in town

D   Wheelchair access no toilet facilities

•   Museum houses R.N.L.I. last rowing lifeboat and carriage - on service until 1957. All lifeboat records plus photos, memorabilia and models.

YORK

Mutton Park

Mutton Lane, York YOU 3UF Tel 01904 489966

£   A £2.80 C (under 5 free) £1.50 Con £2.20 Fam £7.50

P   Free on site

C   Pre-booked school demonstrations, treasure trails

R   Yes cafe

T   Yes

D   Ramps to buildings, toilets facilities, grass and gravel paths may be limiting

•   Three attractions set in 8 acres of grounds. Yorkshire Museum of Farming-rare breeds and collection of farm machinery. Danelaw Dark Age Village- How farmers worked and lived a thousand years ago. Derwent Valley Light Railway-the railway and the farmer.

The Regimental Museum

3 Tower Street, York YOU TSB 01904 662790

£   A £2 C and OAP £1

O   Moon-Sat 09.00-16.30 CL Sun, Xmas, Boxing & NY Days

P   Public car park in town

T   Yes

- The Regimental museum covers over 300 years of the history of two famous Yorkshire Regiments, the collection includes the pageantry of the old Regimental Colours and Standards, the scarlet and gold of uniforms, the glint of weapons and the sparkle of medals.

York Racing Museum

The Racecourse, York YO2 1EX Tel 01904 620911

£   Free if racing on that day

O   Open on racing days - 16 days of the year, other times by appointment

R   Yes on race day

T   Yes

D   Yes

- Small museum, racing silks, trophies, badges and memorabilia.

RKSHIRE

SOUTH YORKSHIRE

BARNSLEY

Cawthorne Victoria Jubilee Museum

Taylor Hill, Cawthorne, Barnsley S75 4HH No tel

£   A 50p C (5-15) 20p
O   Palm Sun-Oct Weekends & BHs 14.00-17.00
P   Limited on site and roadside, car park at Cannon Hall 15 mins walk away
C   'Hands on' facilities for school parties only
R   None on site, tea room at Cannon Hall or garden centre 15 mins walk away
T   Yes
D   Yes
•   A part cruck frame, part post and truss building, housing an interesting 'hotch potch' of a variety of objects. Local history, enthography, by-gones, Victoriana, stuffed birds and animals, wartime memorabilia etc.

Worsbrough Mill Museum

Worsborough Bridge, Barnsley S70 SLJ tel 01226 774527

£   A 50p Con 25p
O   March-Oct Wed-Sun 10.00-17.00 Nov-Feb Wed-Sun 10.00-16.00
P   Car park 100 metres £1
C   Guided tours for parties of 10 or more
R   Drinks, crisps, icecreams etc
T   Yes
D   Yes but no toilet facilities
•   17th Century working water powered corn mill set in 200 acre country park with open farmland and fishing reservoir, Stoneground flour (for sale) produced on the restored machinery

DONCASTER

Miniature World Museum
West Stockwith, Nr Doncaster DN10 4EY Tel 01427 890982
£   A £1.50 C 75p
O   Feb-mid Dec. Wed-Sun 10.00-17.00. Cl Jan.
P   Free car park opposite museum
C   'Can You find' questions on some exhibits
R   Home-made scones, cakes, freshly made sandwiches, tea, coffee and juices
T   Yes
D   Wheelchair access, no adapted toilet.
•   Museum houses 40 period doll's houses, 500 dolls and miniatures through the ages. Antique doll restoration service, teddy bear repairs and free advice. Set in interesting village with a marina.

The Museum of South Yorkshire Life
Cusworth Hall, Cusworth Lane, Doncaster DN5 7TU Tel 01302 782342
£   Free
O   Mon-Fri 10.00-17.00 Sat 11..00-17.00 sun 13.00-17.00 All year, close 16.00 during Dec & Jan Cl Xmas, Boxing Day & Gd Fri
P   Free parking available
C   Study base and Education Officer available for school parties. Holiday activity sheets
R   Tea room
T   Yes
D   Wheelchair access, toilet facilities, chair lift to ground floor
•   Cusworth Hall is a Grade 1 listed 18th Century country house set in parkland, the museum shows how people lived in the South Yorkshire area over the last 200 years.

ROTHERHAM

Clifton Park Museum
Clifton Lane, Rotherham S65 2AA Tel 01709 823635
£   Free
O   All year, Mon-Thur & Sat 10.00-17.00 Apl-Oct Sun 14.30-17.00 Nov-March Sun 14.30-16.30
P   Free on site car park
T   Yes
D   Access to ground floor and toilet facilities
•   Famous Rockingham collection.

The York & Lancaster Regimental Museum
Central Library & Arts Centre, Walker Place, Rotherham S65.1JH. Tel 01709 382121 X 3625
£   Free
O   Tue-Sat 10.00-17.00. Cl Sun. Mon & BHs
P   Pay & display
R   Yes
T   Yes
D   Accessible to wheelchairs
•   Regimental museum collection tells history 1758-1968 and includes uniforms, medals (incl 9 VCs), weapons, equipment, etc. Also incorporates the F.M.Viscount Plumer Collection)

HEFFIELD

City Museum & Mappin Art Gallery
Weston Park, Sheffield S10 2TP Tel 0114 2768588
£ Free
O Wed-Sat 10.00-17.00 Sun 11.00-17.00
P On street parking
) Yes, activity sheets
R Cafe
T Yes
D Wheelchair access and toilet facilities
• City museum displays include cutlery, metalwork, archaeology and natural history. The Mappin Art Gallery has an on-going temporary exhibition programme and a display of Victorian paintings..

Handsworth Parish Centre
Handsworth, Sheffield S13 9BZ. Tel 0114 2692537
£ Free
O By appointment
P Yes
T Yes
• Promotes local history with good selection of photographs, old school and Church records and maps.

Sheffield Bus Museum Trust Ltd
Tinsley Tram Sheds, Sheffield Road, Tinsley, Sheffield S9 2FY. Tel 0114 2553010(daytime only)
£ A £1. Con 50p. Fam £2.
O Sat & Sun, 12.00-16.00. Please phone for dates of 'Special Sunday Open Days' when more attractions and areas of the museum are accessible. Cl Xmas.
P Roadside parking. Limited outside museum.
R On special open days
T Yes
D Access to museum. No disabled toilet
• Displays of buses from 1939 - 1977 and associated artefacts. Small amount of transport related displays.

Fire/Police Museum
101-109 West Bar, Sheffield S3 8PT. Tel 0114 2491999
£ A £2. C £1. Fam £5
O Suns & BHs. Other times by arrangement
P Yes
C Play area. Fire appliances to play on. Uniforms to dress up in. Fireman Sam & engine rides at BHs.
R Yes
T Yes
D Limited access. Toilet
• Largest in UK. Special fire safety/prevention programme.

ACKNOWLEDGEMENTS

Melanie Siddon for all her hard work, research and for putting up with us
Brenda Kinson also for all her hard work and for proof reading
Sacha Mitchell of BA & D
Richard Edgerton of L.E.T.
Meg Holland for being a really helpful friend
Phil Comley for general advice
Jarrold Publishing, Norwich

BIBLIOGRAPHY

Museums Yearbook 1996/97 - used for reference